D0457282

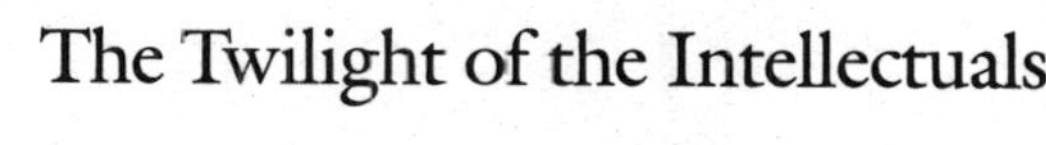
The Twilight of the Intellectuals

HILTON KRAMER

The Twilight of the Intellectuals

CULTURE AND POLITICS IN THE ERA OF THE COLD WAR

IVAN R. DEE
CHICAGO
1999

 For information, address: Ivan R. Dee, Publisher, 1332 North Halsted Street, Chicago 60622. Manufactured in the United States of America and printed on acid-free paper.

Library of Congress Cataloging-in-Publication Data:
Kramer, Hilton.
The twilight of the intellectuals : culture and politics in the era of the Cold War / Hilton Kramer.
p. cm.
Includes index.
ISBN 1-56663-222-6 (alk. paper)
1. United States—Politics and government—1945–1989. 2. Cold War—Soviet aspects—United States. 3. United States—Intellectual life—20th century. 4. Intellectuals—United States—Political activity—History—20th century. I. Title
E743.K69 1999
306.2'0973—dc21 98-45233

To Roger Kimball

Acknowledgments

THIS book is dedicated to my friend and colleague Roger Kimball, who has devoted much time and thought to its preparation and publication. To my other colleagues at *The New Criterion*, past and present, I also owe a large debt of gratitude for their support of endeavors represented in this book. I want especially to thank Christopher Carduff, Marjorie Danser, Jacob Dee, Erich Eichman, Sara Lussier, Robert Messenger, Robert Richman, Maxwell Watman, and David Yezzi. My thanks, too, to Alexandra Kimball for her expert attention to the manuscript and for the preparation of the index. And to my agent, Glen Hartley, and my publisher, Ivan Dee, I am also deeply indebted. To my wife Esta, I owe more than it would be appropriate to mention here.

It is with sadness and gratitude that I also record my enduring debt to the late Samuel Lipman (1934–1994), with whom I founded *The New Criterion* in 1982 and who in the course of our close collaboration offered wise counsel on the writing of the earlier essays in this book.

All but the following essays have previously been published in *The New Criterion*: "The Role of Sidney Hook," "Saul Bellow, Our Contemporary," and "The Flowers on Sartre's Grave" were first published in *Commentary*, for which I thank Norman Podhoretz and Neal Kozodoy; "The 'Apples' of Meyer Schapiro" was first published in *The American Scholar*, for which I thank Joseph Epstein; and "Susan Sontag: The Pasionaria of Style" was first published in *The Atlantic*, for which I thank the editors and James Atlas, who commissioned the essay when he was on the *Atlantic* staff. All are reprinted with the appropriate permissions.

For the judgments expressed in this book I am, of course, solely responsible.

Contents

Introduction: On the Style and Politics of an Intellectual Class

The revolutions of the twentieth century have not been proletarian revolutions; they may have been thought up and carried out by intellectuals.

—Raymond Aron *The Opium of the Intellectuals*, 1955

In any view of the American cultural situation, the importance of the radical movement of the Thirties cannot be overestimated. It may be said to have created the American intellectual class as we now know it in its great size and influence. It fixed the character of this class as being, through all mutations of opinion, predominantly of the Left. And quite apart from opinion, the political tendency of the Thirties defined the style of the class—from that radicalism came the moral urgency, the sense of crisis, and the concern with personal salvation that mark the existence of American intellectuals.

—Lionel Trilling, "A Novel of the Thirties," 1966

WE live today in the aftermath of an immense intellectual upheaval. For much of the twentieth century, intellectual life in the United States—and not only in the United States, of course—has been defined by its response to the politics of the radical Left or to the culture of the modernist avant-garde or to some provisional alliance between the two. Never mind that what Raymond Aron called "the two avant-gardes"—Marxism and modernism, the dream of a socialist utopia and the promise of unending innovation in the arts—have rarely proved to be compatible aspirations. Together, and not withstanding their mutual suspicions and frequent episodes of outright enmity, they have shaped the agenda of modern intellectual life. Their ideas of the good, the true, and the beautiful have exerted so great an influence on the spirit of the age that all intellectual dissent from their authority has been taken to be politically reactionary or culturally philistine or both.

In this last decade of the century, however, the collapse of Communism in the Soviet Union and its satellites and the assault on modernism in the culture of the Western democracies have had the effect of denying these intellectual orthodoxies a large measure of the moral authority they had long enjoyed. Needless to say, there were many important defections from Communist orthodoxy throughout the long, dark decades that preceded the fall of the Soviet empire—the story of one of the most distinguished and most reviled of these defectors, Whittaker Chambers, is recounted in this book—and the ranks of the modernists have similarly produced their share of apostates. Yet individual defections of this kind, though they often did much to advance the cause of moral and intellectual clarity in their respective spheres of influence, are not to be compared to the magnitude of the breakdown that has now occurred in the movements themselves. For the death of socialism as a political ideal and the parallel undermining of modernism as an artistic imperative have clearly marked the end of an historical epoch.

For better or for worse, we now find ourselves confronted by what has come to be called a "postmodern" movement in politics and culture. Whether we regard this development as a deliverance from the baleful illusions of the past or a descent into nihilism and decadence, the fact remains that we have entered an era in which the orthodoxies of Marxism and modernism no longer exert their old authority.

This does not mean that radical impulses which governed the Marxist quest for a socialist utopia have lost their power to inspire intellectual revolt. Far from it. But it is in the nature of this "postmodern" revolt—which is in so many respects a revolt against the basic traditions of Western civilization—to manifest itself as a cultural revolution rather than an open avowal of radical politics. This cultural revolution, which commonly goes by the name of "the culture wars," has, in turn, taken modernism to be one of its principal objects of disparagement and deconstruction. Thus, the "two avant-gardes" that did so much to define the spirit of intellectual life in this century have themselves been so radically deconstructed that they can no longer claim the primacy that was granted them in the period of their ascendancy. It is in this sense that we live today in the twilight of an intellectual era.

The essays and reviews collected in this volume have, as their principal theme, the kind of critical debate that governed intellectual life in this country as the era of Marxist and modernist dominance was drawing to a close and the politics of the Cold War were increasingly transferred to the realm of culture. This is a book about the writers and controversies that shaped this critical debate, about some of the journals in which the debate was conducted, and about some of the ideas that, in one degree or another, had their origin in Marxist and modernist thought.

The Twilight of the Intellectuals is thus, in large part, a book about the intellectual history of the Cold War. It is also, perforce, a book about the impact of the 1930s and the 1960s—the two decades in which the political Left achieved its greatest intellectual influence in this country—and about the role of that influence in shaping the intellectual history of the Cold War. It is one of the paradoxes of this period that the victory of the Western democracies in the Cold War has brought in its wake, in the West, a revolt against the kind of modernist culture which Communism had for so many years targeted for oblivion but never by its own exertions ever succeeded in discrediting. It is in the light of this betrayal of modernism by our own intellectuals that the subject comes up for discussion in this book.

In regard to the intellectual history of the radical Left in the Cold War, it may be appropriate to quote from an editorial, "The Counter-Revolution Abroad, The Cultural Revolution at Home," which was published in the tenth anniversary number of *The New Criterion* in September 1991, two years after the fall of the Berlin Wall. Reflecting on the "collapse of Communism in Eastern Europe, the deconstruction of Communism's political and moral legitimacy in Western Europe for politicians and intellectuals as well as for the public, and its agonizing death throes in the Soviet Union itself," the editors wrote as follows:

> This fateful turn of history, which is as much an event in the moral life of civilization as it is a political victory against the power of totalitarian tyranny, occurred a lot sooner than most of us had any reason to expect. Yet it was not a quick or easy or painless victory for those on both sides of the Iron Curtain who had worked so long and so hard and had sacrificed so much, which for many meant their lives, for such an outcome, while little dreaming that it would finally be achieved before the end of the century that had been dominated by the atrocious enemies of freedom.
>
> In our euphoria over the death of Communism, moreover, it should also be remembered that this was what the difficult and divisive years of the Cold War had always been about. This was what the much maligned champions of the anti-Communist crusade in the Western democracies had always sought to obtain with their pleas for adequate defense budgets, their uphill battles for an informed and intelligent foreign policy, and their steadfast resistance to the many ways in which our Communist adversaries had manipulated the

> intellectual and cultural life of the West to serve their own interests. For the Cold War was always as much a war of ideas as it was a contest for military superiority, and it was a war of ideas in which many talented people in the West—people of intellectual influence and great cultural renown—fought on the side of the political enemy. That, too, should not be forgotten in the wake of this costly and hard-won victory.

And further:

> [I]n the epic struggle between freedom and tyranny in the twentieth century, a large part of the intelligentsia in the West supported the interests of tyranny against the beleaguered defenders of democracy. Already some of the figures who loomed so large in the Cold War period—Jean-Paul Sartre, Bertolt Brecht, Graham Greene, and Bertrand Russell, among others, not to mention their less gifted but no less "committed" American counterparts—have begun to look permanently compromised and discredited because of the vocal and programmatic support they gave to some of the most despicable political regimes in our time, or indeed of any time. Future generations will—if we are lucky, anyway—marvel that it was not the Western defenders of Communist tyranny who suffered so conspicuously from censure and opprobrium in the Cold War period but those who took up the anti-Communist cause.

What must not be forgotten, either, is that, as Robert Kagan wrote in a recent number of *The New Republic*[1] "It was the intransigent idealism of Reagan, not Kissingerian realpolitik, and much less the accommodationism of the liberal establishment, that won the Cold War." But this, too, is a development that the political Left in this country has spent much of the last decade

[1] "Disestablishment," in *The New Republic* (August 17 & 24, 1998).

attempting to deny and misrepresent. It remains to be acknowledged that about all of these issues I write here as an avowed anti-Communist and a partisan—though not, I believe, an uncritical partisan—of the modernism that is under attack. I had never myself been a political radical. From my student days in the late Forties and early Fifties, my political beliefs—to the extent that I held any—were those of a liberal anti-Communist, and when liberalism itself took a sharp turn to the radical Left in the 1960s, I defected to the ranks of the newly emerging neoconservatives, where I happily remain today.

It needs also to be said, however, that my thinking on these issues has been greatly influenced by my close acquaintance with certain figures from the old radical Left. About my relation to one of these figures—Josephine Herbst—I write at length in this book. Here I shall add only that at no time in the years of my friendship with Josie Herbst—a friendship that was sufficiently close for Josie to invite me to become the executor of her estate—did she ever disclose to me the nature of her relation to the Alger Hiss case. That she had been in a position to confirm Whittaker Chambers's charges at the time of the two Hiss trials—but had refused to do so out of loyalty to the Communists in her life and her belief in the merits of Communism itself—was an education in the mentality of Stalinism. For it was the very essence of the Stalinist mentality to regard a renegade like Chambers as expendable precisely because he had dared to tell the truth.

My friendship with Joseph Freeman and his wife, the painter Charmion von Wiegand, to whom Josie introduced me in the early 1960s, constituted another important chapter in my political education. Joe Freeman had been something of a figure in the American Communist Party in the late Twenties and early Thirties. He was a power at the *New Masses*, the CP's monthly cultural journal—he was one of the people responsible for bringing Chambers to the magazine—and one of the organizers of the original *Partisan Review*, which began life as an organ of the John Reed Club. I once repeated to Joe the boast made to me by Philip Rahv that he and William Phillips were the only writers who ever succeeded in stealing a magazine from Joe Stalin. To which Joe replied: "They didn't steal *PR* from Joe Stalin. They stole it from Joe Freeman."

Joe was himself a writer of some talent, and his first chance to make a big name for himself as a writer came in 1936 when he published an autobiography called *An American Testament*. Owing to both the book's lively style—Joe was a born storyteller—and the Party's enormous influence in New York book publishing, *An American Testament* was instantly slated for a huge success. On publication day, copies of it filled the window displays of every commercial bookstore on Fifth Avenue—there were many in those days—and Joe himself was booked for a nationwide lecture and book promotion tour.

Just as his publishers were gearing up for a bestseller, however, word came from Moscow that the book had to be dumped. It was discovered by someone in the Kremlin that *An American Testament* contained an impermissible allusion—I believe it was a reference to Trotsky—that was displeasing to no less an eminence than Stalin himself. So the word went forth for the book to be killed. Overnight it disappeared from the windows of those Fifth Avenue bookstores. The national tour was cancelled, and Joe himself was promptly expelled from the Party. Yet he never uttered a single word in public protest against this treatment, which effectively destroyed his career as a writer.

A quarter of a century later, when I frequently attended dinner parties at the Freemans' Manhattan apartment, stories of this kind—vivid, first-hand accounts of life in and out of the Communist Party, both here and abroad, and about the Party's programmatic dissembling and its ruthless enforcement of whatever "line" the Kremlin found it convenient to adopt at any given moment—were always the principal subjects of conversation. Among the other guests I got to meet at these dinners were figures like the American journalist Louis Fischer—now forgotten but a well-known writer on politics in his day—and the German Dada artist Hans Richter, then married to a wealthy American woman, who always had a droll story to tell about his Communist friends in the Weimar period.

At these dinners Hans Richter and Charmion von Wiegand, for both of whom modernist art was now of far greater interest than radical politics, talked mostly about other artists—though in her younger days Charmion had herself been a foreign correspondent in Moscow plugging away at the Party line. Richter would tell hilarious, affectionate, mildly scurrilous stories about Marcel Duchamp; Charmion talked a lot about Piet Mondrian, to whom she was very close when he lived the final years of his life in New York in the early Forties. Paintings by Mondrian hung on the walls of the Freemans' apartment when I first met them, but most of them disappeared during the course of our friendship as the pictures were sold to meet the Freemans' financial needs.

Mainly, however, these dinners were marathon sessions, especially when Josie Herbst was present, devoted to tales of Stalinist skullduggery and its casualties—tales of betrayal that often ended in the ruin or death of former comrades. Yet to the end Joe Freeman remained publicly silent about these victims of Stalin's perfidy, lest he be stigmatized as a betrayer of the Communist cause. With the example of Whittaker Chambers very much on his mind, he couldn't face the prospect of becoming a political pariah, which would certainly have been his fate among his many liberal friends had he spoken out about what he knew.

It was in the pages of *Partisan Review* that I made my debut as an art critic in 1953, an experience that is discussed in the concluding essay of this volume. On the basis of my contributions to *Partisan Review* I was invited by Clement Greenberg to write for *Commentary* in the mid-1950s, and continued to write for the magazine under Norman Podhoretz and Neal Kozodoy. When *The New York Review of Books* was founded in the early 1960s, I was also invited to write for that journal, which I did for a few years. But I soon withdrew as the *Review*'s virulent anti-American leftism became increasingly distasteful to me. On the occasion of my last lunch with Robert Silvers, who was my editor at the *Review*, he arrived in a state of great excitement to announce that the journal had just scored a tremendous coup: Mary McCarthy had been persuaded to go to Hanoi to write about the war in Vietnam. I knew then that the time had come for me to get out.

In the early 1960s I also wrote for *The Nation*, which was then Stalinist in its political pages but still open to more diverse views in its back-of-the-book literary section; for *The New Leader*, which was anti-Stalinist; and for *The New Republic*, which in those days was an uneasy mixture of both. About the intellectual milieu that is the principal focus of this book, I think it can therefore be said that I have been closely acquainted with it for the better part of half a century.

As to exactly when this milieu may be said to have been dissolved, opinion naturally varies, especially among the surviving members of the intellectual circle that gave it its characteristic style. My own view is that it was as much the culture—that is, the counterculture—as it was the politics of the radical movement in the Sixties that caused the initial breakup of the New York intellectuals as a distinct historical phenomenon. Age had something to do with it, of course, but so did ideas and standards. Whatever their criticisms of their former Marxist beliefs might now be, and however much the New York intellectuals might disapprove of what certain aspects of modernism had degenerated into, it was upon the culture of Marxism and modernism that their own intellectual sensibilities had been formed, and from that perspective the counterculture was viewed as an alien horror.

For many of these intellectuals, the politics of the Sixties were *déjà vu*—something they had already been through. It was the ethos and what might even be called the aesthetics of the counterculture that were anathema—yet these were precisely what, by the mid-Sixties, were coming to be regularly extolled in the pages of *Partisan Review* itself. This really was the treason of the intellectuals in their view. It was, as you might say, to the music of the Beatles—and to the jeers of *their* intellectual champions—that the New York intellectuals left the stage as a group.

Some found temporary refuge in the pages of *The New Yorker*, which itself turned sharply Left in the Sixties. Most continued to write for *The New York Review*, while others woke up to the conservative implications of their own ideas—ideas traditionally considered liberal—and found a home in the neo-conservative movement, which was itself the creation of ex-radicals and ex-liberals. As for what Philip Rahv used to call the "swingers" of the Sixties, they became the darlings of the media, the academy, and mainstream cultural life, where they continue to reign today.

IN THE SERVICE OF STALINISM

Whittaker Chambers: Thinking About Witness

Almost all of the prophecies of Marx and his followers have already proved to be false, but this does not disturb the spiritual certainty of the faithful, any more than it did in the case of chiliastic sects: for it is a certainty not based on any empirical premises or supposed "historical laws," but simply on the psychological need for certainty. In this sense Marxism performs the function of a religion, and its efficacy is of a religious character. But it is a caricature and a bogus form of religion, since it presents its temporal eschatology as a scientific system, which religious mythologies do not purport to be.

—Leszek Kolakowski, *Main Currents of Marxism*, 1978

THE publication by Regnery Gateway of the paperback edition of Whittaker Chambers's *Witness* in 1987 did not, so far as I am aware, cause even the smallest ripple of attention to be paid to this important book. This should not have come as a surprise to anyone. Although *Witness*—a stout volume of some eight hundred pages—was hailed as an event of immense consequence upon its original publication in 1952, the book has in recent decades virtually disappeared from our historical consciousness. It is rare—in my experience, anyway—to meet anyone under the age of forty who has actually read it.

The book has never been without its isolated devotees, to be sure, but these have tended to be readers with special interests either in the history of the radical movement or in the literature of anti-Communism or in the activities of the Soviet espionage apparatus, about all of which, of course, *Witness* has much to tell us. But as a work of more general interest for readers who make a point of keeping themselves informed about the political and cultural world they inhabit—and most particularly, as literature of "a high order," which is how John P. Marquand described it in 1952—*Witness* was long ago consigned to oblivion. The critics never speak of it, the writers of the Eighties have never heard of it, and the older generation—with certain honorable exceptions—has been content to leave its obscurity undisturbed. One can hardly imagine a professor anywhere assigning it to a class as required reading even in a period when the study of autobiography has come to enjoy something of a vogue on American campuses. Yet the truth about *Witness* is that it is one of the classic American autobiographies, and at the time of its publication it was clearly seen to be one even by many of the critics who found much to disagree with in its author's political views.

Since ours seems now to have become a chronically amnesiac culture, it may be worth recalling what the nature of this critical reception was in 1952. And the first and most fundamental thing to be recalled, I suppose, is the great uproar that the publication of *Witness* created not only on the political scene—where Chambers's role in the Alger Hiss case could be expected to generate enormous interest in anything he might write about this fateful event in our history—but in the world of literary and intellectual debate as well. That was, as a matter of fact, the world—or one of the worlds—that Chambers had come from.

Long before the Hiss case came to dominate the nation's headlines and insinuate itself into the political life of the 1950s, Chambers had been known to virtually everyone on the literary Left as a familiar and problematic figure. In the early Thirties he had been—albeit briefly—one of the literary stars of the *New Masses*. In more recent years he had become a controversial figure at *Time* magazine, first as a book reviewer and then as a senior editor, and a well-known contributor to *Life*.

His long sojourn in the Communist Party "underground" seems to have been an open secret to many of his former associates on the literary Left. Most of them knew nothing very specific about what his Party work actually entailed, of course, but they knew it was clandestine—and they also knew that the Party served the interests of the Soviet Union. Neither in his Party days nor during his tenure at *Time* was Chambers universally admired among those who knew or knew about him. But he seems always to have had something of an aura—to have been a man with a talent for commanding attention, causing uneasiness, and dividing opinion. It was, in any case, to his friendships in the literary world, where his skills as a writer and translator were known to be considerable, that he owed his survival when he made his decision to break with the Party, and it was through one of those friendships that he got his job at *Time*. Given this history, it was inevitable that Chambers and his views would become a hotly debated issue in the literary-intellectual world when, in 1948, he found himself in the political limelight as Hiss's accuser. Indeed, owing to the use that Lionel Trilling made of Chambers in creating the character of Gifford Maxim in his novel *The Middle of the Journey*, he had become an issue—though a much smaller one—even in advance of the Hiss case. For Trilling's novel was published in 1947, and anyone who read and really understood *The Middle of the Journey* at that time was more or less prepared for much of what followed when, a few months later, Chambers named Hiss as an underground Communist before the House Un-American Activities Committee. In the somewhat sour critical reception accorded Trilling's novel, we can now see that we were given a polite preview of the far more noisy, hostile, and indeed vicious press that Chambers received when he began his long ordeal of public testimony against Hiss and the Party apparatus they had both served so efficiently.

By the time that he came to write *Witness*, in the immediate aftermath of Hiss's conviction on two counts of perjury, Chambers had ample reason to know that one of his worst fears had been realized. He knew that as far as liberal opinion was concerned—and in the literary and publishing world at least, it was liberal opinion that dominated all discussion—Hiss, though sent to jail for criminal acts that publicly identified him as a Soviet espionage agent, was firmly established as a political martyr. By the same token, Chambers, who had risked his hard-won career and indeed his life by exposing a Soviet spy network at the very heart of the Washington bureaucracy, stood condemned as a turncoat and a villain. In the court of liberal opinion, informing on a fellow conspirator was deemed to be a far greater crime than belonging to a clandestine Communist spy apparatus and stealing government documents for a foreign power.

Thus, in the crazy logic of the case, Hiss—convicted of crimes that showed him to be a liar, a thief, and a traitor—was judged to be innocent even if guilty, and Chambers—the self-confessed renegade who recanted his treachery—was judged to be guilty even if he was telling the truth. For what mattered to liberal opinion was that Hiss was seen to have remained true to his ideals—never mind what the content of these "ideals" proved to be—whereas Chambers was seen to have betrayed them. (It was on this note that Alistair Cooke concluded his hastily written but very influential book on the case—*A Generation on Trial*—in 1950.)

Exactly why Chambers had chosen to do this was never clearly established in the frightful campaign of vilification that was mounted against him. Was he simply a liar? But in two trials, in which Hiss was represented by some of the most illustrious legal talent in the country, twenty out of twenty-four jurors believed that Chambers spoke the truth about Hiss. Was Chambers then an opportunist? But his action against Hiss cost Chambers his job at *Time* and brought the prospect of ruin for him and his family. Was he a psychopath and a forger, as Hiss continued to claim? But the repeated attempts of the Hiss defense attorneys to make those charges stick always turned to ashes.

None of this counted against Hiss—except with the jurors, of course. Whatever the court decreed, liberal opinion had rendered its own irreversible verdict in the case: Chambers, whatever his motives, was found to be a monster, whereas Hiss—whatever his actions—was a man who had been wronged. In 1988, as we approached the fortieth anniversary of Chambers's historic testimony before the House Un-American Activities Committee, the evidence against Hiss was even more definitive than it was in the perjury trials—it had been especially so since the publication of Allen Weinstein's *Perjury: The Hiss-Chambers Case* in 1978—liberal opinion had not been significantly altered in the interim. Which is the main reason, of course, why *Witness* remained a buried classic.

It has to be remembered, then, that even before the publication of *Witness*, Chambers had emerged as a despised, emblematic figure—the archetypal ex-Communist and counter-revolutionary who was not to be trusted, who was to be feared in fact, even when he was telling the truth, and most to be feared, perhaps, when it was no longer possible to deny that he was telling the truth. No doubt there are many reasons that could be adduced to explain this strange situation, and not the least of them was Chambers's own personality. Philip Rahv, who knew him in the early Thirties before Chambers went into the underground, noted in "The Sense and Nonsense of Whittaker Chambers" (*Partisan Review*, July–August 1952) that there was "something in his talk and manner, a vibration, an accent, that I can only describe as Dostoevskyean in essence."

> I thought at the time [Rahv wrote] that he was far from unconscious of the effect he produced. He had the air of a man who took more pleasure in the stylized than in the natural qualities of his personality. Still, whether aware or not, it was

> distinctly the Dostoevskyean note that he struck—that peculiar note of personal intensity and spiritual truculence, of commitment to the "Idea" so absolute as to suggest that life had no meaning apart from it, all oddly combined with a flair for mystification and melodrama.

Lionel Trilling had met Chambers ever earlier—in 1924–25, when Trilling was a senior at Columbia and Chambers, also at Columbia, had just joined the Communist Party. According to Trilling, they had never been friends, but they had friends in common—"young men of intimidating brilliance"—and, as Trilling later reported, "I observed [Chambers] as if from a distance and with considerable irony, yet accorded him the deference which my friends thought his due." When, toward the end of his life, Trilling came to write a new introduction for the reissue of *The Middle of the Journey*, he gave us a very vivid account of what the basis of that "deference" had been. It was not only that "Chambers had a very considerable college prestige as a writer," and, as Trilling added, that "this was deserved." There was the man himself:

> The moral force that Chambers asserted [Trilling wrote] began with his physical appearance. This seemed calculated to negate youth and all its graces, to deny that they could be of any worth in our world of pain and injustice. He was short of stature and very broad, with heavy arms and massive thighs; his sport was wrestling . . . . His eyes were narrow and they preferred to consult the floor rather than an interlocutor's face. His mouth was small and, like his eyes, tended downward, one might think in sullenness, though this was not so. When the mouth opened, it never failed to shock by reason of the dental ruin it disclosed, a devastation of empty sockets and blackened stumps. . . . [T]hat desolated mouth was the perfect insigne of Chambers' moral authority. It annihilated the hygienic American present—only a serf could have such a

> mouth, or some student in a visored cap who sat in his Moscow garret and thought of nothing save the moment when he would toss the fatal canister into the barouche of the Grand Duke.
>
> Chambers could on occasion speak eloquently and cogently, but he was not much given to speaking—his histrionism, which seemed unremitting, was chiefly that of imperturbability and long silences. Usually his utterances were gnomic, often cryptic. Gentleness was not cut out of the range of his expression, which might even include a compassionate sweetness of a beguiling kind. But the chief impression he made was of a forbidding drabness.[1]

In later life, however much Chambers may have changed in other respects, all of the characteristic qualities observed by Rahv and Trilling (and many others) became even more marked in the personality and appearance of this complicated figure. They led many of his associates—including, it is said, the Hisses—to believe that he might be "foreign," maybe even Russian. The fact that he spoke several languages, and even seemed to speak English with an "accent," also contributed to the impression that he was somehow not an American, though in fact he was born in Philadelphia and grew up on Long Island. The Dostoevskyean note became, if anything, an even more ingrained element of Chambers's outlook and manner of utterance as he grew older.

[1] The edition of *The Middle of the Journey* with Trilling's new introduction was published by Charles Scribner's Sons in 1976. It should be said that Trilling clearly disliked Chambers and came to dislike his writing, too. Yet at the time of the Hiss case, Trilling supported Chambers and exhibited remarkable courage in doing so. Approached by one of Hiss's lawyers who, as Trilling wrote, "tried to induce me to speak against [Chambers] in court," he not only refused but shocked this attorney by asserting that "Whittaker Chambers is a man of honor." He could still recall, Trilling wrote, "the outburst of contemptuous rage [my remarks] evoked from the lawyer who had come to call on me to solicit my testimony."

The forbidding drabness, too, the unremitting histrionism, the imperturbability and long silences, as well as the eloquence and beguiling sweetness—all came to be remarked upon, though they inspired differing responses in different quarters, by the friends and the enemies who came to know Chambers as an editor of *Time*, as a figure in the Hiss case, as the author of *Witness,* and in the years that remained to him after the publication of *Witness* when, among other things, he was involved in the early development of *National Review.*

In the matter of appearances, at least, Chambers himself was acutely aware of the fact that he was woefully miscast for the hero's role in the Hiss case, and he was not without a certain grim humor on the subject. "You know what the trouble with this case is?" he once asked Bennett Cerf, the publisher of *Witness*. And he answered:

> We're cast wrong. I look like a slob, so I should be the villain. Hiss, the handsome man who knows all the society people, is the born hero. It's bad casting. If it was the other way around, nobody would pay any attention to the story; but because of the way we look, all of you people think he must be telling the truth. That's what has made him so valuable to the other side.[2]

But as Chambers well understood, it was more than a matter of appearances, of "bad casting," however much appearances—and, indeed, his own problematic personality—may have contributed to the overall atmosphere of hostility and suspicion. There was a whole view of the universe at stake in the belief that had been vested in Hiss's innocence, and it was because of the force with which Chambers placed *that* issue at the center of *Witness* that the book caused the furor that it did. For *Witness*

[2] Bennett Cerf, in *At Random*, published by Random House in 1977. In this memoir Cerf, who considered himself a liberal (and was), tells the story of how he came to publish—and believe in—*Witness.*

fundamentally altered the terms of the political and intellectual debate that had been raging within the liberal camp at least since the Moscow Trials in the Thirties: the debate about the relation in which liberalism stood not only to Communism and Stalinism but to socialism and other modalities of Marxist and "progressive" thought.

That debate—essentially a debate among disabused liberals over the future of liberalism—had reached what seemed to many a kind of watershed in the fierce divisions and acrimonious quarrels caused by the Hiss case and the other revelations of spying, treason, and disloyalty in the late Forties and early Fifties. The "innocent" liberalism of the Thirties was now seen to be hopelessly compromised by its inability (or refusal) to resist the corruptions of Communist influence. Something else—a "new" liberalism—was needed to take its place. Liberals had entered upon a vast effort to set their own intellectual house in order, and it was proving to be a formidable task.

Liberalism, it turned out, was not to be so easily dislodged from the whole morass of illiberal doctrines and beliefs in which, under the influence of Marxism, it had become so deeply embedded, and every attempt to effect such a separation raised the question of whether, in what survived this process of political surgery, there was still something that could legitimately be called liberalism. Over the whole of this worthy enterprise, moreover, there hovered a great fear—the fear of being thought "reactionary," the fear of being relegated to the Right. Even the most disabused liberals believed in their hearts that they still belonged to the Left. The very thought of being accused of collaborating with "reaction," as it was still called, was a liberal nightmare, and there was no shortage of Stalinist liberals (as I believe they must be called) to bring the charge of "reaction"—which might mean anything from outright fascism to perfectly respectable political opposition to certain New Deal initiatives—at every infraction, or suspected infraction, of "progressive" doctrine.

Among the revisionist liberals I speak of, conservatism in this period did not loom as a viable alternative. This was the period, after all, in which Lionel Trilling, in his Preface to *The Liberal Imagination* (1950), famously observed that "in the United States at this time liberalism is not only the dominant but even the sole intellectual tradition."

> For it is the plain fact [Trilling continued] that nowadays there are no conservative or reactionary ideas in general circulation. This does not mean, of course, that there is no impulse to conservatism or to reaction. Such impulses are certainly very strong, perhaps even stronger than most of us know. But the conservative impulse and the reactionary impulse do not, with some isolated and some ecclesiastical exceptions, express themselves in ideas but only in action or in irritable mental gestures which seek to resemble ideas.[3]

In the same year that *The Liberal Imagination* appeared, Diana Trilling published an important essay called "A Memorandum on the Hiss Case" in *Partisan Review*, which was one of the principal journals—the others were *Commentary* and *The New Leader*—in which the revisionist liberal debate was conducted. Of the several significant points that Mrs. Trilling was concerned to make in this essay, the following now seem especially notable both in themselves and for the light they cast on the reception of *Witness* (whose publication still lay two years into the future).

Of the duties that now devolved upon anyone who, as Mrs. Trilling wrote, "thinks Hiss guilty but would still think of himself as a liberal," the first, she argued, was "that he separate him-

3 *The Liberal Imagination* was published by The Viking Press in 1950. Since he believed himself, with just reason, to be writing as a liberal, Trilling was said to have been considerably shaken when Joseph Frank wrote an article in *The Sewanee Review*, in 1956, entitled "Lionel Trilling and the Conservative Imagination." The article was occasioned by the publication of Trilling's *The Opposing Self* (1955).

self from his undesirable allies." She was quite specific about what this meant.

> In the Hiss case, [the] enforced alignment between anti-Communist liberals and reactionaries is particularly open and distasteful [she wrote]. Who brought Hiss's perfidy to public issue, except the one agency in Washington most suspect for its political motive, the un-American Activities Committee? What is the anti-Hiss press, except the usual rabble-rousers and Redbaiters? What party has most to gain from his conviction, except the Republican Party, and the Republican Party in its most retrograde wing? It is scarcely an attractive company, and the liberal must make a clean break with it.

In this respect, it is worth noting that Mrs. Trilling's essay was, in part, a review of *Seeds of Treason* by Ralph de Toledano and Victor Lasky, who were certainly writing from the Right, and not of A *Generation on Trial* by Alistair Cooke, who was writing from the liberal Left. Mrs. Trilling left her readers in no doubt that she was appalled to find that de Toledano and Lasky regarded Chambers as "a hero of our times, a martyr to principle and to the security of the nation," and she condemned such a judgment as "an unthoughtful and dangerous attitude."

Second, about the relation that had obtained between liberalism and Communism, Mrs. Trilling was perfectly clear and properly troubled, and she well understood that the challenge of separating the liberals from their disbelief in Communism's malevolent character would be immense. "But the task of persuading the liberal who is not afraid of Communism," she wrote, "that he should be afraid of it is a gigantic one, and one which involves changing a climate of opinion and feeling over the whole of our culture." Yes, we might add, and the task was no less gigantic in 1988, alas, than it was in 1950. The great difference, of course, is that by the late 1980s there were no Trillingesque liberals left to aid in the task.

Third, there was the reflection that Mrs. Trilling offered on the source of the "idealism" that Hiss was believed by so many to have represented.

> If we can say, as I think we can, that before this century the source of all political idealism was (however remotely) religion, I think we can also say that in our own century the source of all political idealism has been socialism, and, since the Russian Revolution, specifically the socialism of the Soviet Union. I do not mean that whoever has worked for political progress has necessarily been a socialist. I mean only that it has been from socialist theory that political progress has chiefly taken its inspiration, and from socialist example its practice.

What Mrs. Trilling wrote in this passage is largely true, but what is striking about it in retrospect, and especially in relation to *Witness*, is its bland, untroubled acceptance of the momentous event it speaks of. Socialism had indeed supplanted religion as the source of "political idealism," and from that fateful shift there have flowed many of the horrors of the modern age. This was to be one of the philosophical issues that Chambers placed at the center of *Witness*; it had already served, on a more modest scale, as a key element in Lionel Trilling's portrayal of Gifford Maxim in *The Middle of the Journey*. Yet in her "Memorandum on the Hiss Case," Mrs. Trilling did not pause to consider its implications. It clearly did not impress her as a subject that needed to be addressed on that occasion. It might even have seemed that, in addressing it, she would have been in danger of appearing to have something in common with "undesirable allies." She turned instead to a criticism of President Roosevelt for his failure "to see the reality of the Red threat and its menace to democracy."

Mrs. Trilling then went on to express the hope "that if this case is to serve any purpose in our lives there must be salvaged from it a better notion of liberalism." One of the things this meant, she insisted, was that "the case will have been useful, I think, if it helps us to detach the wagon of American liberalism from the star of the Soviet Union." In what ways the wagon of American liberalism remained firmly attached to the idea of socialism, however, and what *that* meant, was nowhere discussed. It obviously did not occur to Mrs. Trilling—or to the anti-Communist liberals who shared her views—that if socialism remained the source of "political idealism," then liberalism itself might be doomed.

This, I believe, is what we have seen happen in the decades since Mrs. Trilling wrote her essay: liberalism—in substance, if not in name—has, in our political institutions, our governmental policies, and in what Mrs. Trilling called the "climate of opinion and feeling over the whole of our culture," ceded more and more ground to the kind of political outlook that is anchored in the socialist vision. You can observe the results in our universities, you can see it in the media, you can hear it in the speeches of the Democrats who run Congress and who are running for the Presidency. In many respects it is now the liberal impulse that expresses itself "only in action and in irritable mental gestures which seek to resemble ideas," for as an intellectual tradition liberalism is bankrupt. Liberalism dares not openly acknowledge, even to itself, its surrender to socialist ideology, for everybody knows that the American voter will not elect a frankly socialist government. And so the rhetoric of liberalism, no matter how threadbare and transparent, must be continually repaired and refurbished and made re-usable until the prize can be won.

I have focused on Mrs. Trilling's essay because it encapsulates so many of the ideas and fears that characterized the most enlightened liberal minds of her generation—those that came to be identified as liberal anti-Communists. It was that sector of the liberal community—staunch in its opposition to Communism and very knowing not only about its underground operations but about the spell it had cast over the whole of our culture—that played a crucial role in the critical reception of *Witness*.

The intellectual uproar over *Witness* occurred on two principal fronts. It was to be expected that the "progressive" Left—those still under the sway of Stalinism and the Popular Front mentality—would attempt to bury the book with the same vicious methods that had been employed in the campaign to discredit Chambers's testimony and render Chambers himself a moral leper. (The term "leper" was actually used in court by Hiss's most celebrated defense counsel, Lloyd Paul Stryker, one of the famous liberals of his day.) As Chambers wrote in *Witness*: "This personal assault upon me was the only real defense that Alger Hiss and his supporters ever developed," and the assault was renewed with added venom when his book was published. If, in the short run, this effort on the part of the orthodox Left failed to impede the immediate success of *Witness*—it was a Book-of-the-Month Club selection and a big bestseller in its day—the long-run effect was nonetheless to keep the book from having much of a literary afterlife. In the world of *The New Yorker*, which was solidly pro-Hiss,[4] *The New Republic*, whose editor in those days was subsequently revealed to have been a member, earlier on, of another underground Soviet apparatus,[5] and other such staunch liberal journals, the barriers were erected and Chambers was stripped of his literary standing.

The response of the liberal anti-Communists to *Witness* was very different—and far more honorable, of course—yet the effect was also in the end to place Chambers outside the boundaries of enlightened intellectual opinion. Because they believed that Chambers was telling the truth about Hiss—and indeed about

[4] A. J. Liebling, *The New Yorker*'s celebrated press columnist, served as an unpaid volunteer for the Hiss defense while pretending to write about the case as an objective reporter. See Allen Weinstein's account of this unlovely episode in *Perjury* (Alfred A. Knopf, 1978), pages 166-167.

[5] I refer to Michael Straight. His later role in identifying Anthony Blunt as a Soviet spy is described in *Conspiracy of Silence: The Secret Life of Anthony Blunt*, by Barrie Penrose and Simon Freeman (Farrar, Straus & Giroux, 1987).

Communism—it became the primary task of the liberal anti-Communists in dealing with *Witness* not to defend Hiss but to rescue liberalism from Chambers's sweeping attack on it. And because they recognized that the author of *Witness* was, as even Philip Rahv acknowledged, a "born writer" and that the book itself was, as Bennett Cerf said, "superbly written," the liberal anti-Communists were concerned, above all, not to challenge Chambers's literary gifts but to diminish the impact which his powerful testament might have on the political and moral status of liberalism. The whole effort of the liberal anti-Communists in regard to *Witness* thus became an exercise in what we would now call damage control.

Rereading the criticisms of *Witness* that were written by some of the outstanding liberal anti-Communists of the early Fifties, what is particularly remarkable in retrospect is the way they managed to combine a genuine admiration for Chambers's achievement with a fundamental rejection of his views. Take, for example, the review-article written by Arthur Schlesinger, Jr., in the *Saturday Review* ("Whittaker Chambers & His 'Witness,'" May 24, 1952). Schlesinger was full of praise for *Witness* as a contribution to American literature:

> Whittaker Chambers has written one of the really significant American autobiographies. When some future Plutarch writes his American Lives, he will find in Chambers penetrating and terrible insights into America in the early twentieth century. Nor need he search long for a parallel life; just as Henry L. Stimson's *On Active Service* is the powerful counterstatement to Henry Adams's *Education,* so Whittaker Chambers's *Witness* is the counterstatement to that book so influential twenty years ago, the *Autobiography of Lincoln Steffens.*

Nothing could have been better calculated to impress upon the readers of the *Saturday Review* the idea that *Witness* was a book of immense importance than to have placed Chambers in the company of Adams, Stimson, and Steffens at that particular moment in history. But there was more:

> In part, *Witness* is an extraordinary personal document—a powerful and compassionate story of a middle-class family broken on the shoals of life in middle-class America, until the surviving son rejects his class and enlists in the ranks of the proletarian revolution. But, like the other great autobiographies, *Witness* is much more than a personal document. It is also a political document and a philosophical document. Its weight and urgency as a personal document are likely to win acceptance for its politics and its philosophy. But the politics and the philosophy, in my judgment, raise basic issues which deserve independent and critical examination.

Schlesinger then went on to belittle the role that espionage and Communist influence might have played in American foreign policy in the Roosevelt era and, what was even more important in his view, to defend the New Deal against the harsh and categorical criticisms that Chambers had made of it in *Witness*.

This was no surprise, of course. Schlesinger was writing less as a disinterested historian than as a partisan of the Democratic Party and a pillar of the "new" liberalism, and it was impossible—philosophically as well as politically impossible—for any champion of the New Deal who also aspired to a position of influence in the Democratic Party to accord any real importance either to Chambers's charges of Communist influence or to his strictures on the vast changes that the Roosevelt administration has brought to the governing of the nation.[6] Given this disposition

[6] The appalling record of the Roosevelt administration in dealing with charges of Communist influence and spying is still almost unbelievable. In the immediate aftermath of the Hitler-Stalin pact in 1939, Chambers had taken his information about Hiss and other Soviet spies to Adolf A. Berle, who is described in *Liberal: Adolf A. Berle and the Vision of an American Era* by Jordan A. Schwarz (The Free Press, 1987), as the man "who then ad-

to reject and condemn Chambers's political analysis on partisan as well as philosophical grounds, it must also be noted that in those days liberals like Schlesinger conducted this debate in a rather higher-minded intellectual style than was later to be the case. There hadn't yet occurred that coarsening and softening of the mind that has been so evident in Schlesinger's writings—and not his alone, alas—since the emergence of the Kennedy machine in the Sixties.

Another important review of *Witness* by a leading liberal anti-Communist was Sidney Hook's in *The New York Times Book Review* ("The Faiths of Whittaker Chambers," May 25, 1952). This, too, described Chambers's book as "one of the most significant autobiographies of the twentieth century."

> It is not among the hundred great books [Hook wrote]. Yet it throws more light on the conspiratorial and religious character of modern Communism, on the tangled complex of motives which led men and women of goodwill to immolate themselves on the altars of a fancied historical necessity, than all of the hundred great books of the past combined. . . . [*Witness*] contains interesting vignettes of the Communist movement, a record of religious conversion, the saga of a farm, an account of desperate courage alternating with moods of spiritual despair—all knit together by the essentially mystical and romantic personality of the author. . . . The literary quality of the writing is impressive.

---

ministered State Department intelligence." "For reasons he never felt he needed to give," writes Schwarz, "Berle did nothing with Chambers' information until he turned it over to the FBI in 1941 for an investigation of Chambers' charges. While Chambers' list surfaced in the State Department in 1943 again, nothing was done until Chambers showed up once more in 1948 to repeat his charges to the House Committee on Un-American Activities." Berle regarded the whole subject, according to Schwarz, as "not really important."

Hook also said of *Witness* that "this book, even more than the verdict of the [Hiss] trials, may well be called the vindication of Whittaker Chambers."

> Its pages [he continued] show that [Chambers] has long since atoned for his own complicity in conspiratorial work by his suffering at the hands of Hiss's friends whose outrageous smears against his personal life and that of his wife surpassed in virulence anything known in recent American history.

Still, Hook too was adamant in voicing the most categorical rejection of Chambers's political and philosophical interpretation of his own experience. About the New Deal, in Hook's case, there was plenty of political sympathy but no partisan defense—he wasn't writing with a view to an appointment in some future Democratic administration. Yet the best explanation that Hook could come up with to explain how it had happened that the Communists had had such a free ride in the Roosevelt administration—in *Witness*, Chambers quotes J. Peters, his boss in the Soviet spy apparatus, as saying that "even in Germany under the Weimar Republic, the party did not have what we have here"—was not very persuasive. "Most of Chambers' facts are rendered intelligible by a less sinister hypothesis than the one he offers," Hook wrote. "It is that stupidity is sometimes the greatest of all historical forces." Now, stupidity certainly played its part in this story; it usually does in human affairs. But to elevate it to the status of one of "the greatest of all historical forces" as a way of accounting for the New Deal's failure to take the Communist issue seriously is tantamount to abandoning the whole question. Mrs. Trilling's analysis of the relation in which the New Deal liberals stood to the kind of Communist "idealism" which Hiss represented had at least the merit of placing the question firmly in the realm of political reality.

What bothered Hook the most about *Witness*, of course, were its author's religious views. These he condemned in toto, declaring that "it is not unlikely that the [secular] humanistic spirit may be the best defense on a world scale against the Communist crusade because it can unite all human beings who, despite their religious differences about first and last things, value truth, justice, kindness and freedom among men." Now, over a third of a century later, I think it would be accurate to say that the "spirit" so fondly invoked by Sidney Hook in his review of *Witness* has not proven to be much of a defense at all. However problematic Chambers's religious views may still be for those readers of *Witness* who are non-believers, he wasn't wrong in his diagnosis that "faith is the central problem of this age." The liberal mind, so comfortable in its own articles of faith, shied away from such an idea, as if from the most dreaded of heresies, and went merrily to its doom in the Sixties when that "impassioned longing to believe," which Lionel Trilling spoke of as the presiding impulse of the Thirties and Forties, reasserted itself in even more virulent forms and with more lasting consequences.

History, as a matter of fact, has proved Whittaker Chambers to have been right about many things, and *Witness* remains not only one of the few indispensable autobiographies ever written by an American—and one of the best written, too—but the very thing that Sidney Hook said it wasn't: "an intelligent guide" to the victory of freedom over Communist tyranny. It is the only great book on the Communist experience to have been written by an American, and it deserves to be recognized as a first-class achievement. Yet there is no reason to believe that this new edition of so important a book will succeed in winning the readers or in exerting the influence it should have. On the contrary, over the whole of our cultural and intellectual life today there reigns an atmosphere that is deeply inimical not only to Chambers's ideas but to his moral gravity—the sense he had that it was not only our political future but our whole civilization that was at stake in the momentous issues he lived through and wrote about so eloquently. Forty years after he brought his first public charges against Alger Hiss, Chambers remains in the liberal mind—which is more than ever the mind that dominates the universities, the media, and the literary world—the monster that Hiss's defenders shamelessly made him out to be. And he remains, too, a writer denied his proper literary standing, And Hiss? Well, among other things, he has been given the distinction of having an academic chair named in his honor at Bard College—a chair in, of all things, the humanities. And as far as I know, it hasn't been funded by the KGB, either. It is, I suppose, supported by that same brand of "idealism" that inspired Alger Hiss. *Plus ça change . . .*

March 1988

Whittaker Chambers: The Judgment of History

No one who has, even once, lived close to the making of history can ever again suppose that it is made the way the history books tell it. With rare exceptions, such books are like photographs. They catch a surface image. Often as not, they distort it. The secret forces working behind and below the historical surface they seldom catch.

—Whittaker Chambers, *Witness*, 1952

You have not come back from hell with empty hands.

—André Malraux to Whittaker Chambers, 1952

NEARLY half a century has passed since the fateful day in January 1950 when a jury in a Federal court in New York City found Alger Hiss guilty on two counts of perjury. That verdict effectively confirmed the charge brought by Whittaker Chambers that Hiss, his former comrade in a Soviet espionage apparatus in the 1930s, had betrayed his country as a Communist spy while serving as a high official in the U.S. State Department. Hiss, who had been with President Roosevelt at Yalta, had participated in the founding of the United Nations in 1945. He was president of the Carnegie Endowment for International Peace when Chambers first publicly identified himself as a Communist before the House Un-American Activities Committee in August 1948. He went to jail as a convicted felon. Yet for the remaining forty-six years of his life—Hiss died in November 1996 at the age of ninety-two—this once highly respected member of the liberal establishment continued to insist upon his innocence. What is more remarkable, a great many intelligent people—those whom Chambers characterized in *Witness* as the "best people"—continued to believe him, or profess to believe him, even in the face of the mounting post-trial evidence that confirmed his guilt. This is how Chambers described the situation at the end of *Witness*:

> No feature of the Hiss Case is more obvious, or more troubling as history, than the jagged fissure, which it did not so much open as reveal, between the plain men and women of the nation, and those who affected to act, think and speak for them. It was, not invariably, but in general, the "best people" who were for Alger Hiss and who were prepared to go to any length to protect and defend him. It was the enlightened and the powerful, the clamorous proponents of the open mind and the common man, who snapped their minds shut in a pro-Hiss psychosis. . . . It was the great body of the nation, which, not invariably, but in general, kept open its mind in the Hiss Case, waiting for the returns to come in. It was they who suspected what forces disastrous to the nation were at work in the Hiss Case, and had suspected that they were at work long before there was a Hiss Case, while most of the forces of enlightenment were poohpoohing the Communist danger and calling every allusion to it a witch hunt.

It was, moreover, an inevitable corollary of this ardently held belief in Hiss's innocence that his accuser had to be stigmatized as a disreputable liar and fraud, if not indeed a malevolent madman. In that pernicious endeavor, which has persisted in some of the "best" circles down to the present day—hence the continued neglect of *Witness*, an autobiography of great literary and historical distinction—Hiss's liberal champions enjoyed an immense advantage. For upon the archetypal figure of the informer there has always been associated something odious and unclean. Americans, in their innocence, tend to be particularly unforgiving in this respect—more unforgiving, in this case, than about evidence of espionage. This, too, was a calamity that Chambers had clearly grasped when he put his life and his career at risk by informing on Alger Hiss.

That in his own self-interest Chambers need not have incurred that terrible risk is not something much appreciated even among people familiar with this celebrated case. It was, after all, within Chambers's power to have sidestepped the entire catastrophe. He could have refused to testify against a former comrade, and in the "best" circles he would have been lavished with praise for defying an unloved Congressional committee. It is worth recalling that in 1948, as a writer for *Time* and *Life*, Chambers was enjoying an immense success in the only decent—and decently paid—job he ever had in his life. He was a happily married man with two young children and a farm in Maryland. He certainly knew what it was likely to cost him if, in naming Hiss as a Communist, he turned informer—and not only in public opprobrium.

"Some ex-Communists are so stricken by the evil they have freed themselves from," he afterwards wrote in *Witness*, "that they inform exultantly against it. No consideration, however humane, no tie however tender, checks them." His own view of the informer's fate was quite different. "By temperament," he wrote, "I cannot share such exultation and stridency, though I understand both. I cannot ever inform against anyone without feeling something die in me. I inform without pleasure because it is necessary."

Everything we know about the Hiss Case—including Chambers's sometimes misguided attempts to shield Hiss himself from the worst charge of all: espionage—attests to the truth of this assertion. Yet the "best people" were so eager to shield themselves from the awful implications of the Hiss Case that they refused to see in Chambers anything but a caricature of irrational anti-Communist wrath. With that caricature firmly established by liberal demonization, the reality of the man himself was effectively removed from enlightened discussion. So, for that matter, was the real Alger Hiss, who, for the "best people," remained safely concealed behind the mask of a New Deal pinup boy, an exemplary figure of virtue and rectitude.

"I always felt that Whittaker was the most misunderstood person of our time," wrote Arthur Koestler at the time of Whittaker Chambers's death in 1961. "When he testified he knowingly committed moral suicide for the guilt of our generation. . . . The witness is gone, the testimony will stand." And so the testimony still stands a half-century later, with added corroboration turning up with greater and greater frequency from hitherto secret archives in Washington, Moscow, and Prague, with every passing year.

Yet Chambers himself has remained an elusive—indeed, an unknown—figure, and *Witness* an unread book. Alger Hiss had pronounced his former comrade "a psychopath," and many of the "best people" continued to believe Hiss—even, it must be said, as their own belief in his innocence began to suffer some damaging doubts. Whatever the nature of those doubts, however, Hiss himself continued to be treated with a level of respect that was rarely accorded to Chambers outside the conservative anti-Communist press. You could sense that aura of respect in the obituaries and death notices occasioned by Hiss's passing in November. In keeping with its liberal orthodoxy, *The New Yorker* published a sentimental, down-home eulogy by Hiss's son, and in *The Nation*, which for decades has made Hiss's innocence an article of faith, Victor Navasky called him "a model citizen." In a great many other accounts of Hiss's death, Chambers remained the usual caricature.

This is but one of the many reasons that the publication of Sam Tanenhaus's *Whittaker Chambers: A Biography* (Random House, 1997) is a capital event. For with this marvelous book a gifted writer of a generation too young to have any personal memories of the Hiss Case has undertaken to give us a life of Chambers that is not only scrupulously documented and dispassionately composed, but also governed by precisely the kind of historical intelligence that has long been absent from critical accounts of its subject. *Whittaker Chambers: A Biography* is neither Cold War melodrama nor anti-Communist hagiography. It is the riveting story of a man of remarkable talents and remarkable suffering (remarkable flaws, too) who had the great misfortune to have "lived close to the making of history"—in his case, the history of the Communist movement in America.

It is thus, among much else, one of the best books ever written about the Communist experience in America—a narrative, as compelling as a good novel, that exhibits a profound understanding of what made a young man of Chambers's literary and intellectual gifts a Communist in the first place, what moved him to make his shattering break with the Communist Party, and then, faced with the horrific implications of the Hitler-Stalin pact in the summer of 1939, begin his long ordeal in attempting to alert the U.S. government to the operations of the underground espionage apparatus that had already penetrated the ranks of its own bureaucracy at astonishingly high levels of responsibility.

Tanenhaus's book is also a chronicle of three troubled families caught up in the vortex of the political traumas of their time: the dysfunctional and somewhat disreputable family into which Chambers himself was born; the family he created when he married Esther Shemitz, a painter he met at gatherings of the John Reed Club in 1929, the year of its founding; and the Hiss family—Alger, his wife Priscilla, and their children—to whom Whittaker and Esther Chambers were far more closely attached than either Alger or Priscilla Hiss could ever bring themselves to acknowledge, lest the fiction of Alger's innocence be seen to be the spectacular act of mendacity it was.

Not the least of Tanenhaus's many accomplishments in this biography is the mastery he brings to his vivid accounts of the very disparate social milieux that shaped Chambers's life—and indeed, his character. To scenes as different as Columbia College in the 1920s, where Chambers formed his friendship with Meyer Schapiro, and the Communist bohemia of the late 1920s and early 1930s, where he met and married Esther Shemitz, and the atmosphere of the *New Masses*, the Communist journal in which Chambers made his first literary reputation; to the nether world of the Soviet underground apparatus in Washington and the frantic regimen this imposed upon Chambers and his family, the terrors involved in his flight from Party discipline, his emergence as a writer for *Time* and his subsequent involvement with William Buckley's *National Review*—to these and a good many other diverse subjects essential to his story Tanenhaus brings a first-rate narrative gift and an undeceived grasp of political nuance. The cast of characters he is obliged to deal with is enormous, and enormously varied. In what other biography are we likely to find figures as different as Meyer Schapiro and Richard Nixon? Yet Tanenhaus somehow manages to give us a persuasive account of all of them without allowing them to divert his narrative from its central focus on Chambers himself. At times even his footnotes contribute something essential to the narrative without interrupting it.[1]

[1] This one, for example, about the fate of Lionel Trilling's novel, *The Middle of the Journey* (1947), in which the character of Gifford Maxim was based on Chambers, whom Trilling had met when they were undergraduates at Columbia in the 1920s: "It puzzled Trilling for many years that his publisher, Viking, did not reissue the novel in 1948–49. Since the book bore many intriguing parallels to the Hiss Case, it was likely to excite fresh interest. Unbeknownst to Trilling, Viking's publisher, Ben Huebsch, was a Communist and had quietly offered his services to the Hiss defense."

It is, however, in its account of the Hiss Case and its aftermath that Tanenhaus faced his greatest challenge, for the story of the two Hiss trials has been brilliantly recounted at least twice before: first in *Witness* and then in Allen Weinstein's *Perjury: The Hiss-Chambers Case* (1978). Yet on this subject, too, the challenge is triumphantly met in Tanenhaus's narrative. For one thing, he brings to it a spare, unornamented prose that renders the complexity of the courtroom drama with a clarity and concision it has never before been given. There is nothing here of the anger and remorse and bitter disappointment that colored Chambers's own account of the trials in *Witness*. At the same time, there is no need—as there was in Weinstein's *Perjury*—to conduct an uphill battle against liberal opinion by piling on an overabundance of incriminating detail. Tanenhaus takes nothing for granted in his account of the Hiss trials, yet at this distance in time and after his own deep immersion in the evidence that was at issue, he well understands that history has already rendered its judgment in the Hiss Case, and tells the story accordingly.

He well understands, moreover, that the judgment of history has effectively reversed the judgment of the "best people" at the time of the trials themselves. Then it was Hiss, the convicted felon still proclaiming his innocence, who was deemed to be the hero and martyr of the affair, and Chambers, who had rendered his country a great service, who was put down as a turncoat and a villain. Now, at last, it is more widely recognized with what cold contempt for his country and for the truth Hiss continued to lie—to his loyal supporters as well as to us.

Writing about the effect of the Hiss trials on Chambers, Tanenhaus recalls:

> No one seemed to acknowledge that he too was a casualty of the case, with an "incurable wound." Scarcely a word was written about Chambers's tribulations—on the career he had lost; on the manifold indignities he had withstood, the gossip, the strenuous defamations; on the pain to his family. Instead,

> he remained for many the monster conjured up by Lloyd Paul Stryker, "bland, dumpy, and devious," in one assessment.

About the refusal of the liberals to acknowledge Hiss's guilt, Tanenhaus is also very persuasive in recalling us to the views of the anti-Communist Left at the time of the trials and its immediate aftermath:

> This failure, suggested one shrewd analyst, the literary critic Leslie Fiedler, grew out of "the implicit dogma of American liberalism," which inflexibly assumed that in any political drama "the liberal per se is the hero." For Hiss's supporters to admit his guilt also meant admitting "that mere liberal principle is not itself a guarantee against evil; that the wrongdoer is not always the other—'they' and not 'us'; that there is no magic in the words 'left' or 'progressive' or 'socialist' that can prevent deceit and abuse of power."

About the trials and their aftermath, too, Tanenhaus's summary is definitive: "Every major question was met and answered. What sets the Hiss Case apart, then and now, was not its mystery but the passionate belief of so many that Hiss must be innocent no matter what the evidence."

Reading the account of Chambers's last years in Tanenhaus's book, I was reminded of the final chapter in Arthur Koestler's autobiography, *The Invisible Writing* (1954). Quoting from an attack upon his work by Raymond Mortimer, the former literary editor of *The New Statesman* and *The Nation*, who had written that "if I find Mr. Koestler's writing unlikeable, it is because he accepts as normal what I believe and hope is abnormal," Koestler responded as follows about the experience of his own generation, which was also Whittaker Chambers's:

> It was entirely normal for a writer, an artist, politician or teacher with a minimum of integrity to have several narrow

> escapes from Hitler and/or Stalin, to be chased and exiled, and to get acquainted with prisons and concentration camps. It was by no means abnormal for them, in the early Thirties, to regard Fascism as the main threat, and to be attracted, in varying degrees, by the great social experiment in Russia. Even today, about one quarter of the electorate in France and Spain, and a much higher percentage among the intellectuals, regard as "normal" to vote for the Communist Party. Even today the displaced persons, the scum of the earth of the post-war era, number several millions. Finally, it was quite normal for six million European Jews to end their lives in a gas chamber. . . . Yet the majority of well-meaning citizens . . . believe and hope that prisons and firing squads and gas chambers and Siberian slave camps just "do not happen" to ordinary people unless they are deliberately looking for trouble.

This was the kind of knowledge of history that Chambers, too, brought to his mission as an informer in the Hiss Case and, as a writer, in *Witness*. It is a similar command of the history of our time that makes *Whittaker Chambers: A Biography* essential reading for the present generation.

February 1997

Who Was Josephine Herbst?

Condemn the fault and not the actor of it?

—Measure for Measure

THERE is a passage in an essay by Henry James—it occurs in the obituary article he wrote on "Dumas the Younger" in 1895—which defines very exactly the feeling we are likely to experience when, at a certain age, we see the people we have known and who have meant a good deal to us pass away and become in death something very different from what they were in life, both in their own lives and in ours.

> One of the things that most bring home his time of life to a man of fifty [James wrote] is the increase of the rate at which he loses his friends. Some one dies every week, some one dies every day, and if the rate be high among his coevals it is higher still in the generation that, on awakening to spectatorship, he found in possession of the stage. He begins to feel his own world, the world of his most vivid impressions, gradually become historical. He is present, and closely present, at the process by which legend grows up.

For the past year or so I have had reason to ponder this passage a good deal as I have read—first in manuscript, then in galleys, and finally in its published form—*Josephine Herbst* (Atlantic Monthly Press/Little Brown, 1984), the biography which Elinor Langer has devoted to my old friend. When Josie Herbst died in 1969, I wasn't yet, to be sure, a man of fifty. I was almost ten years younger than that. Nevertheless, both her death and its aftermath gave me for the first time and to an extent unequaled by the passing of any other writer or artist I have known precisely the perspective, with all of its attendant nuances, that James spoke of. They gave me, that is, my first experience of seeing "the world of [my] most vivid impressions, gradually become historical." And now, with the publication of Elinor Langer's book these fifteen years later, I have the distinct feeling of finding myself "present, and closely present, at the process by which legend grows up." For if I read the signs correctly, Josie Herbst is about to be readmitted—and with a certain fanfare, too—to the public arena of literature and politics where, before her fall, she had passed so much of her adult life. It will not be primarily as an admired author, however, that she will now be rediscovered. Almost all of her writings have long been out of print, and few of the enthusiasts who are now eagerly preparing to assist in her elevation to stardom can be expected to have read them. This time it will not be as a novelist or journalist or memoirist that Josie Herbst will be welcomed into the company of the elect—not yet, anyway—but as a radical heroine and martyr of the feminist movement. Which, if this should come to pass, would tell us—as all such acts of canonization do—a good deal more about the strange times in which we are now living than it would about the tormented life and the failed work of the woman herself.

To the world that presides over canonizations of this sort—the world where reputations are made, influence wielded, and significant sums of money dispensed—Josie Herbst had become a ghostly figure in the years that I knew her, the last dozen years of her long life. Although recognized by name in the councils of the literary establishment, she was nonetheless shunned and "forgotten"—a writer who, though she might still be expected at some future date to make a comeback, was pretty much left to make it on her own. Except to a small circle of (mostly younger) friends and admirers and an even smaller circle of survivors from her own generation, she had dropped out of sight. Whether this constituted a withdrawal on her part (which to some degree it was) or an outright rejection by her contemporaries (which in part it also was) is a matter likely to be a subject of debate and speculation now that her life and career are up for reexamination. For all practical purposes, however, she was in the years that I knew her an "unknown" figure. She was ignored, she was unread, and she was very poor—living, as a matter of fact, largely on handouts from her friends, a few of whom had some money but most of whom were, like myself, just getting by on modest salaries and makeshift incomes. More often than not in those days she was reduced to wearing hand-me-down clothes, and she spent much of her time, especially in winter, since her house in Pennsylvania had neither central heating nor indoor plumbing, residing in one borrowed apartment after another. She was not only broke, she was broken—shattered by the burdens of an unhappy life that she was desperately attempting to come to terms with and never quite succeeding.

That she was also in those years a woman of tremendous vitality and spirit, a sparkling talker and articulate storyteller possessed of a vivid personality, an appealing sense of humor, and a genius for making herself interesting and even endearing; a woman, moreover, for whom the glamour and the hardship of the old literary life had never lost their magical spell—all of this only added to the high drama of her situation and the terrible poignancy of her shattered hopes. For make no mistake about it, it was as a failure and as a peculiarly significant failure—as a failed writer and as a failed woman—that some of us knew her in those last years. Call her, if you like, a heroine and a martyr—that, certainly, will be the approach of those now bent on enlisting Josie Herbst in their various causes—but to do so is, among much else, to sentimentalize a tragedy. It was, in any case, as an example of a certain kind of failure that we knew her, and as a failure, oddly enough, that she made her claim upon us.

In the biography that Elinor Langer has now given us—the first to be devoted to Josephine Herbst—no attempt has been made to soften this sense of failure or to shift responsibility for it onto others. Langer understands very well that, whatever else may have been involved, the principal cause of Josie Herbst's undoing was Josie Herbst herself, and she doesn't flinch from disclosing a good deal of ugly detail—much of which will be a revelation even to those few who think they know the subject well—in the course of telling her absorbing story. There are villains in the book, and some surprising ones, too, and no shortage of mean-spirited and even horrific actions, all meticulously recounted. But it is one of the virtues of this book that its author never attempts to disguise or to mitigate the role played by Josie herself in some of the most terrible episodes of her life. Langer is an unsparing writer, and a very gifted one, too, and it is a mark of her candor that the tale that is told in *Josephine Herbst* is almost unrelievedly grim. She not only has a keen grasp of the wretchedness that dominated so much of Josie Herbst's life, but she also has had the skill to so arrange the narrative that many of the most horrifying events are told in Josie Herbst's own words—though not, of course, from her point of view alone. Langer maintains her own authorial voice throughout, and while her sympathy for Josie Herbst is openly stated and deeply felt, in biographical matters it does not blind her—except in one outstanding regard—to her subject's more egregious failings.

On only one issue—but one that is absolutely central to the life of Josephine Herbst—can Langer be said to have failed, and failed utterly, to take hold of her subject with the requisite tough-mindedness and deal frankly with its implications. That issue is politics, about which Langer appears to share so many of the illusions that disfigured Josie Herbst's life and work that she can no more bring herself to deal with them than Josie herself could. As a result, Langer is obliged to lapse into a kind of silence or else take refuge in a kind of innocence or insouciance about the one phenomenon which, more than any other, caused the woman she is writing about to become a casualty of her time. That phenomenon, of course, is Stalinism in all of its many manifestations, political and cultural. About the role of Stalinism, then, both in Josie Herbst's life and in Elinor Langer's book, there is much to be said, and I shall address that issue here in its appropriate place. Astonishingly, Langer leaves the subject untouched. Yet the life of Josephine Herbst cannot really be understood in isolation from the Stalinist ethos that shaped so crucial a part of it.

In writing about Elinor Langer's *Josephine Herbst*, however, I cannot pretend to speak as a disinterested observer. I must declare my interest, which, both in relation to Josie Herbst and in regard to Langer's book, has been a very close and somewhat paradoxical one. It is not only that I knew Josie Herbst and spent a great many hours in conversation with her over a period of years, or even that I felt—despite our many differences—a deep affection for her. There is more to it than that. Shortly before her death, Josie Herbst made an arrangement with Yale University for the sale of her papers, and as a result an extensive Josephine Herbst archive was established at Yale's Beinecke Library. At the time she made this arrangement, Josie asked me to serve as the executor of her estate in the event of her death. This I agreed to do. When she died, I therefore found myself with the sole responsibility for granting access to her papers. This meant, among other things, that no serious biography of Josephine Herbst could be written without my cooperation. Perhaps I should add that restrictions had to be placed on the papers in the interest of protecting the privacy of many living persons. All her life Josie had been a tireless correspondent.

Often, especially in her later years, she made copies of her letters. In some cases her letters were later returned to her en bloc. Her correspondence with certain writers she had known—Katherine Anne Porter, for example—was copious. Friends frequently confided their innermost secrets to her; perhaps at times they even invented some for her benefit. It was not unusual for casual acquaintances, people she hardly knew but upon whom she had made an emphatic impression, to bare their souls when writing to her—especially in response to her own letters, which were often marvelous. In addition to the letters there are also notebooks. Some of these, too, deal with intimate affairs, her own and others'. Josie appears to have kept everything. The papers are voluminous. Obviously some sort of limit had to be placed on access to them, and I made certain that this would be done. I have never myself read through the entire archive; as far as I know, Langer is the only person to have done so. But in the period immediately following Josie's death I read just enough in these papers to acquire a pretty good notion of what their potential might be for causing pain, embarrassment, or worse to a great many people. I took it as part of my task as executor to ensure that this would not happen.

Exactly why Josie Herbst selected me for this task is not a question to which I can give a definitive answer. I frankly don't know for certain. She had several friends with whom she shared political confidences (I now realize) she never shared with me; and there were others she was closer to in other ways. She certainly knew there were many political issues about which we disagreed categorically, and she was well aware, too, that there were many aspects of her life about which she had been less than candid with me. The painful truth is, she lied much and she concealed much. (But this, of course, I did not discover until after her death.) I can only assume that about the things that mattered most to her at that time she trusted my judgment, and that in any case she wanted an executor who would allow the truth to be told about her life when the time came to tell it. I think it was important to her, too, to know that her literary affairs would not fall into the hands of an academic. She had a very low opinion of the way the professors of literature were coming to deal with writers of her generation. (Carlos Baker's biography of Hemingway, whom she had known well in earlier years, was a particular object of scorn; she could rail about it for hours. And some of the interpretations then being made of the work of her friend Nathanael West prompted similar outbursts.) About all that, anyway, we were agreed; it was a subject we discussed many times. That she was also fond of me I knew, and that no doubt contributed to her decision. Perhaps being childless, she had come to think of my relation to her as somehow filial. (She was thirty-six years my senior—roughly the same age as my mother. Her first novel, *Nothing Is Sacred*, was published the year I was born.) As far as I know, moreover, she never spoke ill of me. This, alas, was unusual with Josie. She had a volatile temper, and was not always in control of it. She also had a nasty habit of saying—and writing—terrible things about her friends, not only those she had for some reason broken with, but even some who remained close and who were important to her survival. Some of this was mere gossip and banter, but some of it was designed to cause pain and it did. Whatever the reason, I appear to have been among those exempted from this disagreeable practice. We never quarreled.

Very soon after her death I faced the first test of the trust she had placed in me. Obliged to go through the things she had left in the little stone house in Bucks County that had been her home since the Twenties—but which she had never owned—I discovered, buried under a pile of old clothes at the bottom of an ancient steamer trunk in the attic, a parcel of papers neatly wrapped in brown paper. On the outside was written, unmistakably in Josie's own hand, the word "Destroy." It frankly never occurred to me for a moment that I should follow this injunction, or indeed was meant to. Josie had lived in that house for forty years with a wood-burning stove in the living room, and she had ample opportunity to consign to its flames whatever papers she wished to destroy. I assumed—and Langer's biography seems to confirm—that Josie could not bring herself either to destroy or to take responsibility for preserving what this parcel contained. What it contained, as it turned out, were the letters, which had been returned to her, that chronicle one of the key episodes of her life. This was the love affair with another woman, Marion Greenwood, that led directly to the breakup of Josie's marriage to John Herrmann—an event that had caused her the deepest unhappiness of her life, and from which in fact she never recovered.

These letters proved to be important in another respect. For they did much, though far from everything, to explain one of the mysteries of Josie's later years: why it was that, despite years of work on what she well understood was the best writing she had ever done in her life and the strong and repeated encouragement of her friends—Saul Bellow and Alfred Kazin among them—Josie could never bring her own volume of memoirs to completion. She had a publisher ready to produce the book, and everyone who read the completed portions of it expected it to be a masterpiece—her first, by the way. Yet it was never finished, and I now realize that there was never any possibility of its being finished. For Josie could never deal with either the sexual or the political events that had destroyed her life, and neither could she deny them. But on this matter, too, I shall have more to say here in the appropriate place. Like so much else in Josie Herbst's life, it brings us back to the ugly issue of Stalinism, which came to play an important role in her marriage, in its breakup, and in the life she lived thereafter.

She was born in Sioux City, Iowa, on March 5, 1892. (The year is worth noting, for beginning in the Twenties Josie gave 1897 as the date of her birth.) Her parents were poor, respectable, small-town people who had migrated to Iowa from their native Pennsylvania with two baby daughters. Josie's father, who had a farm implement business that failed, was amiable but unambitious. Her mother, whom Josie adored, was a more spirited character, interested in reading and an avid storyteller herself, and never quite reconciled to life in the Iowa provinces. It was from the stories that she told of her family and its travails that Josie drew much of the material for her fiction.

Josie was the first of the Herbst daughters to be born in Iowa. Her younger sister Helen followed three years later, and they both grew up sharing their mother's contempt for Iowa and its benighted ways. Like a good many American writers of her generation who came out of the Middle West, Josie had determined from an early age to leave it. But this was not a mission easily accomplished. Lacking money, she was in and out of college for eight years, working at one small-town job or another to pay for her education, and desperately lonely and unhappy the whole time. She first attended Morningside College while living at home, then the University of Iowa and the University of Washington until, at the age of twenty-five, she made it to Berkeley, where she graduated from the University of California in 1918.

She seems always to have wanted to be a writer, and it was at Berkeley that she was first encouraged in that ambition by one of her professors. It was there, too, that for the first time she found a radical milieu hospitable to her own rebellious spirit. "I always knew," Josie wrote her mother at this time, "that somewhere in the world were people who could talk about the things I wanted to talk about and do the things I wanted to do and in some measure at least I have found them."

> Nothing Josie did with her friends in San Francisco [writes Langer] seems very remarkable now. They listened to speeches and climbed Mount Tamalpais and shared festive bohemian dinners . . . or just sat around . . . arguing about the war and capitalism and wondering what was going to happen next.

All the same, it marked the real beginning—a late, hard-won beginning—of Josie's adult life, and not only because of what it contributed to her political or literary outlook. "For the first time in her life," writes Langer, "she was comfortable with men."

Despite this initiation into radical bohemia, however, Josie had still never had a real love affair when she arrived in New York in the fall of 1919, and it was never her fate to be lucky in love. When she did have her first affair, she was twenty-eight years old, and it ended badly. Her lover was Maxwell Anderson, who was later to achieve renown as a playwright but who was then an editorial writer for the *Globe,* a New York newspaper. The problem was he was married. It was through his wife, in fact, that Josie had met him soon after arriving in New York. For him the affair was a diversion and he soon ended it, but for Josie it was love. When, after the breakup, she discovered she was pregnant, she wanted to have the baby, but Anderson opposed it and persuaded her to have an abortion. It was a decision she bitterly regretted.

The novel that Josie afterwards wrote about this experience—it was never published, or indeed publishable—was pretty grim, a tale in the Dreiserian mode, but the real life story had an epilogue that even Dreiser might have hesitated to write. As she was recovering from the abortion, Josie was suddenly bombarded with appeals from her beloved younger sister. Like Josie, Helen had been determined to get out of Sioux City, but she hadn't yet made it. She had married her Sioux City boyfriend, who shared her worldly ambitions—he was later to have a distinguished career as a newspaper editor—and they had been desperately saving money to make their getaway. But now she found she was pregnant and she didn't want to have the baby. It would ruin their lives, she thought. Josie thought so, too, and so without ever disclosing to her sister (or to almost anyone else) the nature of the ordeal she had just been through herself, she encouraged Helen to have an abortion. Helen did, and she died as a result.

Overcome by guilt and remorse, Josie suffered something of a breakdown in the aftermath of her sister's death, and while she eventually pulled herself together it was an event that had a permanent—and damaging—effect on her life. Langer is right, I think, in observing that "when [Josie] lost Helen she lost part of herself and the most important relationships of the rest of her life were attempts in one way or another to bring her sister back." But there is more to it than that. For what this whole episode revealed was a fundamental fissure in Josie Herbst's character—a refusal of honesty and responsibility that turned out to be one of the deepest things about her. This was the hardest thing for Josie's friends to come to terms with after her death. It was certainly the hardest for me, especially since her whole personal style—both in private conversation and in her extraordinary letters—gave the impression of achieving a degree of candor and self-revelation that was both unusual and exemplary. The mask—or what Langer calls the "performance"—was so appealing that many of her friends have to this day refused to abandon their belief in it, preferring the fiction to the reality. And so great is their need to believe in that mask—for it is now theirs as well—that I doubt if even the revelations of Langer's biography will do much to modify it.

Despite the ordeals that Josie suffered in New York in the early Twenties, it was there that her literary career began in earnest, and there too that she became an active participant in the literary-radical-bohemian world which remained her spiritual home for the rest of her life. In 1920 she landed a job with H. L. Mencken and George Jean Nathan—not, by the way, on *The Smart Set*, but working on some of the "sleazier publications," as Langer correctly calls them, which they were also producing at that time. This led to the publication of her fiction in *The Smart Set*, and won her Mencken's support when she later tried to find a publisher for her novel about the Anderson affair. Her friends in this period included Genevieve Taggard, Mike Gold, Joseph Freeman, Floyd Dell, Jessica Smith, Alex Gumberg, Max

Eastman, and Albert Rhys Williams, all of whom were already ardent and active supporters of the Bolshevik Revolution. When she went to Europe in the spring of 1922, having saved enough money for the trip, she spent the summer traveling with Eastman and Williams, who then went on to Moscow while Josie herself settled in Berlin. There she remained for the better part of two years, working on the novel that she hadn't quite finished when she went off to Paris and met John Herrmann—"a young and beautiful boy," as she described him to Genevieve Taggard—with whom she instantly fell in love.

Herrmann was twenty-three; Josie was thirty-two, but passing for twenty-seven. He was extremely good-looking; she had never been beautiful. Like herself, he had just spent two years in Germany—in his case, Munich, where he had gone to study art history but where he had devoted himself instead to working on a novel. They were both Midwesterners. He was from Lansing, Michigan, the son of a prosperous, strait-laced businessman with whom he could not get along and not quite get along without. John was weak and Josie was strong. He was also already an alcoholic. On the day she was introduced to him at the Café du Dome in Montparnasse, he was suffering from a severe hangover. "Everything that was true when they parted," Langer writes, "was true when they met. Josie was ambitious and John was not ambitious, he preferred the company of the cafés and she preferred the solitude of the typewriter, he had confidence in his charm but not in his book and she had confidence in her book but not in her charm. But what became difficult oppositions when things were dissolving between them were magnetizing complements at the time they began."

In France their whirlwind romance had been an idyll of sorts, but when they returned to the United States, which they promptly did, there was trouble, of course. John was still dependent on his despised parents. He was also an incorrigible womanizer—he seems never to have been faithful to Josie for very long. What Josie wanted most was for them to live in rural

Connecticut, near writer-friends of hers, where they would live simply and work on their books. She was nothing if not determined to have her way. The only obstacle was money, and she solved that problem by blackmailing Maxwell Anderson, whose love letters she had kept. Langer doesn't use that ugly word, but that is what it came to—and John knew all about it. It was not, perhaps, the soundest basis for a serene relationship.

Off they went, then, to a small farmhouse in New Preston, Connecticut, in the fall of 1925. Josie afterwards called this period "The Hour of Counterfeit Bliss," and it was undoubtedly the happiest time in her life. But it was soon over. John's mother got wind of the fact that her son was living in sin, and she hired a private detective to investigate. As a result, since John could not resist the pressures of his family and there was always the hope of getting some money out of them, he was forced into marrying Josie. This was not what they had planned on doing. Josie always spoke of it, with varying degrees of humor, resentment, or sarcasm, as her "shotgun marriage"—though in truth, she wanted very much to be married to John Herrmann. And the hope of getting some money out of it was not unfounded—though, like everything else, this, too, didn't turn out as they had hoped. John's parents were persuaded to put up twenty-five hundred dollars for the old stone house in Bucks County that Josie wanted to buy—she had found it, as Langer writes, in "the eastern Pennsylvania countryside she had been hearing about from her mother all her life"—but John's father kept the deed in his own name. That house was to be the only home Josie had for the rest of her life, but it was never her house, and she had to fight hard to remain in it after the marriage had dissolved.

Still, they were together and they were living the literary life they wanted. In 1927, just before they moved to Pennsylvania, John's novel, *What Happens,* was published by Robert McAlmon in Paris, and it was refused entry into the United States on grounds of obscenity. (Morris Ernst took the case, and lost.) Josie's first published novel, *Nothing Is Sacred*, followed in 1928.

Hemingway and Ring Lardner provided the blurbs, and Ford Madox Ford and Katherine Anne Porter reviewed it favorably. Josie and John were both publishing in the magazines, too, though she more than he, and among the visitors they welcomed to Pennsylvania were Malcolm Cowley and Kenneth Burke. They spent some time with Hemingway in Key West.

By that time, however, they were being drawn into the political movement that came to play a dominant role in their lives. In 1930, at the suggestion of Mike Gold, they went to Russia to attend the International Congress of Revolutionary Writers in Kharkov. Langer describes this trip as "more of a lark than a pilgrimage," but "lark" doesn't strike one as quite the *mot juste* for it. In any case, John emerged from the experience a complete convert to Communism, and a dedicated supporter of the Soviet Union. Josie, though she expressed private doubts (as she always would), was also enthusiastic. "Perhaps as early as 1931 he joined the Communist Party," writes Langer. "It was something that Josie never did."

She was still primarily a writer; John was now less interested in literature than in political action. Josie's response to the political atmosphere was to re-interpret the story of her family's history in Marxist terms, and this is what she did in the trilogy of novels that was her main work of the Thirties—*Pity Is Not Enough* (1933), *The Executioner Waits* (1934), and *Rope of Gold* (1939). John's response, in the beginning at least, was to become a public speaker for Communist Party causes, but before long he was drawn into the Communist underground where, if the word of his widow Ruth Herrmann is to be believed, he achieved the historic distinction of being the man who introduced Whittaker Chambers to Alger Hiss.

Before that fateful drama was enacted, however, another more personal crisis had intervened to shatter what remained of their disintegrating marriage. Josie met Marion Greenwood. In the summer of 1932 Josie was at the Yaddo colony in Saratoga Springs by herself. John had taken her there, and then gone on to Michigan for the summer. Marion Greenwood, a young painter, very talented and very beautiful, arrived at the colony soon after Josie, and Josie fell madly in love with her. Josie had had romantic attachments to other women, but nothing like this. The affair that ensued quite swept her off her feet, and she was tenacious about keeping it going. And as it progressed she still harbored the illusion that she could keep her marriage going, too. Toward this end she contrived to bring John into the affair after her term at Yaddo was over. The three of them went off to Mexico together where Josie and John took turns, as it were, as Marion's lovers. It couldn't last, and it didn't. As sexually susceptible and as weakwilled as John was, he was clearly humiliated by the whole sordid experience, and he took off. In a panic, Josie chose her husband over her lover. She still couldn't believe her marriage was coming to an end—that, in fact, it was over. She clung to John as long as she could, but it was soon over, anyway.

Politically, the issue that most excited them in this period was the effort of the Communist Party to organize the farmers—to organize them, it is worth remembering, against the policies of the New Deal. John was much involved in this effort, and Josie wrote about it for the *New Masses*. "For Josie," Langer writes, "it was not only her moment of greatest identification with the farmers but of consonance with the Communist Party 'line.' " For John, it proved to be his ticket to the Communist underground. In 1934, he was summoned to Washington by Hal Ware, who presided over the special underground operation which Chambers, among others, was already serving. When Josie followed John to Washington, still hoping for a reconciliation, she lived in his apartment, and was thus in a position to know something—if not everything—about the secret Party work that John was engaged in. She knew Hal Ware, she knew Whittaker Chambers, and she knew at least enough about what they were doing to disapprove of it and ridicule it. Which was not, to say the least, the way to John's heart at that moment, but she did it anyway—

and not because she disagreed with Party policy, but ostensibly because she considered the work ineffective (or so Langer suggests). I think the real reason she disapproved was that she feared that she was losing John to his new involvement in the Party underground—which she was, and in more than one sense. For the woman John married after he finally broke with Josie and with whom he was already involved was his confidant in Party activities. (It was she, forty years later, who told Elinor Langer that John had introduced Chambers to Hiss over a lunch in Washington in 1934.) One of the things that Josie knew, too—it may have been the only important thing she ever knew about the whole operation—was that Alger Hiss was somehow involved. It was this knowledge that placed Josie, at the time of the Hiss case, in a position to change the course of history by revealing what she knew, but she never did. Out of her loyalty to the Left and out of her loyalty to John—with the passage of time, these became virtually identical in her mind—she not only didn't speak up, but she also offered her services to the Hiss defense lawyers. (She also lied a good deal to the FBI, and sent word to John, who had fled to Mexico, about what she had said.) Being a true believer in the ideals of the Left, she proved to be something of an embarrassment to Hiss's lawyers, however. She urged them to encourage Hiss to speak up in court by defending his political beliefs, which she knew to be Communist. But this, of course, would have identified Hiss as a Communist, and it was the whole point of the Hiss defense to deny that he had ever been one.[1] Yet she went along with that, too, and kept her silence—and at considerable personal cost to herself, for Chambers had already given her name, as well as John's, to the FBI, and she was frequently interrogated on the matter. This was no doubt one of the things that led to the denial of a passport when she applied for one in the Fifties.

[1] Allen Weinstein's *Perjury: The Hiss-Chambers Case* (Knopf, 1978) was the first work to provide a detailed account of Josie's role in the case.

There is much more to Josie Herbst's story, of course—the trips to Cuba, Germany, and Spain in the Thirties, the job she took with the Government in Washington after the United States entered the Second World War, and the reason she was fired from it; the breakup of her long friendship with Katherine Anne Porter, and the reasons for that; and the affair with the poet Jean Garrigue that was even more disastrous and far more protracted than the affair with Marion Greenwood—and Langer has told it all very vividly. Yet there is a sense in which it can truly be said that Josie Herbst's life came to an end when John Herrmann walked out of it for the last time, and that what remained in all her later years was a half-life of shadows and chimeras, of concealments and denials and lost hopes, which, though she no longer had the power, for the most part, to turn them into effective literary fictions, she became more and more adept at transforming into a fictional personality for herself, the dazzling mask that enchanted so many of her friends. Only once, in my own acquaintance with Josie, was I ever given a glimpse of the ravaged spirit that the mask so effectively concealed. I had been spending the weekend at the house in Pennsylvania, ostensibly to talk over the manuscript of the memoirs on which she was working. It was clear to me that she was stymied—I thought, of course, temporarily—and she talked about some of the reasons why she was having so much trouble writing this book. Lack of money, lack of time, problems with the house, distractions of every kind—as the litany continued, I could see that even she wasn't convinced by what she was saying, though her life was anything but comfortable or serene. Just before I left—we were standing in the doorway, about to walk down to the car—I said to her: "Josie, you must finish it. Why can't you finish it?" To my astonishment, she cried out: "It's *John*, I can't deal with John!" And she was so overcome with fits of sobbing that it took some time, and some drinks, before she could pull herself together. All I knew about John then was that he had left her for another woman. I knew nothing about his involvement with Hiss and

Chambers and Hal Ware—or Josie's, for that matter. I knew nothing about Marion Greenwood. But from that moment on I was never as confident as I had been that the memoirs would ever be finished.

What few of Josie's friends in her later years understood, I think—and it may be that Langer doesn't quite grasp it, either, though she provides ample evidence for it—is the degree to which Josie's experience as a woman, especially the experiences that she initiated, together with the passions and dishonesties that marked her political life, and the effort involved in concealing, for so much of the time, the true nature of both, had the effect of brutalizing her personality. There was a streak of sheer ruthlessness and brute callousness in her personality that is as observable in her personal relations, especially in her relations with her lovers, as it is in her politics, and it would be a mistake to think that politics was responsible for what finally must be regarded as a defect of character. Politics does not account for her role in Helen's death, for the blackmailing of Maxwell Anderson, or for the way she corrupted—there is no other word for it—her own beloved husband in the Marion Greenwood affair. All her life she was drawn to weak, vulnerable, romantic men and women, whose lives she hoped to overwhelm and control, and she could never quite understand why it was that in the end they always fled.

Yet, if politics does not explain Josie Herbst's character, it nonetheless contributed much to the brutalization I speak of. Which brings us to the question of Stalinism, and its role in Josie's life. It is in the nature of Stalinism for its adherents to make a certain kind of lying—and not only to others, but first of all to themselves—a fundamental part of their lives. It is always a mistake to assume that Stalinists do not know the truth about the political reality they espouse. If they don't know the truth (or all of it) one day, they know it the next, and it makes absolutely no difference to them politically. For their loyalty is to something other than the truth. And no historical enormity is so great, no personal humiliation or betrayal so extreme, no crime so heinous that it cannot be assimilated into the "ideals" that govern the true Stalinist mind, which is impervious alike to documentary evidence and moral discrimination.

Was Josie Herbst a true Stalinist? Despite all the reservations and criticisms she voiced in private and despite her many disagreements with the Communist Party and its policies, I think it must be said that for the most part she was. That wasn't all she was, of course, but in a large part of her mind for an important part of her life she was, all the same. The slaughter of the peasants in Stalin's collectivization campaign, the Moscow trials, the Great Terror and the Hitler-Stalin pact, not to mention a great many later developments in the post-World War II period—however much she may have suffered over them, she nonetheless swallowed them. There was a lot she choked on, but in the end she swallowed it all. Which is why she remained "loyal" in the Hiss case, and in many lesser causes as well. Whatever she disapproved or regretted or even disavowed—Langer cites many instances, and I could describe others—was always done privately, and never where it would make any difference, and always subsumed under the comforting and exonerating rubric of "What went wrong?" There was never an acknowledgment—even privately, as far as I know—that it was the whole political outlook that was wrong. There was no conception of how evil it all was.

It was the process of brutalization that resulted from all this, I believe, that first confused and then immobilized her as a writer once the audience ready to embrace radical certainties evaporated from the literary scene in the Forties. When she started to write again in the Fifties, it was in a very different mode—a mode of Proustian reminiscence in which the old certainties were dissolved in an evocation of cherished experience. In the memoirs even the most painful memories of the past are, so to speak, aestheticized in a style that Josie would have been incapable of commanding in the heyday of her radical involvement and personal rebellion. Upon this whole later phase of her literary work there is to be found, I believe, the influence of Jean Garrigue—the poet she met (again at Yaddo) in the winter of 1949–50, and with whom she promptly fell in love—and the influence of Jean Garrigue's literary tastes. Jean Garrigue had no interest in politics, no interest in social issues, no interest in anything having to do with the radical movement that had shaped Josie's adult life. She was a romantic aesthete, a lyrical poet of considerable delicacy and nuance whose interests were mainly confined to artistic and amatory experience. In all personal matters she was completely irresponsible, and she and Josie managed to cause each other a great deal of pain over the long course of their stormy attachment, but in literary matters Jean's influence proved, I think, to be decisive in the way Josie now conceived of writing her reminiscences. It is precisely their "aesthetic" character that sets them apart from all her earlier writing.

Yet there were some experiences that resisted this new mode of Proustian reminiscence, and they turned out to be the most crucial. The central emotional crisis of Josie Herbst's life was so intimately connected with its central political loyalty that there was no way of separating them. In the end, the late-blooming aesthetic writer of the memoirs lost out to the vanquished, silent survivor of the Thirties.

Josie Herbst's death in January 1969 came at a moment when events in the world of both politics and culture were swiftly bringing in their wake a significant change in attitude toward the radical movement of the Thirties. The emergence of the New Left in response to the Vietnam war and the accompanying eruption of a vigorous anti-government, anti-middle-class counterculture had the effect of casting even the most extreme Stalinist positions of Thirties radicalism in a new and more favorable light. Actions and beliefs which had long been regarded as morally repugnant because of their abject subservience to the interests of the Soviet Union and which, as we know, in some notable cases had led to spying and espionage, began to enjoy the benefit of a sweeping revisionism. Liberals who had once known better, or seemed to, now either tempered or abandoned their opposition to radical militancy, as liberals generally do when the tide is running in favor of the radical position. Even in the ranks of the most stalwart anti-Stalinist intellectuals there were some notable defections—such as Dwight Macdonald's and Philip Rahv's—to this revival of the radical dream. All of this made it possible for Stalinists who had survived the debacle of the Thirties and the investigations of the Fifties to come forward once again to bask in the rosy glow of yet another (promised) red dawn. As the call to revolution beckoned the young and the revivified romance of the Left renewed the celebrity of aging radicals, a kind of sainthood began to be conferred upon almost anyone who had once been identified with Stalinist causes and had not at any time publicly repudiated them.

Josie Herbst died just a little too soon to reap the full benefit of this historic reversal in her lifetime. By the late Sixties, when the new revisionism was beginning to acquire some real momentum and influence, she was too ill, too weak, too demoralized, and too scattered in her efforts to do much more than act as an interested but ineffectual witness to its development. That she welcomed it there can be no doubt. But at the time she was extremely discreet, if not actually devious, in what she said about it and to whom. To friends like myself, whom she knew to be unsympathetic to the radical cause, she often voiced skeptical and even critical views of its conduct. Without exactly denying her loyalty to the radical position—something she would never bring herself to do—she could nonetheless be quite vehement in her criticism of the actions and attitudes it was then engendering. Yet in speaking or writing to dedicated radicals or those she hoped to convert to the radical cause, she was even more vehement and a lot less guarded in her expressions of support. It is possible, of course, that this zigzag course reflected a genuinely divided attitude on her part, but I doubt if that was really the case. Elinor Langer's biography leaves little room for doubt in this matter.

Josie had been dead a very short time when I began receiving inquiries about the Yale archive. Given the political temper of the time, I naturally expected that any new interest in Josie would focus on whatever reputation she had as a radical and, more specifically, on her contribution to the so-called "proletarian" novel in the Thirties. But at the outset this was not usually the case. Most of the inquiries came from graduate students who had little or no acquaintance with the novels Josie had published between 1928 and 1947. Often these students did not even know what she had written. Some may have read an installment or two of the published memoirs. Others, to my astonishment, had read nothing by her. They had simply been given her name as a possible subject for research by faculty advisors who themselves knew little more about her than that she had once been associated with some famous writers—Hemingway, Dos Passos, et al.—in the Twenties and Thirties. Unembarrassed by their ignorance, most of these students were frankly fishing for "original" documents—letters, manuscripts, etc.—that might be turned into thesis material, and they weren't going to do any unnecessary reading until they knew what they had. They seemed to have no larger literary or intellectual interests, or indeed to have read anything that had not been assigned to them in a course. As kindly as I could, I told them that they would first have to read Josie's published work, which included short stories, essays, and a good deal of journalism in addition to the books, and then come back with more specific requests. The majority of them were never heard from again. It was all a ghastly confirmation of Josie's worst fears about the fate of literature in the academy.

Of the people who contacted me about Josie Herbst in the years immediately following her death, the most serious were the young women—there were never more than a few of them—

who had come to their interest in her through an involvement in and partial disenchantment with the radical movement of the Sixties, an experience that had somehow led to a rediscovery of her novels. It was very much as a woman and as a radical that Josie interested them. This was the first indication I was given that Josie's posthumous reputation, if she were to have one, would owe something—I had no idea then how much—to the feminist movement, and specifically to that branch of it in which the residue of Sixties radicalism was quickly finding a home. (For what it is worth, the unserious applicants were all men.) Obviously these young women had been moved—in a way, it must be said, that I had never been—by the portrayal of female experience in the novels and by the sensibility of the female radical who had written them. This response inevitably prompted an interest in Josie herself, for virtually all of her fiction is transparently autobiographical in one degree or another. It didn't take long, moreover, to discover that Josie had herself been a far more compelling character than any she created in her fiction, and this, in turn, led to expressions of interest in writing her biography.

This, more or less, is how Elinor Langer came to write the biography that has now been published nearly a dozen years after she first contacted me, and how I came to play a role of sorts in its preparation. Langer gives an account of how she came to the subject in the very first chapter of the book:

> In 1973, when I first heard of Josephine Herbst, I was living by myself in a small town in Vermont and teaching at a small college . . . . [Y]et what I appeared to be doing and what I was doing were two different things because, like so many people I knew then, I was in retreat from the radical movement of the 1960s, and in reality I was spending most of my time mulling over what had happened to the movement, and to myself, and why. . . . [T]o the extent that it was possible in my immediate

> circumstances I included in my brooding and my browsing as much of the literature of the 1930s as I was able to find—something I had always done, more or less, because the 1930s had felt like family history to me even before the "New Left" was born but which I now pursued with a greater urgency than ever before. On a visit to Chicago, in a secondhand bookstore, on a shelf labeled "Marxism," I found a collection of essays by participants in the events of the 1930s called *As We Saw the Thirties*, and I bought it as a matter of course. The essay on literature had been written by Granville Hicks, and in it . . . was a small, inviting reference to a trilogy by Josephine Herbst. Not much . . . but it was enough to send me to the university library the following morning and home with the novels [*Pity Is Not Enough, The Executioner Waits*, and *Rope of Gold*] that very day.
>
> My notes from my first reading of the trilogy are a cross between a sigh of relief and a shout of joy: as if I were a traveler who had somehow gotten detached from my party, and Josephine Herbst were the rescuer sent out to bring me home. . . . The decades between when the trilogy was written and when I was reading it simply fell away from me as I held it in my hands and I felt as if a conversation brusquely terminated with the turn of the 1970s had suddenly been renewed. . . . Of my literary reactions I was far less certain.

Whatever her disappointments with the radical movement of the Sixties may have been, Langer emerged from the experience with a good many of her radical pieties intact, and it was clearly in the interest of vindicating them, as well as of attempting to gain a greater understanding of them, that she was drawn to the subject of Josephine Herbst in the first place. In this respect, as in others, her book is very much a product of the cultural ethos of the Seventies. For one of the least examined aspects of the political and cultural history of the Seventies may be found in the widespread effort that began to be made in that decade to justify the spirit of the radical movement of the Sixties, its failures no less than its successes, by rewriting the history of the Thirties. In attributing all manner of innocence and idealism to Thirties radicalism, even in its most blatantly Stalinist manifestations, and by minimizing, if not actually obliterating, all trace of its evil consequences, this revisionist historiography succeeded in exonerating Sixties radicalism, too, of its worst elements. This impulse certainly plays a large role in the book that Elinor Langer has spent a decade writing, and there can be no doubt that her book belongs to this literature of exoneration.

That it has also turned out to be something more than that is a tribute to Langer's honesty about and understanding of Josie Herbst's character and the nature of her personal tragedy. A radical feminist herself, at least when she began to work on this book, Langer had clearly intended to cast Josie in the role of a radical feminist heroine, but it couldn't be done. All the evidence—mostly, of course, Josie's own evidence—defeated the idea, and Langer found herself obliged to portray a very different figure. This will not prevent others from drafting Josie Herbst's life into the service of feminist causes, now that the life itself has been so meticulously documented. Ideology, when sufficiently motivated, has a way of overlooking obstructive truths. But Langer, anyway, has escaped most, if not quite all, of the temptations to give ideology priority over truth in this matter.

The same, alas, cannot be said about Langer's handling, or mishandling, of the role of Stalinism in Josie Herbst's life and work. In this matter *Josephine Herbst* does indeed belong to the literature of exoneration. To the whole question of Stalinism and its place in Josie's life Langer devotes exactly one footnote and little more. The footnote (on page 199) reads as follows:

> I have frequently been asked during the course of this work whether or not Josie was a "Stalinist" and there are those who believe, primarily on the basis of her connection with the Communist Party during this period, that she was. If her rela-

> tionship to the American Communist Party and in turn its relationship to the Soviet Union automatically makes her a Stalinist, so be it, but for her long record of independent thought and action—albeit in association with the Communist Party—for my part I find "Stalinism" not only a meaningless, but, indeed, a misleading description.

One could write a lengthy dissertation on the implications of this footnote, and it would begin with an examination of exactly what is meant by its reference to Josie's "long record of independent thought and action—albeit in association with the Communist Party." *Albeit*, indeed. As if the Communist Party had ever, in Josie's lifetime, accorded a place for independent thought and action in its programs or policies or in the use it made of writers like Josie! There were, as I have noted, many instances in which Josie criticized the Party and opposed its course of action. But when she was overruled and told, in effect, to shut up, she shut up and she stayed shut up, however much she may have suffered in the process. One wonders if Langer really understands what the word "independent" means in this context.

The sad truth is that Langer cannot deal with the issue of Stalinism and the history that lies behind it. Even on the question of Alger Hiss's guilt, though the evidence—especially Ruth Herrmann's revelation of John Herrmann's role in introducing Hiss to Chambers in 1934—has obliged her to agree that Hiss was indeed lying and that he *was* working for the Communist underground, just as Chambers claimed, she still cannot quite face the basic truth of the matter. Hiss even lied to *her* about John Herrmann, as she candidly reports in her book, and yet she goes on to write about the case as follows:

> The Hiss case is one of the greatest miasmas of American politics. . . . There are no arguments which have not been shaken, there is no evidence which has not been obfuscated,

there have been no sentences either uttered or written that have not been parsed into nonsense.

Now this is simply not true. Despite massive and protracted legal attempts to have Hiss's conviction for perjury reversed, the verdict has stuck because the evidence could not—despite Hiss's best efforts—be obfuscated. It has withstood every challenge. To write about the Hiss case in this manner is not an attempt to deal with the historical truth—never mind the moral truth—but an attempt to escape it.

And this, finally, is what Elinor Langer attempts to do with the whole question of Stalinism, both in Josie Herbst's life and in itself—escape it. To have faced it, I suppose, would have meant facing something in her own radical past that she has not yet come to terms with. And so, in yet another generation of disenchanted but nonetheless loyal radicals, the posture of innocence is invoked as a screen against the political realities of our time. It is sad to see this perpetuated in a new generation of writers—and especially in a writer as good as Elinor Langer—but that too, I am afraid, must be counted as an important part of the legacy that Josephine Herbst's silence has bequeathed us.

September 1984

The Life and Death of Lillian Hellman

I am not interested in the degree to which she told the literal truth.

—Marsha Norman, *The New York Times*, 1984

I never took Lillian's politics very seriously.

—Robert Brustein, *The New Republic*, 1984

OF the many remarkable things to be noted about the life of Lillian Hellman, who died on June 30, 1984, none was more remarkable than the quality of the sentiment that greeted its end. Even as the obligatory eulogies were delivered, they seemed to contain an unmistakable note of embarrassment—a grudging awareness that at the time of her death the reputation of Lillian Hellman was well on its way to becoming a shambles. Only in Robert Brustein's bizarre tribute in *The New Republic*, however, was this note given explicit expression.

> Previously characterized by enemies as a fellow traveler who continued to embrace Stalinism long after most other American intellectuals had abandoned it [Brustein wrote], Lillian was now being called a liar and a bully. Herself a victim of blacklisting, she was now thought to be engaged in muf-

> fling the free expression of others, leading some to say that she embraced the First Amendment only in her own defense. It was a miserable epilogue to what should have been a respected old age.[1]

Yet even Brustein found something to admire in what he called "her anger," which in the end, as he described it, "became a freefloating, cloud-swollen tempest that rained on friend and foe alike." It did not rain on friend and foe with the same consequences, of course. As *The New York Times* reported, "Miss Hellman's $2.25 million suit [against Mary McCarthy] cost Miss McCarthy $26,000 in legal fees."[2]

Lest that picturesque reference to a "cloudswollen tempest" mislead us into imagining the aged Lillian Hellman as a kind of liberal King Lear—possessed, as John Hersey quaintly put it, by "a rage of the mind against all kinds of injustice"—it is worth remembering that she was fiercely determined, in typical Stalinist fashion, to silence her critics and, if possible, to bring about their ruin.

Her end was certainly "miserable," as Robert Brustein said, but it was no "epilogue": it was perfectly consistent with the attitudes and activities of a lifetime. Even *The New York Times*, which generally shies away from such esoteric matters, acknowledged that Lillian Hellman's lawsuit against Mary McCarthy "revived the split between American Stalinists and anti-Stalinists of the 1930s." Yet "revived" was not quite the word that was wanted in that sentence; "reflected" or "continued" would have been more accurate. For in the mind of Lillian Hellman, it was a split that was never forgotten or forgiven, and she took her revenge upon her anti-Stalinist adversaries as soon as she felt rich enough and powerful enough to do so.

[1] "Epilogue to Anger," *The New Republic*, August 13/20,1984.

[2] "McCarthy Is Recipient Of MacDowell Medal," *The New York Times*, August 27, 1984.

No one knows this better than Robert Brustein, who less than ten years ago dedicated one of his books, *The Culture Watch: Essays on Theatre and Society, 1969–1974*, to Lionel Trilling—the same Lionel Trilling who was so egregiously maligned in the pages of Lillian Hellman's *Scoundrel Time*. Yet in nothing that Brustein wrote on the occasion of Lillian Hellman's death was there a word said in defense of either Mary McCarthy or Lionel Trilling. It would no doubt have been considered bad taste to invoke "the split between American Stalinists and anti-Stalinists of the 1930s," yet Brustein managed, all the same, to make a veiled reference to it when he spoke sarcastically of "American intellectuals still waging fifty-year-old wars"—a reference that had the effect of mocking the victims of Hellman's malevolent words and actions while appearing to remain "above" such pettifogging interests. In any case, when it came to "waging fifty-year-old wars," Lillian Hellman was herself a veritable field marshal with plenty of loyal troops at her command.

It was to be expected, of course, that she would be praised at the time of her death. The etiquette of the occasion called for panegyric, and there was no shortage of admirers to provide it in ample measure. She had a great many friends in positions of power, influence, and high reputation. She had many political allies who supported her various vendettas. And she had something else, too—the kind of money and position that enabled her to bestow (and withhold) rewards. For a good many years, moreover, it had been an established practice in the literary world for writers to lavish her work with the most extravagant encomiums; and her personal political history—notwithstanding the fact that she was the very model of the American literary Stalinist—had likewise won her a special status as, of all things, a moral heroine. The chorus of acclaim that had become an expected accompaniment to every new turn in Hellman's career had reached its fulsome climax in 1976 with the publication of *Scoundrel Time*—the third volume in the trilogy of her so-called "memoirs," and one of the most poisonous and dishonest testaments ever written by an American author.

It tells us a good deal about the temper of the times that this malicious and mendacious book, written to even old scores with her anti-Stalinist "friends," was widely hailed on its publication as a work of awesome moral probity. Reviewing it on the front page of *The New York Times Book Review*, Maureen Howard was moved to invoke the shades of Emerson and Thoreau as appropriate points of comparison, and ended her catalogue of praise with a reference to Camus—a writer whose entire career as an artist and a moralist represented a complete repudiation of everything Lillian Hellman stood for. Oh, how her friends rallied round that detestable book! John Hersey spoke of Hellman as "a moral force, almost an institution of conscience" in the pages of *The New Republic*—the same *New Republic*, incidentally, whose editor had just rejected a less favorable account of *Scoundrel Time* written by Alfred Kazin. And when Diana Trilling sought to set the record straight by answering the charges made against her and Lionel Trilling in *Scoundrel Time*, her publisher—who was also Hellman's publisher—promptly refused to publish what she had written on this subject, an act that elicited not the slightest word of protest from this "institution of conscience."

Yet it was undoubtedly with *Scoundrel Time* that Lillian Hellman, flushed with money, spite, overconfidence, and the incipient paranoia which dominated her later years, began to overplay her hand. Memories might be short and a sense of moral discrimination nonexistent in the well-heeled literary and theatrical society that had made her its heroine, but elsewhere history—and Lillian Hellman's role in it—had not been entirely forgotten. Writers who had reason to remember what the blight of Stalinism had once visited upon American political and cultural life began to speak up—not only Diana Trilling, but Murray Kempton in *The New York Review of Books*, William Phillips in *Partisan Review*, and Irving Howe in *Dissent*, among others. One focus of Hellman's attack in *Scoundrel Time* had been the anti-Communist Left and the liberals allied with it, and she specifically maligned the editors and writers of *Partisan Review* and *Commentary* for their alleged failure to come to the defense of those who were questioned about their Communist Party activities by Senator McCarthy's committee and other committees of the United States Congress in the late Forties and Fifties. She explained their alleged delinquency in the following manner:

> Perhaps that, in part, was the penalty of nineteenth-century immigration. The children of timid immigrants are often remarkable people: energetic, intelligent, hardworking; and often they make it so good that they are determined to keep it at any cost.[3]

Her explanation, in other words, was the customary Stalinist charge of sellout, only in this case embellished with a touch of snobbery that was distinctly her own.

In his response to this charge, William Phillips wrote:

> Lillian Hellman's question as to why we did not come to the defense of those who had been attacked by McCarthy is not as simple as it appears. First of all, some were Communists and what one was asked to defend was their right to lie about it. My own code was to tell the truth about myself, regardless of the consequences. Another consideration was the feeling, which I am sure was shared by others, that Communists did not have a divine right to a job in the government or in Hollywood—any more than I felt I had a right to a high-salaried job in an institution I believed to be an instrument of capitalist power and exploitation. . . . Frankly, too, I could not take seriously those Communists and fellow-traveling celebrities who were playing with revolution, for it did not seem

[3] *Scoundrel Time* (Little, Brown and Company, 1976), pages 40–41.

> to occur to them that being for a revolution might have consequences. Furthermore, it was not just a case of disagreeing with the Communists. They had branded us as the enemy. They were under orders not to speak to us. Their press called us every dirty name in and out of the political lexicon. And, of course, they were the apologists for the arrest and torture of countless dissident writers in the Soviet Union and in other Communist countries. . . . [H]ow could Lillian Hellman not know these things? And just as she asks how we could not come to the defense of McCarthy's victims, one could ask her how she could not come to the defense of all those who had been killed or defamed by the Communists? How could she still be silent about the persecution of writers in Russia?[4]

She had clearly gone too far and claimed too much. Writing in the aftermath of the Vietnam war and the Watergate scandal, she no doubt felt she could get away with anything—even Garry Wills's wholesale misrepresentation of the history of the Cold War that served as the introduction to *Scoundrel Time.* (It was in that introduction, by the way, that Mary McCarthy was first cited as an enemy because of her public role in opposing the Communist-controlled Cultural and Scientific Conference for World Peace, which was staged at the Waldorf-Astoria in New York in 1949 and for which Lillian Hellman served as a prominent sponsor and spokesman.) Yet favorable as the *Zeitgeist* was to the lies and accusations propounded in the pages of *Scoundrel Time* and its introduction, American intellectual life had not, after all, become so lost to the corruptions of revisionist history that there were not some writers left to remind us of the truth, and they now began to mount their counterattack not only in their own defense, but also in defense of veracity itself.[5]

[4] William Phillips, "What Happened in the Fifties," *Partisan Review*, 1976 (Number 3).

[5] My own contribution to the discussion was "The Blacklist and the Cold War," which is reprinted below on pages 70–80.

In the critical responses of William Phillips, Diana Trilling, et al., to the fabrications and allegations of *Scoundrel Time*, we saw the first round in what was to become, by 1984, a sweeping exposé of the falsehoods that formed the very fabric of Hellman's autobiographical writings— those writings that brought her, as Robert Brustein correctly noted, "renewed fame, wealth, and the respect of the literary community, besides making her a model for independent women everywhere."

It would be tedious as well as unnecessary to rehearse all the voluminous detail that is now on public record to show how often and how profoundly Lillian Hellman misrepresented, distorted, and ignored the truth in writing the autobiographical trilogy that consists of *An Unfinished Woman* (1969), *Pentimento: A Book of Portraits* (1973), and *Scoundrel Time* (1976). The key documents in the case are Martha Gellhorn's "Guerre de Plume" (*The Paris Review*, Spring 1981), Dr. Muriel Gardiner's memoirs, *Code Name: Mary* (Yale University Press, 1983), and Samuel McCracken's "'Julia' and Other Fictions" (*Commentary*, June 1984).

Martha Gellhorn's piece is particularly hilarious and devastating in showing how virtually every word written by Hellman about her adventures in and on behalf of the Spanish Civil War and about her acquaintance with Ernest Hemingway—Gellhorn was married to Hemingway at the time—was sheer invention. Dr. Gardiner's *Code Name: Mary* is an account of her own work in the anti-fascist underground in the Thirties—the work that Hellman not only fictionalized and embellished in her famous "memoir" of "Julia," but in the story of which she falsely claimed to have played a role herself. Devastating, too, is Samuel McCracken's documentary research into the specific circumstantial detail on which the veracity of "Julia" must finally be judged.

To say that Lillian Hellman emerges from this literature as a false and self-serving witness would be an understatement. She stands exposed as a shameless liar, and Mary McCarthy was only stating the truth when she said, in her famous charge on the Dick Cavett Show, that "Every word she writes is a lie."

One final detail about *Scoundrel Time* deserves mention, however, for the light it casts on the way this "institution of conscience" manipulated the "facts" (as she never tired of calling her fictions) in the service of political falsehood. In *Scoundrel Time*, in an episode replete with disingenuous solicitude for the "friend" she was determined to discredit—namely, Lionel Trilling—Lillian Hellman gave us a wonderful example of what can only be called her "method" in dealing with the truth. Reading the introduction that Trilling had written in 1975 for a new edition of his novel, *The Middle of the Journey*, and finding that he continued to stand by his judgment that Whittaker Chambers, upon whom the character of Gifford Maxim in the novel was based, was "a man of honor," Hellman roused herself to set her readers straight about Chambers and the Hiss case. This is the way Allen Weinstein described her performance in his book, *Perjury: The Hiss-Chambers Case:*

> Sections of *Scoundrel Time* took up the argument for Hiss's innocence and his frameup, with Hellman observing that "Facts are facts . . . and there had never been a chance that, as Trilling continues to claim, . . . Chambers was a man of honor." Hellman offered three major sets of "facts" to support her belief in Alger Hiss's innocence: that Chambers hid his microfilms in a pumpkin for a long period of time (every news account in 1948 and all subsequent books on the Case pointed out that Chambers placed the films in the pumpkin the morning of the day he turned them over to HUAC); that "most of the frames of the five rolls of microfilm were unreadable" (also well publicized was the fact that only one roll was illegible, while the two strips of State Department documents were perfectly "readable"); and that the "pumpkin papers"—finally released to Hiss and other researchers in 1973—were found "to contain nothing secret, nothing confidential" (which applied

> only to the non-State Department rolls). Hellman's insistence that she "wasn't a historian" was thus amply vindicated.[6]

This is the writer about whom Robert Brustein could write in his obituary tribute, "I never took Lillian's politics very seriously," and in praise of whom Marsha Norman was given space in *The New York Times* to declare: "I am not interested in the degree to which she told the literal truth."[7]

Yet if we are not to take "Lillian's politics very seriously," and if we are not to put much stock in her capacity to tell "the literal truth" about anything, the question that inevitably arises is: on what basis *are* we being invited to admire either the woman or her work? Her claim to being considered an "institution of conscience" was bogus, for it was based on her political activities and these were wholly devoted to Communist causes in a period when Communism had shown itself to be a system of murder and terror.[8]

The "memoirs" that brought her wealth, fame, and honors of every sort are now shown to have been a fraud. Is it, then, on the basis of her superior contribution to the art of the drama that we are being asked to admire Lillian Hellman? Not at all. Even her friends were too embarrassed to make much of a claim for her on that score. Robert Brustein acknowledged that none of her plays is "of the first rank," and while he went on to suggest that three of them—*Toys in the Attic*, *The Autumn Garden*, and *The Little Foxes*—would "have a permanent place in American drama" (itself a highly equivocal compliment considering the quality of American drama), he concluded by observing that "it may be

[6] Allen Weinstein, *Perjury: The Hiss-Chambers Case* (Alfred A. Knopf, 1978), pages 551-552.

[7] Marsha Norman, "Lillian Hellman's Gift To a Young Playwright," *The New York Times*, August 26, 1984.

[8] The best single account of Lillian Hellman's political history is to be found in Sidney Hook's essay "The Scoundrel in the Looking Glass" in his book *Philosophy and Public Policy* (Southern Illinois University Press, 1980).

that her life, with its strong alliances, combative courage, and abrupt domestic scenes, will eventually be considered her greatest theater."

Marsha Norman, the playwright whose *'night, Mother* won her the Pulitzer Prize for drama in 1983, likewise had little to say for Lillian Hellman's plays in the lengthy *hommage* she published in *The New York Times*. "It was her other writing that called me, her life that moved me," Norman wrote. "Her own story was the most compelling one she wrote, she was her own most significant character." Which in a way, of course, is true—but not in the way that Marsha Norman meant it. For what we are being asked to admire, finally, is that fictional character which Lillian Hellman so adroitly created in her "memoirs" and which she performed so consummately in the "theater" that she had made of her *life*. What we are being asked to admire, in other words, is a carefully constructed illusion.

It is an illusion, however, that can be sustained only if we ignore the facts of her real life and the beliefs that governed it. We were given an interesting glimpse into the latter when *The New York Times* reported the terms of her will on July 20.[9] Lillian Hellman left an estate "valued at about $3.5 million," according to the *Times*, and her will stipulated that half of her residuary estate was to go to the "creation of the Dashiell Hammett Fund." The *Times* story went on to report:

> The fund, according to the will, will make grants "for the promotion and advancement of political, social and economic equality, civil rights and civil liberties."
>
> Miss Hellman asked in the will that the trustees of the fund "be guided by the political, social and economic beliefs—which, of course, were radical—of the late Dashiell Hammett, who was a believer in the doctrines of Karl Marx." Miss

[9] "Hellman Estate to Aid Friend and Trust Funds," *The New York Times*, July 20, 1984.

Hellman lived off and on with Mr. Hammett for thirty-one years.

Robert Brustein may not have taken Lillian Hellman's politics very seriously, but Lillian Hellman did and so must we. In bequeathing so large a portion of her wealth to a fund honoring the *beliefs* of yet another unrepentant Stalinist, Lillian Hellman wrote her own truest epitaph.

October 1984

The Blacklist Revisited

Few among the intellectuals in the Party realized at the time that their mentality was a caricature of the revolutionary spirit; that within the short span of three generations the Communist movement had travelled from the era of the Apostles to that of the Borgias. But the process of degeneration had been gradual and continuous, and the seeds of corruption had already been present in the work of Marx: in the vitriolic tone of his polemics, the abuse heaped on his opponents, the denunciation of rivals and dissenters as traitors to the working class and agents of the bourgeoisie.

—Arthur Koestler, *The Invisible Writing*, 1954

FIFTY years ago, the House Un-American Activities Committee in Washington opened its famous hearings into Communist influence in Hollywood. To mark this anniversary occasion, the Left-liberal establishment in Hollywood has thrown itself into a frenzy of commemorative events. These events are designed to honor the "victims" of the blacklist that resulted from those hearings, and reaffirm the "innocence" of the Communists and fellow-travelers who remained abject in their loyalty to Stalin while refusing to acknowledge their political affiliations and beliefs. They are also designed to vilify the ex-Communists in their ranks who committed the unforgivable "crime" of telling the truth about this shameful allegiance to one of the most bloodthirsty tyrannies of this terrible century. As Patrick Goldstein wrote in "Hollywood's Blackest Hour" (*The Los Angeles Times*, October 9, 1997), "In today's Hollywood, honors are given only to those who were blacklisted."

Needless to say, in this very long article in the *Los Angeles Times* there was no acknowledgment of what it meant to be under Communist Party discipline in the 1930s and 1940s, and no reference, either, to the political terror and the horrors of the Gulag that Hollywood money and influence helped to support during the worst years of Stalin's murderous reign. That it might be considered an even blacker hour in Hollywood's history when so many of its well-heeled talents threw their support to the enemies of American democracy—the enemies, indeed, of the very freedoms that enabled Hollywood itself to prosper—was also nowhere acknowledged. Today it is openly admitted that a good many of the once famous names that were blacklisted in Hollywood half a century ago *were* Communists, and were thus under Party discipline when they put on their ritual show of innocence and victimhood before the House Un-American Activities Committee. But fifty years later, the actualities of the Communist movement in America have disappeared from all discussion of the blacklist.

This climate of denial is not new, of course. For at least a quarter of a century it has been a flourishing enterprise in this country, and it is to remind readers of its earlier history and bring them up to date on the mystifications and misrepresentations now rampant in the current literature on the subject that I am reprinting here the article I wrote for *The New York Times* on "The Blacklist and the Cold War" on October 3, 1976.

At the time that "The Blacklist and the Cold War" was written, I was working at *The New York Times* as the paper's chief art critic and art news editor. I had also served a brief stint in 1972 as the cultural news editor on the daily *Times*, and occasionally written on a broad range of other subjects for the paper. Soon after I returned from my summer vacation in 1976, one of the editors I worked with asked me to attend an advance screening of a movie called *The Front*, which starred Woody Allen. My editor had already seen the movie, and thought it might be something I would want to write about. When I saw the film, I understood why. It was about the blacklist, of course, and came at a time when Lillian Hellman's *Scoundrel Time* was enjoying immense acclaim. No sooner had I seen *The Front* than I attended a screening of another film, the documentary called *Hollywood on Trial*, about the so-called Hollywood Ten who had turned the hearings of the House Un-American Activities Committee into even more of a circus than they already were. It was left to me, however, to write about the subject in my own way. No editor ever told me what could or could not be said in such a piece, and the article appeared exactly as I wrote it—and as it appears below.

When it was published on the front page of the Sunday Arts & Leisure section of the *Times*, the article caused considerable uproar. The revisionist history of the Cold War, which attributed all evil intent to President Truman—and sometimes even to Winston Churchill—and portrayed Stalin as their innocent victim, was in full flower. The radical movement of the 1960s had also brought in its wake a revisionist history of the Communist movement that had flourished in this country from the 1930s until well into the 1940s and even the 1950s. I knew several people who didn't finally break with the Party until the Communist crackdown in Hungary in 1956. The immense power and influence on American cultural life that had been exerted by the Communist Party in the era of the Popular Front had been conveniently forgotten. It was considered bad taste to remind people of Stalin's crimes—or, indeed, of the immense role played by Stalinism in this country's politics and culture. It was still firmly believed by most liberals—the folks who wrote for *The New Yorker*, *The Nation*, and *The New Republic*, for example—that

Alger Hiss was innocent. Many of those people also worked for the *Times*, and one of them tried to get me fired for writing "The Blacklist and the Cold War." It was bad luck for him that the editor he appealed to for my dismissal happened to be the editor who had commissioned me to write the article in the first place.

Letters pro and con poured into the *Times* offices for weeks, some of them quite amazing. Arthur Schlesinger, Jr., for example, wrote to say that "The Blacklist and the Cold War" should be required reading for everyone under the age of forty. Alfred Kazin also wrote a letter praising the piece. But there was no shortage of letters denouncing the article, and there were a few veteran reporters in the *Times* newsroom who never spoke to me again. For a certain liberal mindset, to be anti-Communist was the only truly unforgivable crime.

What caused especial consternation was the reference the article makes to what I called the "other" blacklist—the blacklist drawn up by Communists in Hollywood, Broadway, book publishing, and journalism—that prohibited certain anti-Communists, many of them former Party members who had broken with the Party, from working in their industries. Everyone who worked in those fields was well aware of this phenomenon, but I may have been the first to call it a blacklist—which is what it was, of course. But then, it was in the nature of Stalinism for its followers to lie about everything that impinged upon their political allegiance. We now know, for example, that Lillian Hellman lied when she denied her own membership in the Communist Party. And those denials had a very corrupting effect on the liberals who had been induced to embrace the Stalinist view of the Cold War—Garry Wills, for an egregious example, who, as far as I know, has yet to repudiate the mendacious account of the Cold War he wrote as the Introduction to *Scoundrel Time*.

What follows, then, is the article as it appeared in *The New York Times* of October 3rd, 1976.

The Blacklist & the Cold War

Who would ever have dreamed, a generation ago, that the blacklist and the Hollywood Ten, the sordid proceedings of the House Un-American Activities Committee, and the political vagaries of Joe McCarthy, would one day reemerge as a form of cultural chic? But this unlikely vicissitude, which would have strained the credulity of the Truman and Eisenhower era, is now decisively upon us.

Suddenly, a revisionist history is "in," and not only among the academic historians who, for a decade, have been laboring to persuade us that the Cold War was somehow a malevolent conspiracy of the Western democracies to undermine the benign intentions of the Soviet Union, but among filmmakers, writers, and producers. A new wave of movies, books, and television shows is assiduously turning the terrors and controversies of the late 1940s into the entertainments and bestsellers of the 1970s.

From what we have seen so far, the trend is unmistakable. The past week has brought us the opening of the new Woody Allen movie, *The Front*, which takes as its sometimes comic, sometimes serious theme the blacklisting of writers and actors in the television industry. Even before its release, *The Front* had itself become part of the "history" recounted in an ambitious new documentary movie, *Hollywood on Trial*, to be released later this month. We have already had a volume of letters, *Additional Dialogue*, by the late Dalton Trumbo, one of the Ten heroes of *Hollywood on Trial*, and we shall soon have a Trumbo biography by Bruce Cook. Three weeks ago, Channel 5 in New York broadcast a BBC documentary on the career of Edward R. Murrow that had as its climax the latter's 1954 "See It Now" program on Senator McCarthy, and a new three-hour television movie about a McCarthy-like figure, directed by Jud Taylor, will be broadcast on the NBC network in the spring.

Meanwhile, Lillian Hellman's much-praised memoir of the McCarthy period, *Scoundrel Time*, holds a firm place on the bestseller list for the twenty-first week, and publishers have signed up Murray Kempton, Nora Sayre, Victor Navasky, David Caute, and others for more books on the period. The well-known critic Eric Bentley has already used the transcripts of the House Un-American Activities Committee hearings as the basis of both a play, *Are You Now or Have You Ever Been*, and a thick documentary volume, *Thirty Years of Treason*. How long, one wonders, will it be before some jolly spirit mounts a Broadway musical about J. Parnell Thomas and the Hollywood Ten, or we are given a rock version of the Army-McCarthy hearings?

It is a phenomenon, all right—this wave of revisionist accounts, fictional and nonfictional, historical and mythological, of events that occurred a quarter-century ago—but what is it all about? And why now?

One thing it is about, certainly, is the present. The relation of the 1970s—of social, political and cultural attitudes today—to the 1960s bears a close resemblance to the relation in which the late 1940s and early 1950s stood to the 1930s. And just as the crises of the 1930s—and the values generated by those crises—were reenacted in the investigations and controversies of the late 1940s and 1950s, so the crises of the 1960s—and the values and beliefs generated by them—are now under serious scrutiny and debate.

The Front and *Scoundrel Time* and *Hollywood on Trial*—to judge from the most recent works at hand—are thus as much a part of this reexamination of the 1960s, and especially the radicalism of the 1960s, as they are an attempt to redraw the history of an earlier era along lines—often, alas, fictional lines—that are sympathetic to the present climate of liberal opinion. The point, it seems, is to acquit 1960s radicalism of all malevolent consequence, and to do so by portraying 1930s radicalism as similarly innocent, a phenomenon wholly benign, altruistic, and admirable. Lillian Hellman puts the matter baldly in the last pages of *Scoundrel Time*. Of writers like herself, who for so long defended every Communist shibboleth and falsehood, she says: "Whatever our mistakes, I do not believe we did our country any harm." And of the writers who were anti-Communist she says: "I think they did." They gave us, in her view, the Vietnam War and Nixon.

Another thing these works are about, then, is the Cold War and détente—and very explicitly. *The Front* opens, even before Woody Allen's archetypal schlep-hero is drawn into a scheme to act as a front for a blacklisted writer, with a quick-cut patchwork of old newsreel footage. We are given glimpses of the war in Korea, General MacArthur, President Truman, the Rosenberg prosecution, civilian bomb shelters, the Vietnam War, etc., toward all of which we are expected to take an attitude of complete and unquestioned disapproval. *Scoundrel Time* is similarly prefaced—in this case, by Garry Wills's long essay in historical mystification that depicts "Truman's aggressiveness" as a form of premeditated political villainy and omits all reference to that distant and obscure figure, obviously considered irrelevant to the discussion—Joseph Stalin. Which is rather unfair to Stalin, considering the role that his political influence once played in Miss Hellman's life.

If, for Mr. Wills (and, one must assume, Miss Hellman), it was President Truman who "launched the Cold War in the spring of 1947," then for Arnie Reisman, the author of *Hollywood on Trial*, it was Winston Churchill, and even earlier. Reactions will differ, of course, to the experience of hearing the voice of John Huston, the narrator of *Hollywood on Trial*, mouthing in all solemnity the judgment of Mr. Reisman that in 1946 "Winston Churchill drew an iron curtain across Eastern Europe." Again, it seems awfully unfair to Stalin to deny him proper credit for one of his most distinctive achievements—but that is the way things often are in the fantasy world of revisionist history. The imagery of perfect (Communist) innocence must be upheld, and the historical record adjusted accordingly.

It must be said, in this respect, that the Congressional investigations of Communist influence in the entertainment industry and the blacklisting that resulted from them—the common theme of *The Front*, *Scoundrel Time*, and *Hollywood on Trial*—are subjects almost ideally suited to buttressing this (false) imagery of innocence. The scenario abounds with easily recognized villains, from Congressmen out to grab a headline at any cost, to craven industry executives solely concerned to protect their careers and investments, to former comrades out to save their own necks. The investigations and the hearings were often conducted in an appalling manner. Their very nature created a situation in which informing became a career in itself, and innocent people *were* smeared and even destroyed by false accusations.

From which it does not follow, however, that all the accusations *were* false. Less easily recognized, from the current perspective anyway, are the other villains of the tale—the many wealthy dedicated Communists in the industry who—both because it was the Party line to do so and in the hope of saving *their* necks—denied their true commitments and beliefs, and thereby created an atmosphere of havoc and hazard for the truly innocent. Writing about the Hollywood Ten in *A Generation on Trial* (1952), a book generally sympathetic to Alger Hiss, Alistair Cooke observed that "they refused to say if they were Communists, in a series of hearings that the witnesses, just as much as the Committee, were responsible for turning into a squalid and rowdy parody of a court of law." Despite the best efforts of Mr. Reisman and the director of *Hollywood on Trial*, David Helpern, Jr., to have us think otherwise, the contribution of the Hollywood Ten to this "squalid and rowdy parody" comes through loud and clear in the old film clips of the hearings.

Still, the myth of total innocence must be upheld even where it is contravened by the acknowledged facts. When Dalton Trumbo died last month, *The New York Times* matter-of-factly reported in his obituary that he admitted in 1970, when he was securely restored to Hollywood clover, to having been a member of the Communist Party from 1943 to 1948, and again briefly in

1954—a fact conveniently omitted from the voluble interview with Trumbo that is part of *Hollywood on Trial*. Nor, in its earnest effort to portray the Hollywood Ten as champions of democracy and the underdog, does the film quote Trumbo's own contemptible comment on this commitment: "I never considered the working class anything other than something to get out of."

As for the industry, about which *The Front* and *Hollywood on Trial* are so pious, it responded as industry always responds to any manifest threat to its profits—with whatever mixture of caution, cowardice, prudence, hypocrisy, dissembling, and emergency planning it deemed necessary to its prosperity and survival. This was the ethic of the industry when the Hollywood Ten—and Lillian Hellman, too—were counted among its loyal, pampered, high-priced hacks. It was the ethic of the industry when it put its blacklists into effect. And is the ethic of the industry any different today, I wonder, when many of the former blacklistees are once again pleased to be the beneficiaries of its huge salaries and specious glamour?

The history of this period, dubbed *Scoundrel Time* by Miss Hellman, is anything but simple, but that is precisely what *The Front* and *Hollywood on Trial* urge us to believe—that the issues were all very simple, a matter of good guys versus bad guys, with all virtue accruing to the people who, in principle, denied the government the right to investigate what it judged to be threats to its security, and defied any government process that might illuminate such threats. In *The Front*, with its cartoon characterizations, the character played by Woody Allen gets the girl by defying the committee looking into his connection with the Communist or fellow-traveling writers he has been fronting for. The schlep becomes a moral hero, and the good guys win. In this scenario, as in *Hollywood on Trial*, the only real threat is the government itself, and those opportunists who exploited a climate of fear.

The climate now is very different, of course. Radicals are chic, the FBI is under a cloud, and the old blacklist has become a roll of honor. It is conveniently forgotten that once there were other blacklists. In *Hollywood on Trial*, only the director Edward Dmytryk—one of the Hollywood Ten—alludes to the lists of anti-Communists who were denied work when Stalinist influence was at its height. Unmentioned, too, are the vicious attacks that anti-Communist liberals and radicals were obliged to endure whenever they attempted to reveal the bloody truth about what Miss Hellman delicately describes now as the "sins" of the Stalinist regime. Who could guess, reading the *soigné* prose of *Scoundrel Time*, that Miss Hellman was once one of the most vigorous public defenders of those "sins," which even Khrushchev did not hesitate to call crimes involving the murder of hundreds of thousands, eventually millions, of innocent victims? Perhaps she has forgotten that she had joined in attacking the philosopher John Dewey, a pillar of the liberal establishment, for convening a commission of inquiry into the truth about the Moscow Trials. The climate now is indeed very different—it is a climate of amnesia.

So we are treated, in the course of *Hollywood on Trial*, to a glimpse of the most notorious of Hollywood's pro-Communist films, the egregious *Mission to Moscow*, with its scene of these same Moscow Trials showing us one of the old Bolsheviks "confessing" to being a paid German agent and a sweet-faced Stalin beaming with confidence and wisdom, and we are clearly expected to approve. We are treated to a lecture, in *Scoundrel Time*, on the alleged failure of "the good magazines, the ones that published the most serious writing . . . to come to the aid of those who were persecuted."

William Phillips, the editor of one of the magazines so described, *Partisan Review*, has written an interesting reply to *Scoundrel Time* in the current issue of that journal. He points out, in a reference to the other blacklist, the one that nobody talks about and that Woody Allen will certainly never make a movie about, that "I and other writers who had broken with Communism were kept from writing for various journals and prevented from getting not-so-lucrative university jobs because of the pressure and machinations of the Communists."

"Lillian Hellman's questions as to why we did not come to the defense of those who had been attacked by McCarthy is not as simple as it appears," Mr. Phillips continues.

> First of all, some were Communists and what one was asked to defend was their right to lie about it. . . . Another consideration was the feeling . . . that Communists did not have a divine right to a job in the government or in Hollywood. . . . Furthermore, it was not just a case of disagreeing with the Communists. They had branded us as the enemy. They were under orders not to speak to us. Their press called us every dirty name in and out of the political lexicon. And, of course, they were apologists for the arrest and torture of countless dissident writers in the Soviet Union and in other Communist countries . . . how could Lillian Hellman not know these things?

Such questions were seldom raised in the heyday of the radical movement in the 1960s, which is probably one reason why the myth of Communist innocence in the 1930s can now be propagated with such evident ease. What has been swamped in the new wave of revisionism about both the 1960s and the 1930s is the liberal view that regarded *both* Stalinism and the blacklists as threats to democracy—the view that looked upon the conduct of the House Un-American Activities Committee and the values of the Communist Party as plagues to be resisted.

Sitting through *The Front* and *Hollywood on Trial* and turning the pages of *Scoundrel Time* and reading the endless reviews that lavished it with so much praise, one is haunted by the question once posed, albeit in another context, by William Hazlitt: "Were we fools then, or are we dishonest now?"

November 1997

Nora Sayre's Sentimental "Journey"

It will never be known what acts of cowardice have been motivated by the fear of not looking sufficiently progressive.

—Charles Péguy, *Notre Patrie*, 1905

IT is a pity that no one has yet written a history of the progressive mind in America. We are just sufficiently distant enough from the heyday of progressivism to have a certain perspective on its characteristic ways of looking at the world, yet we are still just close enough to its demise—or its transmutation into something else—to have some vivid first-hand memories of the peculiar intellectual deformations it visited upon our political and cultural life for something like a third of the present century. Entire areas of American life—the media and publishing worlds, the entertainment industry, the Federal bureaucracy, education, the academy, even the churches—cannot be wholly understood without a firm grasp of what the progressive outlook bequeathed to us in the years of its ascendancy, which by my calculations extend from the end of the 1920s to the mid-1960s.

Such histories of the American political Left in this period as we have been given do not really satisfy the need for a study of the progressive mind, which, though anchored in left-wing political ideology, was always a reflection of something more than a set of political positions. The progressivism I speak of was an ethos, a cast of mind, a secular faith that reached into every aspect of living and thinking. It was thus as much a code of feeling as it was a mode of thought. Its loyalties determined everything from literary taste and the choice of spouses to the way children were educated and political events responded to. At the height of its influence, progressivism had an answer—or at least a response—for every question, which is why it could not be dislodged from its position of authority in the lives of its acolytes by specific political events, no matter how shattering, but required for its demise the emergence of an ethos even more radical and comprehensive and compelling in its prescriptions for life than the system of belief it supplanted. It is in this respect that the counterculture of the late Sixties and early Seventies, with its call for a more fundamental personal emancipation, may be said to have devoured the remaining remnants of a once-regnant progressivism and propelled its progeny into a radicalism of a very different sort.

In speaking of the progressive mind in America we must distinguish, of course, between the ideas and attitudes propagated earlier in the century by the reform movements associated with Theodore Roosevelt, Robert M. La Follette, and William Jennings Bryan and the very different kind of progressivism that came to be identified, to one degree or another, with an allegiance to Stalinist fellow-traveling. Used in this latter sense, the word "progressive," once so common in political parlance, isn't much heard anymore in discussions of the radical Left in this country. It seems to have become a casualty of the Cold War.[1] Conservatives, at least those old enough to have become familiar with the term in their youth, shun the very notion of progressivism as a euphemism for Stalinism itself—which, indeed, it

[1] See, for example, *The Reader's Companion to American History*, edited by Eric Foner and John A. Garraty and sponsored by the Society of American Historians, published in 1991. The entry for "Progressivism," written by Robert M. Crunden, makes no reference to the Soviet-oriented progres-

very much still was when I was in school in the late Forties and early Fifties. Many liberals, especially those old enough to have experienced the duplicities of the Communists at first hand, avoid the word for the same reason. Yet even among people on the hard Left, progressive is a term that has lost its luster. It seems dated and a little tarnished—a throwback, perhaps, to an era more receptive to Marxist-inspired political causes than our own. Progressive is, in any event, too old-fashioned a term to serve the up-to-date purposes of the radical Left today, which are more likely to exploit the issues of race, sex, the environment, social welfare, and multiculturalism than to advocate Marxist-Leninist notions of revolution. Revolution of some sort had always, of course, been the subtext of Soviet-oriented American progressivism, but it was a subtext that dared not speak its name too loudly in public lest more moderate liberals, upon whom progressives were dependent for allies and access, be reminded of what progressive politics was really about.

All the same, no other word will do to describe the kind of Left-liberal mentality that once played so large a role in shaping American cultural life and the social thought on which it was based. In its period of maximum influence, progressivism always occupied a much larger place in American cultural life than Communism itself. For progressives, thanks to their liberal allies and patrons, often had easy entrée to milieux where known Communists were not entirely welcome. While all Communists were, in their public utterances at least, progressives, not all progressives were Communists—which is to say, under Communist Party discipline. Progressivism may thus be said to have represented the laity of the Communist movement in the

sivism I speak of here. In this connection, it should also be noted that while the book contains an entry for "Anticommunism," written by Ellen W. Schrecker, there is none for "Communism," though there is a brief, unsigned entry for the "Communist Party."

Stalinist era, and, as with any given faith, the style of obeisance to fundamental articles of belief naturally varied a good deal within its ranks.

Hollywood progressives, for example, differed markedly from their counterparts in the industrial labor movement. Comfortably situated progressives on *The New Yorker*, conforming to the ethos of their own subculture, tended to be more insouciant in their radicalism than, say, writers for *The Nation*. So, too, their respective progressive readers. And so it went. Harvard progressives were often more snobbish than those at City College, while Berkeley produced a community of progressives that differed from both.

Yet despite these differences in style, class, and disposition, what made these progressives an identifiable force in American cultural life were precisely the articles of belief they held in common, and foremost among them was a vision of American life—a vision of life itself—that was largely Stalinist in origin. Never mind what was actually taking place in the real-life Soviet Union in Stalin's time. About that, for the most part, progressives of every stripe were marvelously adept at keeping themselves in a highly adaptable condition of disbelief. What was of compelling concern to them was life in the United States, which progressives viewed almost entirely in terms that were codified by the Communist Party line as it evolved in the course of its many modifications, permutations, and outright reversals to meet the needs of Soviet power. About a whole range of historic events and public figures—from the Sacco-Vanzetti case and the Spanish Civil War to the Alger Hiss conviction and the Hollywood Ten—progressives adopted an iconography and a demonology that have remained impervious to critical doubt or documentary evidence down to the present day. Which is why there has been no discernible impact on what remains of the progressive mind by the revelations lately emanating from the KGB archives in Russia. The verifiable facts of history had long ago ceased to be relevant to the progressives' act of faith.

I have been reminded of all this once again by the new book that Nora Sayre has written about herself, her parents, their friends, her friends, their respective political allegiances, and her own unrepentant attachment to the old progressive sentimentalities. Entitled, somewhat misleadingly, *Previous Convictions: A Journey Through the 1950s* (Rutgers University Press), the book aspires to illuminate a much larger chunk of history than the despised decade in which Sayre herself came of age and upon which she now looks back with so much distaste. For this is a book that eulogizes the Twenties, gives us a kind of Popular Front cartoon version of the Thirties, castigates the Fifties, sentimentalizes the Sixties, and brings us up-to-date on what was left of the progressive platitudes well into the Eighties and Nineties.

About the Twenties, Sayre writes in a spirit of unembarrassed filial piety. The Twenties was the glamorous decade that shaped her parents' lives and thus, in Sayre's view, set a standard for how life should be lived that has never again been met. Her father, Joel Sayre, had worked on the old *New York Herald-Tribune*, made a middling reputation on *The New Yorker*, and, as Nora Sayre writes, "spent about five years in Hollywood, employed on over a dozen film projects." Later he wrote for television. Her mother, Gertrude Lynahan, was also a journalist. Her career, it is said, "was abetted by H. L. Mencken." In the Twenties she worked on *The New York World* at a time when Joseph Mitchell, later a colleague of her husband's at *The New Yorker*, was a copy boy there. John O'Hara was Nora Sayre's godfather. Other members of her parents' circle included Nunnally Johnson, James Thurber, James M. Cain, St. Clair McKelway, S. J. Perelman, Dorothy Parker, and Edmund Wilson, the latter a neighbor of the Sayres on the Upper East Side of Manhattan when Nora was growing up—one of the children, as she writes, "who passed the crackers and cheese and refilled the ice trays" at their parents' cocktail parties and "felt colorless in comparison to our seniors."

> When I remember my parents' friends [she writes], I think of them indoors, in living rooms, laughing, eating salted nuts and drinking whiskey, talking expansively—with a group rather than to one person. The setting would shift from New York to Beverly Hills and Cape Cod, occasionally to Connecticut. And one or two guests might spend the night, perhaps on sofas: next morning there would be the long silent trip to the bathroom, the speechless breakfast, and then a few jokes about hangovers. But no perceptible remorse.

In a show of progressive conscience, Sayre expresses some concern that "it may seem that I've confined myself to an elite" in the writing of *Previous Convictions*, but she hastens to add that "most of the writers of the Twenties and the radicals of the Thirties"—in other words, the figures under discussion in this book—"had made their own way—through their work." In their work, whether for the commercial press in New York or for the Hollywood studios, Sayre believes that these models of progressive virtue scorned commercialism, but her own account of their careers doesn't support such a claim. In her father's case, for example, she makes it perfectly clear that he sought work in Hollywood in order to meet his family's needs. His wife had suffered an irreversible breakdown and needed care. In addition, he wanted his daughter to attend Radcliffe College. Both required more money than Joel Sayre could make at *The New Yorker*. I think he behaved admirably in attending to the needs of his nearest and dearest, but why claim that this deliberate embrace of commercialism was the exact opposite of what Joel Sayre required of himself? Well, because commercialism represents a fall from honor in the progressive lexicon, and so must be denied even where the motive for it is easily explained.

It is in telltale details of this sort—and they become more flagrant and more abundant when Nora Sayre turns to "the radicals of the Thirties"—that we come to understand the peculiar variety of progressivism that pervades *Previous Convic-*

tions, which its author characterizes as both "a memoir of mentalities" and "a book of ruminations." For hers is a progressivism of nostalgia—a progressivism compounded almost exclusively of other people's fond memories and cherished illusions and her own uncontainable envy for a time and a milieu in which an unclouded Left-liberal outlook on politics and a debonair style in art and life were joined in joyous opposition to what was otherwise seen to be a benighted society of ignoramuses and reactionaries. In other words, Menckenism adapted to the needs of middlebrow journalism and radical chic.

The envy which Sayre still harbors for this happy breed of debonair *révoltés* gives to everything she writes a distinct air of belatedness, a feeling that she and her generation arrived on the scene after the partying was over and only the debris—the hangovers, the recriminations, the denials of wrongdoing, the breakdowns—remained as souvenirs of better times.

Feeling dispossessed of those better times, which Sayre identifies exclusively with her parents and their circle, she certainly understands that she was born too late to participate in their experience, yet she seems nonetheless to have adopted their characteristic attitudes—attitudes that became fixed in the Twenties and Thirties—as her own. These, not surprisingly, she soon found to be woefully inapplicable to life in the Fifties, and as a consequence she bitterly condemns the Fifties as "a bad time to be very young, a bad time to enter the early chapters of your life, bad for curiosity or the impulse to explore."

It seems never to have occurred to her—even now, some forty-odd years later—that others, especially those born neither to her advantages nor to her disappointments, might look back on the Fifties with very different feelings, might indeed have reason to look back on the Fifties as better times than any we have seen since. But then, for some of us who were young in the Fifties, the cynosures of the parochial world into which Sayre was born—*The New Yorker* of Harold Ross and the Hollywood of the big studios—did not, after all, represent the summit of human achievement. For that matter, it did not represent the summit of journalistic or cinematic achievement. We read *The New Yorker* for the cartoons, for the criticism of Edmund Wilson and Louise Bogan, and for occasional outside contributors like Rebecca West, W. H. Auden, and V. S. Pritchett. Hollywood movies we went to for entertainment, just as we did when we were kids, not for art or edification, and we went to them a good deal less often once foreign films—movies for grownups, as I came to think of them—were readily available to us. In the arts, the critics whose writings meant the most to us—Clement Greenberg, B. H. Haggin, Virgil Thomson, Edwin Denby, Eric Bentley, Harold Clurman, Manny Farber—never appeared in *The New Yorker*, and most of those who did were better known for their wisecracks than for their critical sagacity. If we made allowances for a writer such as Dwight Macdonald, which in those days we did, it was largely because he had made his reputation in *Partisan Review*, and even in the Fifties his most audacious writing continued to be published by *Partisan Review* or *Commentary*, not *The New Yorker*.

For a sentimental progressive like Nora Sayre, however, the intellectual milieu represented by *Partisan Review*, *Commentary*, *Encounter*, and a handful of literary quarterlies remains enemy territory even in retrospect. For one thing, it was too highbrow in its tastes; its views of popular culture were far more critical than that of the middlebrow contributors to *The New Yorker*. For another, it espoused the wrong kind of politics; it was anti-Communist. Above all, it was merciless in exposing the fallacies of the progressive mind, not only in its political sentiments but for its literary and cultural pieties as well. In the Fifties, writes Sayre in *Previous Convictions*, "her family's friends . . . thought the Cold War anti-Communists were extremely stupid," and over the course of the last forty years this anti-anti-Communist stance—in many respects, the last refuge of progressive orthodoxy—has evolved in Sayre's mind into a moral absolute.

It made her earlier books—*Sixties Going On Seventies* (1973), a collection of journalistic pieces on the anti-Vietnam War movement and the counterculture, and *Running Time: Films of the Cold War* (1982), an attempt to write anti-anti-Communist Hollywood history—little more than progressive caricatures of their respective genres. Except in one respect—Sayre's touching account of her father's life—the same moral imperative makes *Previous Convictions* a repository of all the most discredited progressive myths that have accumulated about the Thirties and the Fifties. In Nora Sayre's progressive "journey" through the Fifties, *Partisan Review* is seen to have sold out to American conformity because of its anti-Communist position in the Cold War, Alger Hiss is thought to be guilty of nothing more than acting like a New Deal liberal, and the real political saints and martyrs of the decade are veteran Stalinist types like Donald Ogden Stewart and his wife, Ella Winter, the widow of Lincoln Steffens, living in comfortable political exile in London, and the Hollywood Ten, some of whom were still under Communist Party discipline. It is in such particulars that the progressivism of nostalgia degenerates into sheer fantasy and denial.

At times, to be sure, it is difficult to know whether Sayre is as flat-out ignorant of some of the figures she admires or is merely—how should one put it?—disingenuous. Malcolm Cowley, for example, is a figure Sayre much admires, and there is indeed something to admire in Cowley's purely literary endeavors. Yet in *Previous Convictions*, Sayre praises Cowley for, of all things, his politics, which in the Thirties were largely party-line Stalinism. She cites two long letters written to Cowley by James Thurber in the Thirties in which the latter, as Sayre writes, "accused the Communists of trying 'to put the artist in a uniform so like the uniform of the subway conductor that nobody would be able to tell the difference,' and of a 'desire to regiment and discipline art.'" Presciently, Thurber even expressed a fear that "the Communists [were] contributing to 'the growing menace of fascism.'"

Yet it never occurs to Sayre to wonder why Thurber would have been writing such things to Cowley at that particular moment in history if, indeed, Cowley was as independent in his politics as she foolishly claims him to have been. No doubt it would have been a violation of progressive piety for Sayre to have reminded her readers that even Edmund Wilson—not your garden-variety Red-baiting reactionary, as even Sayre would concede—was moved to write as follows to Cowley, then still reigning as the literary editor of a very progressive *New Republic*, in October 1938:

> What in God's name has happened to you? I was told some time ago that you were circulating a letter asking endorsements of the last batch of Moscow trials—though you had just published articles in which, as far as I could tell, you were trying to express a certain amount of skepticism. I don't suppose you're a member of the C.P.; and I can't imagine any other inducement short of bribery or blackmail—which sometimes appear in rather obvious forms and to which I hope you haven't fallen a victim—to justify and imitate their practices at this time. You're a great guy to talk about the value of a non-partisan literary review after the way you've been plugging the damned old Stalinist line . . . at the expense of the interests of literature and to the detriment of critical standards in general!

That's why Thurber was protesting to Malcolm Cowley, who was more brutally described by James T. Farrell as the "literary mouthpiece" of the Communist Party in the Thirties, but this is not the kind of historical intelligence that Nora Sayre regards as relevant to her progressive-valentine account of Cowley in the Thirties. Nor does Sayre bother, either, to point out that it wasn't until fifty years later—in the 1980s!—that Cowley deigned to acknowledge that he might have made some mistakes about "Russia" in the Thirties, and even at that late date used the occasion to revive his old quarrel with the anti-Stalinists at *Partisan Review*. For his politics and his illusions, Cowley is clearly one of Sayre's role models.

Another seems to be Lillian Hellman, for there is much in *Previous Convictions* that reads like a distended remake of *Scoundrel Time*, with Donald Ogden Stewart and Ella Winter performing the roles originated by Dashiell Hammett and Hellman herself—the roles of romantic victims of political persecution rather than (what in fact they were) privileged and prevaricating apologists for a terrible political tyranny. As in *Scoundrel Time*, the writers and intellectuals associated with *Partisan Review* and *Commentary* are looked upon in *Previous Convictions* as greater enemies of American democracy than the followers of the Communist Party, for the former are seen to have failed the tests of progressive orthodoxy. Thus fantasy history repeats itself in the form of farce, but there is more than enough in *Previous Convictions* to remind us of what a malevolent farce the progressive mind itself has turned out to be.

February 1996

THE TWILIGHT OF THE NEW YORK INTELLECTUALS

The Edmund Wilson Centenary

HENRY BRANDON: *When you write about literature, do politics influence your selection?*
EDMUND WILSON: *No. There are certain kinds of writers that are more congenial to me than others. . . .*
HENRY BRANDON: *What do you think of the standards of literary criticism today?*
EDMUND WILSON: *I don't think about those things at all! Literary criticism is a department of literature for me, and when I read literary critics I read them as literature; the others I can't read at all. I never think of myself, for instance, as a literary critic; I think of myself simply as a writer and a journalist. I write about things that interest me. . . .*

—*Conversations with Henry Brandon*, 1968

ON the occasion of the centenary of the birth of Edmund Wilson (1895–1972), Jeffrey Meyers has written the first full-length biography of this remarkable writer, *Edmund Wilson: A Biography* (Houghton Mifflin). It doesn't come a moment too soon. If Wilson wasn't the greatest literary critic of his time—a distinction that, in my view, belongs to T. S. Eliot—he was certainly the only American critic whose work can be usefully compared to that of the leading novelists and poets of his own generation. Yet, barely a quarter of a century after his death, Wilson's books are largely unread and the man himself looks more and more like a figure from a distant era. The literary tradition that nurtured him and his readers is in disarray. The literary vocation to which he dedicated his long career had already become an endangered endeavor long before he quit the scene, and in the years since his passing literature itself has suffered a loss of status in American cultural life that would have been impossible to imagine in the period of his influence. It is not only that Wilson has had no successors. The world in which he prospered has passed into history, and what has supplanted it is a degraded, highly politicized literary culture guaranteed to misconstrue his accomplishment and misrepresent its virtues.

As I write, for example, there is in progress in New York City a series of programs marking the Wilson centenary under the rubric of "The Last of the Public Intellectuals." This is a grotesquely inappropriate way to characterize Wilson's achievement, which was primarily that of a man of letters. The term "public intellectual" is a recent coinage of the academic Left designed to subordinate literature to the interests of politics and the adumbration of social policy.

It thus gives priority to what is the least persuasive and most perishable aspect of Wilson's literary corpus—his penchant for indulging in leftist clichés and other crackpot political ideas—while at the same time relegating his principal accomplishment, and indeed the very nature of his talent, to an entirely secondary status. This may seem an odd way to celebrate the life and work of a writer who devoted his talents to the art of literature, but it is entirely in keeping with the current academic practice of making politics a test of literary merit. For the academic Left today, the very concept of the man of letters is looked upon as contemptible.

As Meyers correctly reminds us in the preface to *Edmund Wilson: A Biography*, this happens to be an approach to literature that Wilson himself explicitly condemned in the course of his own career. "If Wilson is somewhat out of fashion today," Mr. Meyers writes,

> it is only because the impressive intellect, knowledge and humane insight that illuminate his books have been lost through the onslaught of rigid ideological conformity, which he opposed throughout his life. As he prophetically wrote in *The Nation* in January 1938: "The young . . . are today not enthusiastic . . . about books: they merely approve when the book suits their politics. . . . I think it is a pity that they do not learn to read for pleasure. They may presently find that an acquaintance with the great works of art and thought is their only real assurance against the increasing barbarism of our time."

It is one of the many virtues of Meyers's book that it recalls us to the centrality of Wilson's literary interests and reminds us of the nature of those interests. For Wilson belonged to a tradition—he may have been its last major representative in America—for which history was itself a branch of literature; and literature, though not finally reducible to the historical conditions in which it is created, nonetheless remained a key to the understanding of history. It was in this respect that Wilson belonged as much to the line of historians like Michelet, Renan, and Taine as to that of a writer like Flaubert—the Flaubert, as Wilson reminded his readers in *The Triple Thinkers*, who wrote to Michelet that "you are certainly the French author whom I have read and reread most." Wilson's own way of dealing with the sometimes conflicting imperatives of history, with its tendency to reduce art to a subordinate status, and those of art itself, which its more militant exponents wish to extricate from history altogether, may be gleaned, I think, in the passage he quotes from the letter in which Flaubert criticized Taine's *History of English Literature*:

> There is something else in art beside the milieu in which it is practiced and the physiological antecedents of the worker. On this system you can explain the series, the group, but never the individuality, the special fact which makes him this person and not another. This method results inevitably in leaving *talent* out of consideration. The masterpiece has no longer any significance except as an historical document. . . . People used to believe that literature was an altogether personal thing and that books fell out of the sky like meteors. Today they deny that the will and the absolute have any reality at all. The truth, I believe, lies between the two extremes.

Wilson did not entirely agree with Flaubert's assessment of Taine. In his essay on "The Historical Interpretation of Literature," Wilson wrote that "the truth was that Taine loved literature for its own sake—he was at his best himself a brilliant artist"—the kind of artist that Wilson himself aspired to be. And it was precisely "between the two extremes" cited by Flaubert that Wilson usually produced *his* best work—including the essay on "The Politics of Flaubert" in *The Triple Thinkers*.

As for Wilson's own politics, I think Meyers has done more to clarify the origin of his essential outlook on "public" issues than any other writer who has addressed the subject. Wilson is commonly thought to have been radicalized by the Marxist movement in the 1930s—a current of political thought and political action in which he did indeed, for a time, become deeply engaged. It is another of the virtues of Meyers's book, however, that it establishes Wilson's war experience in France in the First World War as the crucible in which all his subsequent attitudes toward society and governmental authority had their moral origin. Nowhere else have I seen Wilson so definitively identified as one of the "men of 1914," as they have been called—the generation that emerged from the slaughter of the war with its outlook on life permanently altered, the generation that made "a separate peace" with society itself as a direct result of the war.

Wilson was not involved in actual military combat himself. He served behind the lines assisting in the care of its casualties, and that was nightmare enough. "In July 1918," Meyers writes, "the first mass of wounded Americans poured in after the major battle at Château-Thierry and included many cases of syphilis and shell-shock."

> Wilson spent a month dressing the raw burnt skin of the screaming victims of mustard-gas. He recalled that "their penises were spongy and raw and swollen to enormous size, and bandaging and unbandaging them was extremely painful. There was one doctor, known for his sadism—he liked to kick the enlisted men—who would rip the bandages off. . . . One patient had three-quarters of the surface of his body burned and his lungs partially destroyed."
>
> The hospital was permeated with the stench of rotten flesh and the death-rate was appallingly high.

As Wilson recalled in *The American Jitters*:

> I swore to myself that when the War was over I should stand outside society altogether. I should do without the comforts and amenities of the conventional world entirely, and I should devote myself to the great human interests which transcend standards of living and conventions: Literature, History, the Creation of Beauty, the Discovery of Truth.

To which Meyers adds: "Though he cared little about money and lived very modestly for years, [Wilson] could never have pursued his literary goals by standing outside society." What "outside society" meant, in Wilson's case, was a place well beyond the reach of the kind of well-heeled bourgeois proprieties in which he had been brought up, an only child, by his neurotic father and his uncomprehending mother. "The war," Meyers writes, "cut him off . . . from his conventional upper-middle-class existence, which he had always assumed he would follow."

And further:

> More importantly, his war experience transformed [Wilson] into a lifelong pacifist. It provided the ethical basis not only for his sympathy with the defeated South in the Civil War, but also for his opposition to America's foreign policy: the participation in World War II, the Cold War ideology that justified vast military spending and the disastrous involvement in the war in Vietnam.

I think this puts Wilson's political thought—if it can be called that—at a higher level of ethical reflection than its historical simplifications and moral insensibility can be made to bear. After all, even Wilson's admirers on the political Left shuddered—some publicly but many more privately—over the obtuseness of the political analysis that made his introduction to *Patriotic Gore* such an embarrassment. This was the key passage, written in November 1961:

> I think that it is a serious deficiency on the part of historians and political writers that they so rarely interest themselves in biological and zoölogical phenomena. In a recent Walt Disney film showing life at the bottom of the sea, a primitive organism called a sea slug is seen gobbling up smaller organisms through a large orifice at one end of its body; confronted with another sea slug of an only slightly lesser size, it ingurgitates that, too. Now, the wars fought by human beings are stimulated as a rule primarily by the same instincts as the voracity of the sea slug. It is true that among the animals other than man it is hard to find organized aggression of the kind that has been developed by humanity. . . . The difference in this respect between man and the other forms of life is that man has succeeded in cultivating enough of what he calls "morality" and

> "reason" to justify what he is doing in terms of what he calls "virtue" and "civilization."

Which is itself fairly primitive as a political theory. (Fortunately, the book proved to be far better than its introduction.) But I believe that Meyers is essentially correct in tracing Wilson's basic political attitudes—the pacifist clichés included—to his war experience in France.

Like many other writers of his generation who were similarly moved by the war to reject bourgeois society, Wilson proved unable to bring the same powers of skepticism and disbelief to the myths of the Revolution when they first loomed in the Depression era. But his romance with the Revolution was shorter-lived than that of many of his literary contemporaries in the 1930s, and his nose for Stalinist cant soon separated him from true believers like Malcolm Cowley. Finally, however, Wilson had no talent for politics. The introduction to *Patriotic Gore* is, in this respect, a confession of his abiding incomprehension of the political life of his time.

Wilson famously wrote about an amazing variety of subjects and cultures, yet when we go back over his work it seems to me that almost all of his best writing was devoted to the prose literature and the intellectual history of the nineteenth and twentieth centuries. I am not in a position to judge the merits of *The Scrolls from the Dead Sea*; and about poetry—except for certain things in *Axel's Castle* and the essay on Auden—I find Wilson's criticism unpersuasive. He needed a subject about which he could tell a story, and he was a better storyteller in his critical and historical writing than in his attempts at fiction. Thus his best writing was, as he intended it to be, essentially narrative writing about people, events, and ideas. This is what gave his criticism its immense appeal to his readers, at least until the late 1960s, when—it is my impression—he was no longer read with the same avidity. After that, the number of readers who could enthusiastically respond to the kind of priority which Wilson gave literature and learning in his writing began to dwindle. In my own student days in the late 1940s and early 1950s, you could be pretty sure that everyone with an interest in writing would have read Wilson's weekly article in *The New Yorker* by the time they turned up at parties on the weekend. (In those days, the magazine came out on Thursdays.) When I was teaching at Yale in the mid-1970s, however, the only thing I could be sure my students had read every week was Pauline Kael's movie column in *The New Yorker*. The world had changed, and literature could no longer be counted on to command the same allegiance. We had entered the era of "good trash," as it was sometimes called, and the "new sensibility." One consequence of this change was that Wilson's trade publishers allowed some of his best books—*The Triple Thinkers*, *The Wound and the Bow*, and *The Shores of Light*—to go out of print. When these books were reprinted in the 1980s, they were issued by the Northeastern University Press—a tacit acknowledgment that they were not expected to have a significant readership.

Wilson always insisted that he was, first and last, "a writer and a journalist," which is a very different thing from a "public intellectual." His principal models, as Meyers reminds us, "were Edgar Poe, Hippolyte Taine, George Saintsbury, Van Wyck Brooks, and H. L. Mencken." With the exception of Poe, these are writers who are now very little read by serious students of literature, and even Poe is very little read as a critic.

It is depressing to think that Wilson may now be fated for a similar obscurity, but the chances of his escaping it do not look good. The attempt made by the very academic Lewis Dabney a few years ago to produce a *Portable Edmund Wilson* did nothing to revive an interest in Wilson as a writer. It had the character of a mausoleum to be visited on ceremonial occasions—than which, of course, there is no better way to seal a writer's fate. The book set out to satisfy too many interests, and its refusal

—or was it only an inability?—to distinguish between what might be of enduring interest in Wilson's *oeuvre* and what has already proved to be perishable made the book a poor introduction for readers coming to Wilson for the first time. It simply packaged Wilson for classroom consumption, which, given today's academic atmosphere, itself amounts to a death sentence.

Nor have the early responses to Meyers's biography been any more encouraging. I was particularly appalled to see in Elizabeth Hardwick's review in *The New Yorker* that Wilson's diaries were said to be "among his principal achievements." I very much doubt that this mistaken judgment was intended by Elizabeth Hardwick to add another nail in the coffin of Wilson's reputation as a literary critic, but that was inevitably its effect. So is the notion that Wilson's "greatest subject" was "his own life." Are we really being invited to believe that Wilson's diaristic accounts of the societies he frequented on Cape Cod and in upstate New York—or even on his European travels—are more important than, say, the essays and portraits he devoted to Joyce or Hemingway or Fitzgerald, to John Jay Chapman, Christian Gauss, Justice Oliver Wendell Holmes, or Ulysses S. Grant? This seems to me a strange way to pay tribute to Wilson's accomplishments. I, certainly, would rather reread him on Flaubert and Michelet and Dickens—even on Harriet Beecher Stowe—and on the literary battles of the 1930s, than to endure once again the deadly chronicles of Wilson's compulsive sex life, which in the later diaries are rendered in a manner that is not significantly different from the dreary accounts of his visits to the dentist and the late-night drinking bouts. There are, to be sure, some very affecting *literary* moments in the late diaries—his account, for example, of what it meant for him to reread Macaulay's *History of England* as his own life and work were drawing to a close. But even these remain isolated episodes, and leave us wishing that Wilson had lived long enough to devote full-scale essays to their subjects.

On the subject of Wilson's sex life, Meyers again puts the

matter exactly right when he observes that "for Wilson, as for Pepys and Boswell, no seduction was complete until he had recorded its details in his diary." Yet I doubt if even Elizabeth Hardwick would want to claim that Wilson's diaries are in a class with either Pepys's or Boswell's. Wilson's life, apart from his writing and the intellectual labor that went into it, just wasn't that interesting. "He defined his own cyclical behavior," Meyers writes, "as dedicated toil followed by an orgy," and the details of the "orgy," or seductions, that he was concerned to record were often remarkably unappetizing. With his customary powers of application, Meyers has researched Wilson's half-century of sexual activity—from his loss of virginity in the arms of Edna St. Vincent Millay at the age of twenty-five to his drunken encounter with Penelope Gilliatt at the Princeton Club at the age of seventy-five—with a thoroughness that leaves little to the imagination. Meyers is not without a sense of humor in recounting this chronicle of Wilson's transformation from the "man in the iron necktie," as E. E. Cummings once described him, "into one of the great literary fornicators of all time," but it is a story that was often far less amusing for those who were nearest and dearest to Wilson himself. For anyone who knows what a sodden wreck Penelope Gilliatt had become when she succumbed to Wilson's charms in his old age, the story isn't really amusing at all—it is sordid. And what Elena Wilson—his fourth wife and the only one he seems to have loved very deeply—was obliged to endure on this score isn't a pretty story, either. It is no wonder that in the immediate aftermath of Wilson's death in the summer of 1972, Elena Wilson's first thought was: "Where are the diaries? Where are the diaries?" She had plenty to be apprehensive about.

Wilson's career as a fornicator, like his forays into politics, will in the end contribute nothing to secure his literary reputation. About Wilson's life, it seems to me that Meyers has now said everything that is of any conceivable interest for us to know, and more at times than we need to know. He has done particularly good work in correcting the record of Wilson's embattled marriage to Mary McCarthy—a story that McCarthy herself shamelessly lied about in the self-serving autobiographical sketches she wrote in the last years of her life, and which her most recent biographer, Carol Brightman, proved to be remarkably credulous about.

Yet biography—especially as biography is now written—tends not to serve as an inducement for its readers to turn from the life of a writer to his work. It may even serve as a substitute for an experience of the work itself. If this is what happens in Wilson's case, it would be indeed an irony, for it was a large part of his success as a writer that he used the biographical portrait as a means of recalling his readers to a writer's merits as well as to his place in history.

That was certainly one of the sources of the influence he exerted on my own career as a writer. When I was a student, it had become very much a fashion in the highbrow literary world to dismiss Wilson as a superficial critic, a mere popularizer or journalist. In *Partisan Review*, Delmore Schwartz had written an attack on his work, and then Stanley Edgar Hyman launched an even more vicious assault on Wilson in *The Armed Vision*. What I soon discovered, however, when I began to frequent the literary milieu in which these attacks had occurred, was that Wilson was actually more admired than these attacks suggested, and that the attacks themselves were more expressions of envy than of disinterested criticism designed to serve some higher literary purpose. It was Lionel Trilling who, in 1952, broke the ice that had pretty much sealed off Wilson's reputation from prospering in the literary quarterlies when, on the occasion of the publication of *The Shores of Light*, he spoke with admirable candor about what Wilson's example had meant in his own case. When I decided against an academic career, moreover, it was precisely Wilson's career as an intellectual journalist that served me as a model of what might be possible. Now, more than forty years later, the old condescending attacks on Wilson are forgotten, and Wilson's own writings are in danger of being forgotten, and even a writer as intelligent as Elizabeth Hardwick can seriously suggest that his life was his "greatest subject." I hope that Jeffrey Meyers's biography might do something to reverse the momentum of this loss—a loss in our collective cultural memory—but the signs, as I say, are not promising that it will. For the effect of this biography—so far, anyway—has been to turn the writer into a "character," whose contributions to literature and history are now of secondary interest.

May 1995

The Follies of Dwight Macdonald

THERE is a passage in Hazlitt's *The Spirit of the Age*—it comes in the essay on "The Late Mr. Horne Tooke"—that defines not only its eponymous subject but also an entire class of failed writers. "He generally ranged himself on the losing side," wrote Hazlitt, "and had rather an ill-natured delight in contradiction, and in perplexing the understandings of others, without leaving them any clue to guide them out of the labyrinth into which he had led them. He understood, in its perfection, the great art of throwing the *onus probandi* on his adversaries, and so could maintain almost any opinion, however absurd or fantastical, with fearless impunity."

Writers of this class are remembered for their follies, rather than their wisdom, for their follies have a representative character. What they illuminate is not the distilled intelligence of their time but its shibboleths and chimeras. These they have the talent to make so entertaining that their writings seem for a while audacious and even original. It is only later, in the sober light of retrospection, that we come to understand that the "ill-natured delight in contradiction" in such writers had only succeeded in trivializing every important subject they touched upon. In the end this ability to "maintain almost any opinion, however absurd or fantastical," turns out to have been an act, a performance, a role that never required the writers themselves to live by any of the ideas they so easily espoused. There was always a new role to play, or an old one to be revived, or a holiday to be taken when no suitable parts presented themselves.

It has long seemed to me that the American writer Dwight Macdonald (1906–1982) was a figure of this kind. "All he wanted was *negative success*," Hazlitt said of Horne Tooke, and then added: "to this no one was better qualified to aspire. Cross purposes, *moot-points*, pleas, demurrers, flaws in the indictment, double meanings, cases, inconsequentialities, these were the playthings, the darlings of Mr. Tooke's mind." The same could be said of Macdonald's. In that coterie of New York intellectuals that first made its presence felt in the pages of *Partisan Review* in the late 1930s and early 1940s—the circle in which Macdonald achieved his initial reputation as a writer—delight in contradiction was elevated to a vocation, and Macdonald was its most amusing practitioner. Yet in politics he always remained something of a fantasist and a lightweight, an amateur passionately in love with extreme positions and unworldly strategems. "For him," wrote William Barrett in *The Truants*, "every venture into politics was a leap toward the Absolute." Hence his addiction to "almost any opinion, however absurd or fantastical," so long as it remained safely distant from any possibility of compromise or realization.

That he commanded a gift for intellectual entertainment is undeniable, and it was all the more appreciated because it was a gift rarely found in the leaden world of radical debate. His high-spirited prose was often fun to read. If not for his radicalism, he might have become the Mencken of his generation. Yet in Macdonald's case, the amusement his writings offered tended to be in inverse proportion to the seriousness of his subjects. About figures easily ridiculed, whether in politics, literature, journalism, or popular culture, he could be devastating as well as hilarious. This is an example from his little book *Henry Wallace: The Man and the Myth* (Vanguard Press, 1948), published the year that Wallace, who had been Vice President in the the third Roosevelt administration, broke with the Democratic Party to run for the presidency as the candidate of the Progressive Party, a Stalinist creation:

> Wallaceland is the mental habitat of Henry Wallace plus a few hundred thousand regular readers of *The New Republic*, *The Nation*, and *PM*. It is a region of perpetual fogs, caused by the warm winds of the liberal Gulf Stream coming in contact with the Soviet glacier. Its natives speak "Wallese," a debased provincial dialect.

When Macdonald traded his jester's cap and bells for the costume of a thinker, however, he always ran the risk of turning himself into a target of satire. This was particularly true when he took to rehearsing some untenable political posture. At such times, real issues and momentous events were recast as episodes in a private drama of choices so absolute that they no longer bore much relation to the realities which had prompted them. In the realm of politics, Macdonald's position was often that of a writer in a kind of free fall where the gravity of history was suspended in favor of sheer weightlessness.

Here, by way of examples, is a sampling of Macdonald's characteristic political utterences between 1941, when he was quarreling with his colleagues at *Partisan Review* over America's role in the Second World War, and 1953, when he finally conceded that he had lost interest in the whole radical enterprise:

> In the war or out of it, the United States faces only one future under capitalism: fascism. (*July–August 1941*)

> No, whatever leadership towards social progress may exist in the world, it is not to be found in this country. (*July 1944*)

> It may be there is no exit from the blind alley, but surely the first condition for finding one is to give up the superficial lesser-evil approach, with the support it implies for a future war

> against Russia, in favor of a more radical and basic approach, be it pacifist or social-revolutionary or perhaps some new combination of both. (*March 1946*)
>
> Let us admit at once—let us, indeed, insist on the point—that all the criticisms made of U.S.S.R. could also be made of U.S.A. (*Spring 1948*)
>
> During the last war, I did not choose, at first because I was a revolutionary socialist of Trotskyist coloration, later because I was becoming, especially after the atom bomb, a pacifist. Neither of these positions now appear valid to me. (*Winter 1952*)
>
> Perhaps there is no solution to these agonizing problems. . . . This is one reason I am less interested in politics than I used to be. (*1953*)

That Macdonald was *ever* taken seriously as a political thinker is less a reflection of any sagacity he commanded on the subject of politics than a measure of the intellectual desperation that afflicted the non-Stalinist radical Left once the myth of a socialist millennium had collapsed and radicals had to make do with purely rhetorical substitutes—a commodity that Macdonald was certainly well equipped to supply.

This view of Macdonald is, of course, very much at odds with his reputation as a radical, a Marxist, a Trotskyist, an anarchist, a pacifist, a champion of revolution, a partisan of the 1960s New Left, and the rest of the folderol about his career as a "revolutionist." With Macdonald, I believe, we must distinguish between the roles he assumed—there were quite a few of them, after all—and the fundamental loyalties that governed his life, his style, and his moral temper. In my view, anyway, he was always at heart a bourgeois literary aesthete—a bit of a snob, too, as aesthetes tend to be, a patrician rebel, and a cultural elitist—who was able to sustain an interest in politics, *any* politics, only when its choices presented themselves to his mind as high drama for the happy few. His spiritual affinities, if we may call them that, were closer to those of the literary culture of the 1890s and the 1920s than to the political culture of the 1930s and 1940s, though it was the latter, of course, that provided him with the roles that won him his reputation as a radical. Macdonald was thus an example of a cultural phenomenon too rarely studied: the aesthete who carries into politics a disdain for compromise and even common sense that is more appropriate to the rarified air of Parnassus than to the contingent conflicts of the social arena.

It is worth remembering in this connection that the aesthete's mind is also one that is enamored of absolutes, and in the absence of absolutes—the most dreaded of all conditions for the aesthete and the radical alike—the ordinary interests of art or politics or life itself lose their savor. Boredom looms as the only alternative, and some variety of intellectual ennui is the punishment that follows in its wake. This was the condition that overtook Macdonald in that long furlough from radical polemics that separated the first phase of his political engagement in the Thirties and Forties from his second and final plunge into the politics of revolution in the Sixties and Seventies. It was a furlough spent mostly at *The New Yorker*, which he had once denounced in *Partisan Review* as the "accurate expression of a decaying social order," but where his own bourgeois snobberies were now easily accommodated, and where, ironically enough, the politics of revolution acquired a kind of chic at the very moment when the aging Macdonald was abandoning the magazine to ascend the rhetorical barricades for the last time.

Macdonald himself has left us a poignant clue to his sensibility in a dispirited memoir called "Politics Past," which he published in *Encounter* in 1957 during his long furlough from the radical ranks. This was intended to be his swan song to politics, and would have been if he had not been lured out of political retirement by the events of the Sixties. Looking back on the 1930s from the perspective of the Cold War of the 1950s, he wrote in defense of his own failed efforts as a political writer that "an interest in *avant-garde* politics was expected of every proper intellectual. Those few who were 'unpolitical' were *déclassé*, accused of Escapism, Living in an Ivory Tower, etc. Even so unpolitical a type as Edmund Wilson signed *Culture and the Crisis*, a celebrated pamphlet-manifesto, in support of the Communist candidates in the presidential election."

The most telling word in this passage is, I think, "*avant-garde*," which in this context nicely conflates the impulses of radical politics with those of modernist art and literature. But the whole passage mixes up the language of the literary avant-garde with that of the radical movement in a way that suggests a closer acquaintance with *Axel's Castle* than with *Das Kapital*. (The notion that Edmund Wilson was somehow "unpolitical" before 1932 isn't accurate, either.) And the entire memoir acquires added resonance when we learn from Michael Wreszin's biography of Macdonald, *A Rebel in Defense of Tradition: The Life and "Politics" of Dwight Macdonald* (Basic Books), about his student days as an aesthete at Exeter in the 1920s. Wreszin writes:

> Dwight became part of a circle of bookish young men who saw themselves as set apart from the majority of the students. . . . Within that group, Dwight, Justin O'Brien, and Dinsmore Wheeler founded their own inner circle, the Hedonists. Mencken, Baudelaire, George Jean Nathan, and Oscar Wilde were their patron saints. Their motto: "*Pour épater les bourgeois*." Their notepaper bore the slogan "Cynicism, Estheticism, Criticism, Pessimism." They sported monocles and batik ties and carried canes on their walks in the surrounding countryside. They were, Dwight later admitted, "frightful snobs."

From the aestheticism of the 1920s, with its motto, "*Pour épater les bourgeois*," which pretty much remained Macdonald's intellectual banner during his undergraduate years at Yale, to the "*avant-garde* politics" of the Thirties was not, for a man in his privileged position, that big a leap. It was *épater les bourgeois* all the way, while for a good deal of the time there was no need to forgo bourgeois comforts or a steady income. The problem for a radical/aesthete like Macdonald, however, was to decide exactly which of the many varieties of "*avant-garde* politics" on offer in the Thirties—and later on, too, for that matter—was sufficiently pleasing to his taste to command his allegiance.

The new biography by Michael Wreszin, a historian who teaches at Queens College and the City University of New York, makes fascinating reading in this regard. For it happened that Macdonald, once he discovered the pleasures of the Left's capacious ideological smorgasbord, managed to sample just about every dish that was served up, defending each in turn with absolute conviction and tolerating no alternatives or modifications. Professor Wreszin gets the matter exactly right when he says of Macdonald that "expediency, pragmatic compromise irritated him. He was attracted not so much to abstract ideological frameworks as to commitment, enthusiasm, dedication to one's beliefs."

But what *were* Macdonald's beliefs? He had so many in the course of his career, and they were so frequently subject to sudden shifts. In less than a decade he moved from a commitment to the Communist Party, which he discovered while researching an article for *Fortune*, where he was making a five-figure salary during the Depression, to the embrace of Trotskyist anti-Stalinism before settling for a vaguely defined mixture of anarchism and pacifism during the Second World War. It was wholly in character, moreover, that during his Communist phase he was a fellow-traveler rather than a party member, that during his Trotskyist period he quarreled with Trotsky, and that during his anti-war anarchist-pacifist period he adamantly refused to acknowledge that there was something more at stake in the war than a defense of American capitalist imperialism.

For Macdonald, it was always enough to be against the

government, opposed to American society, and scornful of capitalism. That was what made radical politics fun for him, and when it stopped being fun, he turned his talents to debunking American middlebrow culture, an endeavor that satisfied both his intellectual elitism and his distaste for his own class, the American bourgeoisie. As a critic, however, he was careful to steer clear of great writers. He seemed instinctively to understand that they were beyond his range. Popular culture, on the other hand, offered rich opportunities for sarcasm and condescension. Attacking it was almost as much fun as attacking Henry Wallace or Harry Truman.

It was not as if Macdonald had ever acquired any special affection for the toiling masses or their ill-bred champions in the labor movement even in his most radical period in the Thirties. He was still too much of a snob for that. Professor Wreszin tells an interesting story in this regard about the summer of 1934. Macdonald was then employed at *Fortune*, and would soon marry Nancy Rodman, a wealthy debutante turned radical who was already further to the Left than Macdonald himself. It was on her trust fund that they lived when he quit *Fortune* to devote himself full time to radical journalism.

> On a hot Saturday in July, Dwight, the photographer Walker Evans, and Geoffrey Hellman, who was a staff writer for *The New Yorker*, drove up to Westchester County to visit Nitgedaiget "(Yiddish for 'not to worry')," a Communist Party training and recreation center. Dwight reported to Nancy, still vacationing in Dublin, New Hampshire, that visiting the camp almost "made a fascist" out of him. He had discovered in himself an aristocratic revulsion—"as to bathing in a slightly dirty pool with the other comrades and eating off slightly soiled plates with the other comrades and applauding mass-level violin solos with the other comrades"—that surprised him. He added by way of justification that he had a "fundamental dislike for living as one of the herd. The comrades

> were $99^{44}/_{100}\%$ pure Yiddish and they had that peculiar Yiddish love of living in each other's laps that you can observe any day at Coney Island." Dwight must have been slightly defensive about these class and ethnic slurs, for he quickly added that he felt "disgusted by humanity, whether Yiddish or Racquet Clubbish, when it presented itself as a squirming mass." In any event, he and his cohorts could not stand the camp beyond Sunday noon, brunch time, so they beat a hasty retreat to the Westchester Embassy Club, where Geoffrey Hellman was a member, and they "bathed in a clean capitalist pool and drank a couple of Tom Collinses in capitalistic solitude."

Nancy, however, was ready to place Dwight's experience in a proper—which is to say, a politically correct—context. Professor Wreszin continues:

> Nancy did not seem to take offense at this glib, Waspish mockery, responding that she could well understand how he "might have turned Fascist" by attending the camp. "My stomach is often turned at continual radical meetings and dirty radicals and self-interested radicals." But she was quick to add, "Still I believe in communism as the only way out of the political disruption that is going on nowadays." Nancy had just read Ella Winter's *Red Virtue: Human Relationships in the New Russia*, which she thought very good. Winter's Russia sounded pretty idyllic despite the hardships. "There at least everyone has some definite goal. An attempt is made to let everyone do work for which they are fitted and to adjust those that are not fitted. And stupid conventions are forgotten and everyone has a personal freedom that we never dreamed of."

Mercifully, the Macdonalds were soon disabused of this version of red virtue, rescued by the predominantly Jewish intellectuals who were attempting to publish *Partisan Review*, which had been founded as an organ of the Communist Party, as an anti-

Stalinist, pro-Trotsky, Marxist literary journal. "Dwight, with his enthusiasm for debate, was charmed by the aggressiveness of his new associates and impressed with their learning and serious literary interests," Professor Wreszin writes. Macdonald even found a patron for the new magazine in George L. K. Morris, the painter who had been his classmate at Yale and with whom he had briefly published a literary journal called the *Miscellany*. Nancy Macdonald served as *Partisan*'s business manager. Yet, when the war erupted and real political choices had to be made, Macdonald found these "new associates" insufficiently radical, and so he broke with them to start his own journal, *Politics*. Macdonald was never one to allow political reality to hamper his style.

Appropriately, Professor Wreszin calls the hundred-page section of his biography that is devoted to Macdonald's political furlough at *The New Yorker* "Criticism as a Substitute for Politics." With the collapse of *Politics*, moreover, he broke up his marriage to Nancy Macdonald, grandly declaring that "the only responsibilities, duties, obligations I will accept are those that I want to, those I choose to, freely and spontaneously"—the last remaining vestige, perhaps, of the anarchist philosophy he had adopted during the war but which he now pretty much abandoned along with the wife who had supported his anarchist journal. Inevitably, this section of Professor Wreszin's book has its longueurs. Macdonald's most ambitious intellectual effort of this period was his essay called "Masscult and Midcult," a study of popular culture in which all of the author's snobberies are on full display and which contains little, if any, understanding of what the loss of middlebrow culture would mean when it was supplanted by the degraded simulacrum that has now taken its place.

Except for its account of the shenanigans surrounding Macdonald's brief attachment to *Encounter* and his quarrels with the Congress for Cultural Freedom, Professor Wreszin's book doesn't get going again until it is time to tell the story of Macdonald's return to politics as a born-again radical in the Sixties. This story really *is* an example of history repeating itself as farce, and rather a grim farce at that.

1965: "Dwight was quick to give his support and name to an Artist Protest Committee, which published a large ad in the *New York Times* with over 630 signatures. The ad called on all Americans to end their silence and speak out against the war. Dwight's name could be found among the likes of the screenwriter Alvah Bessie, the actor Howard Da Silva, Howard Fast, and Corliss Lamont, all of whom he had seen as contemptible apologists for Stalin a little over a decade earlier."

1968: "The clincher was a phone call Dwight made to Fred Dupee to inquire about the situation [at Columbia University]. Dupee responded with enthusiasm: "You must come up right away, Dwight. It's a revolution! You may never get another chance to see one." . . . Dwight loved it. It was as though a "Victorian father had been removed from his family's bosom (or neck)." Later when he saw [President] Grayson Kirk on television complaining of student anarchy and barbarism, he felt his image was on target."

1970: "On Thursday April 30 he made the trip to New Haven to show solidarity with the liberal-left elements on [the Yale] campus. . . . He came away feeling good about the entire affair. Defending his activities and alliance with the New Left to the harshly critical Nicola Chiaromonte, Dwight stoutly defended his support of the Panthers. . . ."

It was *épater les bourgeois* to the end. And in the end the only thing that survives is the literary anthology called *Parodies* (1960), in which the aesthete in Macdonald kept faith with the spirit of the Hedonists circle at Exeter in the Twenties. But then, of course, Macdonald's career was itself a parody of the radical vocation in our time.

April 1994

Mary McCarthy & Company

What is missing is a certain largeness of mind, an amplitude of style, the mantle of a calling, a sense of historical dignity

—Mary McCarthy, "The Vassar Girl," 1951

WHEN a writer with a large reputation and a strong public personality quits the scene after many years in the limelight, there inevitably follows a period of uncertainty in which posterity—the cruelest of all critics—has not yet determined its verdict, and briefs for the defense are given every opportunity to dominate the discussion. The eulogies sound the appropriate note of piety and praise; the remaining manuscripts, ceremoniously augmented by glowing testimonials, are rushed into print; the favor of a friendly assessment is more or less assured; and the author's name is everywhere draped in respectful mourning. The literary world makes its obeisance to one of its own, and even the writer's enemies refrain from casting doubt upon the manufacture of encomia.

Nowadays, moreover, there is likely to be added to this chorus of acclaim a promptly produced biography of the subject, for today's biographers gather their materials long before the body is buried and are no longer deterred by a sense of delicacy about the feelings of the immediate survivors. It might even be said that the timely publication of such a biography, precisely because it is certain to raise even more questions than it answers, is likely to bring this period of respectful mourning to a close. For biography, especially as it is practiced today, is a genre that specializes in laying bare its subject's imperfections and delinquencies, and it is these, rather than the tale of achievement that is the ostensible *raison d'être* of such books, that commands attention. Biography of this kind, no matter how respectful its intention, is therefore bound to clear the air of incense and restore its subject to the realm of reasonable debate.

In the case of Mary McCarthy, who died in 1989 at the age of seventy-seven, the customary rituals have all been lavishly observed. Even before her death, she had been hailed as America's "First Lady of Letters," quite as if this were an official position in our national cultural life that had been owed to her. It hardly mattered that McCarthy had spent a lifetime ridiculing such honors, or that the national cultural life of which she was now to be thought an ornament was something she held in very low esteem. She embraced her elevation with an evident sense of vindication—the bad girl of American letters, who had always been forgiven her misdeeds, had again gotten away with it this one last time—and this feeling of vindication, which had an important political dimension to it, was clearly shared by her many admirers. So it came as no surprise that McCarthy's passing would bring an amplification of a sentiment so patently at odds with the character of her writing and the spirit of her temperament, and she would be presented to us in retrospect as a paragon of literary probity, intellectual independence, and political sagacity.

Now the expected biography has appeared with a promptitude that is all the more remarkable because of its exorbitant length. Carol Brightman's *Writing Dangerously: Mary McCarthy and Her World* (Clarkson Potter) is by no means the longest book of its kind to come off the press, but it does run to some seven hundred pages, which is rather a lot about a writer who never produced a single major work. For Brightman, however, McCarthy is clearly more interesting as a figure of history than as a writer per se. This no doubt has a good deal to do with the specific historical circumstances under which the biographer first met her subject. It was during the Vietnam War, and Brightman, as she says, "had become a foot soldier in the revolution"—that is, a writer-activist in the antiwar movement. "I had left a fledgling career as a film and book reviewer to start an antiwar magazine, *Viet-Report*," she writes, and it was in this capacity that she was introduced to McCarthy in 1967 by Robert Silvers, the editor of *The New York Review of Books*. McCarthy was about to leave for Hanoi on a political reporting assignment for the *Review*, and Brightman, who had just returned from Hanoi, was brought in to advise "the famous author of *The Group*" on what she would find there. *Hanoi*, the book that resulted from that political pilgrimage, idealized the Vietnamese Communists in the most sentimental fellow-traveling fashion, characterizing their regime as a "virtuous tyranny" to be admired, and castigated both the American prisoners-of-war and America itself with that mixture of snobbery, condescension, and self-aggrandizement McCarthy had perfected thirty years earlier in her caustic reviews of lousy Broadway plays. It was the most shameful of all her books, and proved to be distasteful even to her buddies on the Left—even, alas, to Dwight Macdonald, who had a strong stomach for such political nonsense.

It should be understood, then, that it is the bond once established between Brightman and her subject in that halcyon moment of radical solidarity that provides the basic historical *donnée* from which *Writing Dangerously* is written. Which is to say, it is a book about an earlier generation (what Brightman calls "the granddaddy generation") of the American intellectual Left written by a member of the Sixties radical Left who, though still loyal to the ethos of the Left, is now trying to make sense of the debacle that has overtaken its most cherished articles of belief and left its sacred ideology in ruins. In this respect, the book that *Writing Dangerously* most closely resembles is Elinor Langer's *Josephine Herbst* (1984), an earlier attempt on the part of a disaffected Sixties radical to look for answers as well as absolution in the failures of her predecessors.

There are great differences, of course, between the two books and the two subjects. Josie Herbst was a Stalinist, and McCarthy was not (though she gave a good impersonation of one in *Hanoi*). Herbst would never attack the Communists in public, however much she criticized them in private, whereas McCarthy was (shall we say?) more adaptable to the needs of the moment, allying herself with the anti-Communists and the anti-anti-Communists according to the shifting fortunes of the radical Left and her own career. *Josephine Herbst* is therefore the story of a failed life as well as a failed ideology, whereas *Writing Dangerously* is a tale of worldly success in which the heroine survives every misfortune—a wretched childhood, an army of discarded lovers, three disastrous marriages, bad books, political misadventures, and even a famous law suit—to achieve in the end both literary fame and fortune and bourgeois marital bliss. There is also another important difference: whereas Josie Herbst was the kind of radical who lost everything as a result of her actions and her beliefs, McCarthy was always the kind of smart, Left-leaning opportunist who managed to turn every personal attachment and every shift in the *Zeitgeist* to her own advantage. She had a knack for escaping the wreckage unscathed.

It is for this reason, by the way, that the title of Brightman's biography—*Writing Dangerously*—strikes me as ridiculous, for McCarthy's were the kind of "risks" that, in life as well as in literature, always advanced her career. Indeed, the more pain she inflicted by means of her pen, the more she betrayed her friends, her lovers, and her husbands, the more praise she reaped in the process. (*Hanoi* was virtually the only exception.) In a century in which many writers better than Mary McCarthy have put themselves in real danger through their writing—the danger of poverty, the Gulag, and even death—it demeans the whole idea of literary risk to place her in their company, and it is a measure of Brightman's identification with her subject and what may fairly be described as her infatuation with the glamour of McCarthy's career that she does not seem to understand this. On this issue, as on others—McCarthy's three failed marriages, for example, and the writings on Vietnam—she lapses into the role of "authorized" biographer, suspending judgment in favor of her subject. As Brightman herself acknowledges, she felt "the tug of McCarthy's personality" in the interviews that were conducted with her subject—eighteen in all—and the sway of that personality makes itself felt on every page of the book, which is not always to the book's advantage.

Still, it is Brightman herself who introduces the theme of failure in writing about McCarthy and her generation of New York intellectuals. Although she speaks admiringly of this generation as "the last one to sustain an imaginative and critical involvement with the world around it"—which means, I suppose, that she still approves of what they made of their politics—she adds that "I wanted to understand how and why its writers pulled back from their early promise." I think she is right about the unfulfilled promise of that generation, which is what we mean by failure, but we don't actually hear much more about it in *Writing Dangerously,* which tends in the course of its lengthy narrative to dissolve into a series of vivid vignettes of personalities, political debates, literary projects, love affairs, publishing arrangements, and intellectual social life, not to mention the sex life of McCarthy herself, without ever coming to grips with the nature of the "promise" or the reasons for its failure.

To account for this omission, which leaves a moral and intellectual void at the center of Brightman's very long book, it is necessary to examine exactly what she means when she speaks so approvingly of the "imaginative and critical involvement with the world" that she attributes to McCarthy's generation of New

York intellectuals. McCarthy herself was never a leader in the intellectual and political initiatives of that generation. She took her cues from the men in her life: lovers, mentors, colleagues, who were themselves deeply divided in their attitude toward the world they wished to engage in their work. While on the one hand they tended to be rebels of the Left who were fiercely critical of American society and bourgeois life, they were also, on the other, ambitious to secure a place of preferment in the American cultural establishment they looked down upon with a good deal of intellectual scorn and political distaste. In the beginning—that is, in the Thirties, and to a lesser extent in the Forties—the greatest obstacle to their success was their opposition to Stalinism, which in its cultural manifestations dominated the literary world that held the keys to preferment. Stalinism was, in its literary and artistic standards, philistine and middlebrow, whereas the writers in *Partisan Review,* the principal organ of the anti-Stalinist Left, were ferociously highbrow. McCarthy herself made her literary debut as the drama critic of *Partisan Review* by playing—and brilliantly, too—the highbrow scourge of a Broadway theater still firmly tethered to the standards of Stalinist philistinism.

What changed all this, oddly enough, was the Cold War. It was the Cold War that gave this generation of New York intellectuals—McCarthy included—its entrée to the larger cultural stage that it both coveted and condescended to. Suddenly there were jobs in universities, in publishing, and in the mainstream media that had formerly been closed to writers of their persuasion. There were fellowships, subsidies, conferences, contracts, and the other emoluments of an established intellectual class. The irony was, of course, that the New York intellectuals now qualified for the mainstream because of their politics—that is, their anti-Stalinism—at the very moment when the actualities of the political situation, the military threat coming from the Soviet Union, greatly diminished their radical commitment. It was discovered that in an increasingly perilous world, the United States could no longer be considered the principal enemy and might even be worth defending against the libels and slanders of the European—especially the French—Left, which placed itself in militant opposition to American interests.

As was her custom in such matters, McCarthy enthusiastically joined in this reversal of opinion, writing essays on "America the Beautiful" and "Gulliver en Amerique" (an attack on Simone de Beauvoir's criticism of America) that some readers believed marked a "conservative" turn in her thinking. Later on, of course, when a radical critique of America was once again the intellectual fashion of the Left, she returned to the subject with a far more savage criticism of America than "Gulliver" had ever been able to muster. McCarthy had become, so to speak, a political pen for all seasons.

What has to be understood about the political demeanor of the New York intellectuals at the height of the Cold War was that they were never entirely comfortable in the support they rendered to—and received from—the United States in its struggle with the Soviet Union. While fully availing themselves of the benefits of their new position, they could never really give up the idea that political virtue was still in some sense the preserve of the radical Left. They remained, emotionally even more than intellectually, secret believers in the radical dream. This made them extremely touchy about and indeed vulnerable to attacks from the Left—especially those of Norman Mailer, Harold Rosenberg, Irving Howe, et al.—which they publicly scorned but which privately caused them a lot of grief. I saw a good deal of Philip Rahv in the Fifties, when I first began writing for *Partisan Review*, and I was always struck by the great gap that separated his private conversation from his public pronouncements on these matters. He had a morbid fear of being nailed as a renegade.

This split came to be symbolized for me in what was said privately about Lionel Trilling. No writer was more highly esteemed by the readers of *Partisan Review* than Trilling was in the

Fifties. Yet his appearances in the magazine were frequently accompanied by a campaign of disparagement that was conducted behind his back, and often by the very people who were publishing him in the magazine. Trilling was seen to have completely severed his ties with the radical ethos. He was considered too bourgeois, too respectable, too square, too "conservative," yet because *Partisan Review* seemed to need him, he could not be expelled from its pages without causing a scandal that would have cost *PR* some of its support. Some of this anti-Trilling sentiment was publicly expressed by Delmore Schwartz, Harold Rosenberg, and Irving Howe, but the really vicious talk was carried on *sotto voce* in a way that absolved its speakers from responsibility. They didn't really get up the nerve to dump Trilling until many years later when, owing to the resurgence of radicalism in the late Sixties, it no longer cost them anything.

It was the radical movement of the Sixties that brought the New York intellectuals back into the political limelight as avowed partisans of the Left. It didn't happen all at once, and there were many poisonous feuds to be negotiated along the way. Rahv, for example, abominated both Norman Mailer and Susan Sontag, who had emerged as the intellectual darlings of the radical movement, and his relations with Irving Howe were none too cordial, either. He had also split with *Partisan Review* and started a magazine of his own called *Modern Occasions*. (One of his first priorities was to commission a blistering attack on Trilling.) But under the diplomatic auspices of Robert Silvers at *The New York of Books*, which had now supplanted *Partisan Review* as the principal intellectual organ of the highbrow Left, all was smoothly accomplished. Rahv re-emerged as—in Frederick Crews's wonderful phrase—a "born-again Leninist," and Dwight Macdonald, too, after years of political sleepwalking through the pages of *The New Yorker*, rediscovered the pleasures of radical militancy.

Right on cue, Mary McCarthy followed suit. If not exactly a "born-again Leninist" herself—years earlier she had confessed that "it was too late for me to become any kind of Marxist. Marxism, I saw . . . was something you had to take up young, like ballet dancing"—she nonetheless knew how to mimic the gestures and ideas that went with the position, and harness them to the rhetoric of social snobbery, which was her principal instrument as a political writer. In this respect, the Vietnam War should have been an ideal subject for her gimlet eye, allowing her to exercise the gift for caricature that she had used on her intellectual friends in *The Oasis,* on her Vassar classmates in *The Group*, even on the art and culture of Venice in *Venice Observed*, and on the hapless American military personnel in Saigon and Hanoi. But it turned out not to be such an ideal subject, after all. It couldn't be turned into a social comedy of manners—the material was too stark—and the art of caricature doesn't, in any case, live on easy terms with the kind of bathos she brought to her account of the "virtuous tyranny" she professed to adore in North Vietnam. The bad faith of the whole enterprise had finally capsized her style,which was the only thing she had brought to it in the first place.

In the end, Mary McCarthy's politics were like her sex life—promiscuous and unprincipled, more a question of opportunity than of commitment or belief. Because the author of *Writing Dangerously* is herself writing from inside the ethos of the radical movement that must be elucidated and judged if her subject's relation to it is to be understood, she cannot really deal with the central questions of McCarthy's life and work or with those of the intellectual generation to which McCarthy belonged—the so-called "last one to sustain an imaginative and critical involvement with the world around it." Brightman is in many respects a good writer, a diligent researcher and readable prose stylist who knows how to shape a narrative. But she has been disarmed by her experience and her pieties from asking the deepest questions about her material. (This was the problem with Elinor Langer's *Josephine Herbst,* too.) About neither McCarthy nor her generation does she ever discover "how and why its writers pulled back from their early promise." The subject is simply lost in a blizzard of anecdote and annotation.

Because she cannot see her subject from the outside, Brightman's book also fails on other counts. For one thing, she misses the comedy of Mary McCarthy's career. It was only in writing about herself that McCarthy ever struck a really authentic note, and it is for this reason that the only books likely to survive are *The Company She Keeps* and *Memoirs of a Catholic Girlhood.* (By the time she came to write *How I Grew* and the unfinished *Intellectual Memoirs* it was too late. She had lost touch with her material, and was inclined to prevaricate.) I don't regard *The Company She Keeps* as good fiction, but it is excellent social reportage and written on a scale appropriate to the very small compass of the author's talent. When she tried to do something larger in the same vein—*The Group*—it was a literary failure modeled on the clichés of the bestseller list of the day. Which is why the only thing ever recalled from that book—unless you are a Vassar alumna—is the account of Dottie and her pessary, which is very much in the vein of *The Company She Keeps.*

As for the later novels, I doubt if they will ever be reread by anyone who isn't paid to do so. *Birds of America* is particularly awful, and underscores what I mean by the comedy of McCarthy's career. When it came to her account of American society and its interest in food, which looms very large in that book, she simply didn't know what she was talking about. The whole country was in the grip of a culinary revolution while *Birds of America* was being written, and Mary McCarthy simply didn't know anything about it. She thought a pot of basil in the kitchen window was some sort of challenge to convention when the magazines and newspapers were already crowded with tips on what to do with it. It was the same, really, when she turned to the subjects of Venice and Florence—subjects far beyond her depth. She was never again the writer she had been in her early contributions to *Partisan Review.* Without intending to, of course, she too had "pulled back" from that "early promise," but Brightman has left it to the reader to figure out why and how.

January 1993

The Role of Sidney Hook

OF the writers who belonged to the original "family" of the now much chronicled New York intellectuals, Sidney Hook was in several important respects the most unusual. In a circle of writers who prided themselves on their insiders' knowledge of Marxism and for whom, indeed, Marxism was long held to be the central issue of the day, Hook was the only one who was a recognized authority on the subject. Whereas the others were all, in varying degrees, amateurs of the Marxian dialectic—brilliant amateurs in some cases, but amateurs nonetheless—it was Hook alone who early on established his reputation as a professional scholar in this field and wrote the books—*Towards the Understanding of Karl Marx* (1933) and *From Hegel to Marx* (1936)—that helped to shape the agenda of intellectual debate. He came to the subject, moreover, not only out of a partisan political interest—this was true of all the New York intellectuals—but as a trained philosopher who brought an intimate knowledge of Marx's writings and their philosophical sources to bear on the incessant factional disputes and divisive ideological claims and counterclaims that have loomed so large in the intellectual life of his time.

In the early Thirties, when Hook was vigorously espousing Marxist causes, the authority he brought to the subject made him a formidable and influential figure—admired by radical intellectuals as much for his courage as for his perspicacity. He was said to be the only avowed Marxist to serve on the faculty of a major American university—he had already begun his long association with the department of philosophy at New York University—and, in this period, no less an eminence than Earl Browder, then head of the American Communist Party, had invited him to set up a Communist spy apparatus. This was distinction indeed! Browder had called on the wrong man, however. Even as a Marxist, Hook showed a disturbing tendency—some would say a compulsion—to act as an independent thinker. Although an inveterate joiner of boards and committees who was always ready to enlist in a cause he believed in, Hook was politically unclubbable. And this tendency to independence, which in the course of the Thirties brought him into fierce and open conflict with the Communists and their sympathizers, soon made him a figure of another sort—a despised renegade, and at times a pariah, who became for many liberals and radicals an unquestioned symbol of political perfidy and whose example, for that very reason, even some of his faint-hearted intellectual associates and admirers feared to emulate too conspicuously lest they, too, be consigned to the outer darkness. In this role, as well, Hook was often unusual, if only for the intensity of the abuse he was made to suffer for his frankly stated and scrupulously argued beliefs.

It was not exclusively to the world of the intellectuals, however, that Hook directed his voluminous writings and his many-sided political activities. He was also unusual among his confreres in the New York intellectual world for electing to play a public role. The determination and tenacity which Hook brought to the task of initiating and pursuing public debate over a whole range of political questions, with himself often occupying an unpopular position, was one of the salient characteristics of his career. While, for the most part, it remained the practice of the New York intellectuals to conduct an intramural, highly factional debate about such political questions—at least until the

1960s, when *The New York Review of Books* and *The New Yorker* provided some of them with the means and the opportunity to reach out to a larger readership—Hook habitually adopted a more public role in his campaigns to distinguish historical truth from political falsehood. From the time of his break with the Communist party, which occurred in 1933–34 in the immediate aftermath of Hitler's coming to power—an event in which he clearly perceived the role of Stalin and his policy of the-worse-the-better—Hook seems to have understood the importance of acting as an embattled citizen of the democracy with which, as an independent radical, he still had many quarrels, to be sure, but which he nonetheless embraced as a cause to be energetically defended. It was this civic dimension to the many tasks he set himself that so often placed Hook at odds with his fellow intellectuals, who, in their attachment to the ethos—if not always to the specific political doctrines—of the Marxist legacy, so frequently refused to identify their interests with the survival of bourgeois democracy. Oddly enough, Hook still called himself a "socialist"—a matter to be discussed—but it was unmistakably as a champion of bourgeois democracy that he was long locked in public combat with the true believers in socialism.

Though often accused of being a zealot and a die-hard, especially in his opposition to Communism and its liberal apologists, Hook was actually a good deal more forthright and reasonable about the shifts he made in his political outlook over the years than many of his accusers have been about their own. Hook's shifts, moreover, were never tethered to the winds of fashion—he never had a taste for what was chic—nor were they tailored either to serve the interests of a political party (or a political candidate) or to win for Hook himself an appointment to political office. Agree with them or not, Hook's views and the arguments given to support them were reasoned and informed responses to the central political events of this century, and much of the time they resulted in highly unpopular opinions. As he remarks in the closing pages of *Out of Step* (Harper & Row, 1987), his long and aptly titled volume of memoirs:

> Almost always I found myself in a minority. . . . I have always been somewhat premature in relation to dominant currents of public opinion. I was prematurely antiwar in 1917–21, prematurely anti-fascist, prematurely a Communist fellow-traveler, prematurely an anti-Communist, prematurely, in radical circles, a supporter of the war against Hitler, prematurely a cold warrior against Stalin's effort to extend the Gulag Archipelago, prematurely against the policy of détente and appeasement, prematurely for a national civil-rights program and against all forms of invidious discrimination, including reverse discrimination.

The book that Hook gives us in *Out of Step* is, in effect, the political chronicle of an American intellectual dissident, and it has the great virtue of reminding us, again and again and again, that Communism has been the principal cause of the author's dissent from received intellectual opinion because Communism and the illusions it has generated have played so important and so disheartening a role in the intellectual life of our time. Communism is not, to be sure, the only subject discussed in this book—far from it—nor was it the only subject on which Hook took a critical position, but it is certainly the main one. For this reason, *Out of Step* is not a book to be recommended to those who are easily wearied by lengthy accounts of the polemical battles that intellectuals have waged with one another on the issue of Communism and the nature of Soviet power. Since he had devoted so much of his long life to opposing the views of those who either defended the Communist cause because they wished to see it triumph or mistakenly discounted the threat it posed to the survival of freedom and democracy because they failed to grasp the true dimension of that threat, this chronicle of Hook's intellectual career inevitably places a greater emphasis on this issue than on any other. I think it is proper that it does so, and the result is a book that must be counted as a major contribution to the literature of anti-Communism—the most important contribution by an American writer, I think, since Whittaker Chambers's *Witness*. It is not a book without serious flaws—some of which will be noted here—but it is nonetheless essential reading for anyone who aspires to an understanding of the place that Communism and the opposition to Communism have occupied in American intellectual life.

The historical scope of Hook's chronicle is a broad one, reaching from the period of World War I to that of the Reagan administration, and its cast of characters includes, among many other distinctive figures in the intellectual and political world of his time, John Dewey, Bertrand Russell, Bertolt Brecht, Albert Einstein, Arthur Koestler, Whittaker Chambers, Morris Raphael Cohen, Max Eastman, Norman Thomas, V. F. Calverton, Malcolm Cowley, James Burnham, Edmund Wilson, and the writers of the *Partisan Review* circle. About some of these figures—Dewey, Russell, Einstein, and Cohen—Hook writes at length, while others—Cowley, for example, who is depicted solely for his work as an outstanding literary apologist for the Moscow Purge Trials—are given little more than walk-on roles. Some are discussed with an impressive spirit of generosity—Dwight Macdonald, for example, with whom Hook fought some crucial political battles in the Forties and Fifties. In other cases—Philip Rahv's, most particularly—old scores are settled with an all too evident rancor. (Hook was no doubt correct in his assessment of Rahv's character, but he was dead wrong about Rahv's literary and intellectual gifts.)

Not surprisingly in a book of this sort, Hook also avails himself of an opportunity to respond to the many false and unfair charges that were brought against him in other writers' memoirs—Alfred Kazin's and Irving Howe's, among others—and in these passages we are given a glimpse of the various ways in which even such renowned literary figures have, like so many lesser mortals, often edited their memories to suit the needs of the day. If at times there is a certain bitterness in Hook's devastating attacks on his critics, there is also a certain humor—and it wasn't Hook, in most cases, who had initiated the controversy. Again and again, his positions had been misrepresented and his motives maligned, and it was not to be expected that he would endure such treatment with a saintly indifference. In all of this "gossip," there are important issues at stake, and Hook is naturally concerned to set the record straight as well as to defend his own honor. I think he succeeded in doing both.

Out of Step is not a book primarily concerned with personalities, however. It is a book about history, and it is in its account of certain key episodes that Hook's memoirs are likely to have a permanent historical interest. The most important of these episodes are recounted in the chapters that Hook devotes to the Dewey Commission of Inquiry, which was organized by John Dewey, Hook, and others in the Thirties to investigate the truth about the Moscow Trials; the Cultural and Scientific Conference for World Peace, which took place at the Waldorf-Astoria in New York in 1949 and was a Cominform effort to enlist American intellectuals in the defense of Soviet foreign policy; the activities of the American Committee for Cultural Freedom and the Congress for Cultural Freedom in the Fifties, and the reasons for their demise; and the collapse of his own university in the late Sixties (described in painful detail in the chapter called "*Walpurgisnacht* at New York University: The Academic Ethic in Abeyance").

In the events recounted in these chapters, though spread out over a period of thirty-odd years and involving many different figures, the essential historical drama is the same: American intellectuals, representing the political conscience of the Western democracies, found themselves challenged by a widespread and well-organized campaign to falsify the political record and the political goals of the Soviet Union and other Communist regimes for the purpose of advancing the interests of those regimes. In the ways in which our intellectuals responded, or failed to respond, to these historic challenges, much of the political history—and, alas, the moral history—of American intellectual life since the Thirties was written. It was a mark of Hook's distinction that he was deeply involved in all of these events, and always on the right side, upholding a standard of truth and a commitment to democracy in the face of Communist mendacity and the support it so often received from fellow-traveling liberals.

The chapters that Hook devotes to the American Committee for Cultural Freedom and the Congress for Cultural Freedom make particularly interesting reading in the light of the many slanders which have been hurled at those organizations, often by writers who did not hesitate to benefit from them when they were flourishing. Hook staunchly defends the morality of the now-famous CIA subsidy to the Congress, but freely acknowledges that it was nonetheless a political blunder of considerable magnitude to have accepted the subsidy. At the same time, he recalls for his readers the political atmosphere in which the work of the Congress was undertaken:

> We were already in fact, if not *de jure*, engaged in a defensive war with Communism—the war was actually raging in Korea—and our fears [were] that its flames would spread and engulf Western Europe. We were in daily contact with a stream of refugee intellectuals, whose harrowing tales of persecution not only moved us deeply but gave us a sense of guilt. . . . Our conviction that in all likelihood we would soon be involved in a European war, triggered by the advance of the Red Army or an attempt by the Communist party in France or Italy to take power, accounted for the stilling of uneasiness about our funding.
>
> If it was permissible to help keep free trade unions from being overwhelmed by the Communist trade unions with access to the unlimited resources of the Kremlin, if it was per-

> missible to aid democratic political parties in Western Europe to carry on a political struggle in opposition to the Communist parties funded by the Soviet Union, certainly a case could be made for the legitimacy of aid to those who were attempting to keep the alternative of a free culture open to the intellectuals and opinion makers in the same areas.

Beyond this, Hook offered his readers a list of twenty actions taken by the Congress between 1951 and 1956 that will no doubt come as a surprise to those whose mental picture of the Congress's political agenda has been derived from the writings of Christopher Lasch and other left-wing critics. Beginning with 1951, the first item on the list is the following: "Protested against the execution of 17 Negroes in Martinsville, Virginia, and the local system which punished men differently according to their color for the same crime." For 1952: "Protested the admission of Spain in UNESCO." For 1953: "Protested to the Peron government [of Argentina] against the arrest of Victoria Ocampo and Francisco Romero." For 1954: "The American Committee produced a book entitled *McCarthy and the Communists*, exposing the nature of McCarthyism." And so on. The history of the Congress for Cultural Freedom remains to be written, but until it is, Hook has given us the best account of it that we have.

In reading *Out of Step*, the question that inevitably arises about its account of Communism is: does Hook exaggerate the extent of its influence in American life? The charge has often been made that he does, and it was made again by Arthur M. Schlesinger, Jr. in his review of *Out of Step* in *The New Republic* (May 4, 1987):

> Looking back, Hook considerably exaggerates the power of American Communists—an overestimate that, ironically, he shares with the young historians of the New Left. He speaks of Communist influence in the Thirties as "so strong that it amounted to domination of key areas of American cultural

> life, in literature, art, and movies." The Communist Popular Front organizations, he writes, "dominated the cultural, literary, and in part the academic landscape." And again: "The climate of opinion in American liberal and literary circles with respect to the [Moscow] Trials, until the Nazi-Soviet pact of August 1939, remained overwhelmingly favorable to the Soviet Union." *All this gives the Communists far too much credit.* [Emphasis added]

Schlesinger concluded by dismissing Hook as one of those people—obviously to be pitied—who "are transfixed by the Communist issue for all their lives."

This, I think it is fair to say, was now the received opinion about Sidney Hook among those liberal intellectuals who, though they may once have served—and served with distinction—in the anti-Communist ranks, no longer wish to be identified as "Cold-War liberals," and do everything in their power to shed the anti-Communist label. Liberals of this persuasion—born-again liberals, as I tend to think of them—are not to be confused with the kind of doctrinaire leftists who emerged in the Sixties as the unashamed champions of Marxist ideology. Born-again liberals tend to be older and to know more about Communism than the Sixties types, and they wouldn't dream of baldly defending the aspirations of Marxist-Leninist regimes. All the same, they have been profoundly affected by the anti-anti-Communist and anti-American attitudes of the Sixties and by the wave of historical revisionism—especially as it had been applied to the history of the Cold War—that these attitudes brought in their wake.

This, too, is a subject that awaits its historian. The subject is certainly a fascinating one, full of dramatic reversals and personal disavowals, and its dramatis personae are a rather distinguished, even a glamorous, lot. George F. Kennan, Mary McCarthy, and Theodore Draper must be counted among the group's intellectual superstars, and so, also, must Arthur M. Schlesinger, Jr.

Each has exorcised his anti-Communist identity at a time and place of his own choosing: Kennan upon returning to America from his diplomatic duties abroad; McCarthy on arriving in Hanoi, where she discovered that the real enemy in the Vietnam war wasn't Communism but the United States; Draper—well, that is a tale too long to be told here. Schlesinger seems to have undergone the requisite rite somewhere in the vicinity of Hyannis, around the time that Robert Kennedy was making his ill-fated bid for the Presidency. Moving to the Left in the heady days of the antiwar movement, Schlesinger was more effective than any of the others in transforming himself from the very archetype of a Cold-War liberal into the newer, more stylish, born-again model. His categorical censure of Hook on the issue of Communism and its influence is therefore worth some attention, for it clearly defines the shift that has occurred in liberal thinking about the Communist issue over the last two decades.

In his review of *Out of Step* in *The New Republic*, Schlesinger acknowledges that he "was at Hook's side in some of those battles [against Stalinist influence] after the war, and I rejoiced with him as he struck down the infidel." He is speaking of the late Forties, but he never quite explains why he thought it important to join Hook in this political battle, for he now describes the power of the American Communists after the war as consisting of little more than "a mild influence in the labor movement and the intellectual community." This is not exactly the position that Schlesinger upheld at the time, however.

In 1949, a decade *after* the Nazi-Soviet pact, the issue of Communist influence was still sufficiently compelling in his eyes for Schlesinger to devote an entire chapter to "The Communist Challenge to America" in *The Vital Center*—a book designed, in significant part, to the task of winning American liberals away from the influence of the Communist movement. A year earlier the Communist party had succeeded in taking over a candidate—Henry Wallace—for the American Presidency. In the very year that *The Vital Center* was published, the Cominform mounted the Waldorf conference, enlisting the services of prominent American scientists, writers, and academics on behalf of the Soviet Union. The two leading liberal weeklies, *The Nation* and *The New Republic*, were still following the Stalinist line on most political matters, and one of them, *The New Republic*, was still owned and operated by a man who, as he subsequently acknowledged, had earlier been recruited by Anthony Blunt to serve as a Comintern agent.[1] In 1947, Alger Hiss was still a high official in the U.S. State Department, and then, until his resignation in 1949, president of the prestigious Carnegie Endowment for International Peace. Somehow the word "mild" does not suffice to describe the phenomenon Schlesinger was alluding to.

There is, moreover, another interesting connection between *The Vital Center* and Schlesinger's review of *Out of Step*. In his attack on American radicalism in *The Vital Center*, Schlesinger invoked the character of Hollingsworth, the utopian reformer in Hawthorne's *Blithedale Romance*, as an example of the kind of totalitarian mind that liberalism should resist. He even attacked the literary historian V. L. Parrington for his sarcastic dismissal of Hawthorne—no doubt in this matter reflecting the influence of Lionel Trilling, who in 1940 had published the first version of the classic critique of Parrington that was to receive a wider readership when it became part of the essay called "Reality in America" in *The Liberal Imagination* (1950).[2] "Parrington evi-

[1] I refer, of course, to Michael Straight. In a book on the Blunt affair—*Conspiracy of Silence: The Secret Life of Anthony Blunt* by Barrie Penrose and Simon Freeman (Farrar, Straus & Giroux)—we are reminded that it was to Arthur Schlesinger, Jr., then a member of President Kennedy's White House staff, that Straight confessed his involvement with the Soviet espionage apparatus. Kennedy had offered Straight the chairmanship of a new agency, the Advisory Council on the Arts, and Straight knew what would happen when the routine check by the FBI was carried out. Schlesinger then arranged for Straight to tell his story to the FBI, and it was Straight's confession that led to the unmasking of Blunt as a Soviet agent.

[2] See "Parrington, Mr. Smith, and Reality," in *Partisan Review*, January–

dently thought that in Hollingsworth," Schlesinger wrote, "Hawthorne was portraying a George Norris or a Bob LaFollette. We know today that he was portraying a Zhdanov." Schlesinger went on:

> And if . . . the Parringtons were caught off guard, if nothing in their system prepared them for totalitarianism, how much more unprepared were the readers of the liberal weeklies, the great thinkers who sought to combat Nazism by peace strikes, the Oxford oath, and disarmament, the ever hopeful who saw in Soviet Communism merely the lengthened shadow of Brook Farm! . . . This was in a real sense a *trahison des clercs*.

It is bracing to recall what a good writer Arthur Schlesinger once was about these matters, but it tells us something important about the character of born-again liberalism to see what use he made of Hawthorne's Hollingsworth in his review of *Out of Step*. For it is no longer a Zhdanov that Hollingsworth calls to mind for Schlesinger, but—Sidney Hook! It is in this facile and unconscionable equation of anti-Communism with Communism itself that the true face of born-again liberalism is to be seen. A writer who has devoted much of his life to opposing Communist influence in the name of freedom and democracy is placed on a par with a representative of the Stalinist terror. And Schlesinger wondered why Hook was at times so bitter about his intellectual contemporaries!

The truth is, it is the born-again Arthur Schlesinger, not Sidney Hook, who was guilty of distorting the issue of Communist influence, and the method he employed in doing so was all the

---

February 1940. It is interesting, in the present context, to consider Sidney Hook's role in Lionel Trilling's intellectual development. According to Mark Krupnick, in his book *Lionel Trilling and the Fate of Cultural Criticism* (Northwestern University Press, 1986), "All through the Thirties [Hook] had been the single greatest influence on Trilling's political attitudes."

more ignoble in being the work of a renowned historian who could be expected to know something about historical evidence. When Hook wrote that "the climate of opinion in American liberal and literary circles with respect to the [Moscow] Trials, until the Nazi-Soviet pact of August 1939, remained overwhelmingly favorable to the Soviet Union," was he right or wrong? Schlesinger does not actually say. He simply declares that "too much credit" is given the Communists. But, it must be asked, how much is "too much"?

The Moscow correspondent of the liberal *New York Times* in the Thirties wrote approvingly of the Trials, as Schlesinger well knows, and the American ambassador whom the liberal Franklin Roosevelt installed in Moscow was likewise favorably disposed toward them. (Hollywood even produced a popular movie celebrating the fact.) On the literary scene, Hook cited the case of Malcolm Cowley—the literary editor of *The New Republic*, then one of the leading organs of fellow-traveling liberal opinion—who wrote repeatedly in defense of the Trials, even going to the trouble of favorably "reviewing" the published transcripts, and not as fiction, either. Is all this ancient history that can now be forgotten, even by renowned historians? Well, not exactly. For it was not until 1984, nearly fifty years after the Trials, that Cowley finally got around to acknowledging his shameful role in this affair—and even then, though admitting that his writings on this subject "did have some effect on American liberals as a result of the reputation I had earned for being moderate," he rather grandly exonerated himself from exerting any harmful influence. He then went on, in characteristic Stalinist style, to denounce the "Trotskyists" (meaning, I suppose, the writers who pilloried him in *Partisan Review*) as "imperialists themselves [who] tried to lead a struggle against Communism in any form, in any country, with Senator McCarthy as their embarrassing ally."[3]

[3] See "Echoes of Moscow: 1937–1938" by Malcolm Cowley, in the *Southern Review*, Spring 1984.

Even now, it is only in Sidney Hook's chronicle that we are given a truthful account of this episode.

There is a great deal more to be said about the distortions to be found in Schlesinger's review of *Out of Step*, but I will cite only a single further example of his curious way of dealing, or not dealing, with Hook's criticisms of his contemporaries. For Schlesinger, Hook is clearly guilty of an act of *lèse-majesté* in writing harshly about intellectuals, especially born-again liberals, if they have achieved literary celebrity. Thus, he quotes a remark about Mary McCarthy—"an almost infinite capacity for self-deception"—as an example of what he called Hook's "resentment," but says nothing about McCarthy's own political writings, which are the basis of Hook's judgment. But how is one to account for the pernicious inanities that Mary McCarthy has written on some of the gravest political issues of our time? Her attack on George Orwell in *The Writing on the Wall* is easily explained, for she clearly understood how loathsome Orwell would have found her apologia for the Communist regime in North Vietnam. "I can hear [Orwell] angrily arguing," she wrote, "that to oppose the Americans in Vietnam, whatever their shortcomings, is to be 'objectively' pro-totalitarian." Orwell might indeed have so argued, and would he have been wrong to do so? How can one explain her gushing praise for that totalitarian regime except by reference to her capacity for self-deception? Open any page of Mary McCarthy's *Hanoi*, and you find something like this:

> No cultural revolution would be thinkable here, since culture—the accretion of the past—is the guarantor of Vietnamese independence. The delicate position of Pham Van Dong's government is that it is bent on preserving Vietnamese traditions but it is also bent on preserving the sacred tradition of socialism, i.e., watchful central planning. On the one hand, it proceeds with an almost tactile sense (*cf.* Dr. Tung's surgical fingers) of what its people—and their history—will accept or

> reject. On the other, it insists on what is "good" for them; this is a moral, ascetic government, concerned above all with the quality of Vietnamese life.

One weeps to think that these are the words of a writer now held up to us as an exemplary literary figure—"Our Woman of Letters," as Michiko Kakutani recently called her in an article of that title in *The New York Times Magazine*, an article in which (needless to say) no reference is made to *Hanoi*. A writer of conscience—a Camus, say, or a Silone, not to mention Orwell himself—might have felt obliged to return to the subject of Vietnam in the light of the catastrophe that overtook the country in the wake of the American withdrawal, but Mary McCarthy was never that kind of writer.

Whereas Hook candidly addressed such matters in *Out of Step*—matters that occupy as large a place in American intellectual life today as they have done in the past—Schlesinger merely sidesteps them by fatuously announcing that "there are indeed more things in heaven and earth than are dreamed of in the anti-Communist philosophy."

There is an irony to be noted about this line of attack on Hook, for it attempts to discredit him precisely where he was least vulnerable—in the history he gave us of the political attitudes and the political actions of the American intellectual Left in its relation to the Communist movement—and it leaves unaddressed what may very well be the weakest and least persuasive aspects of the positions Hook espoused. I have already observed that Hook made his first reputation as an authority on Marxism, and it is as a writer on Marxism and its influence on American intellectual life that he made his most important contribution to American thought. But at the same time, he has also been the vocal exponent of another philosophical tradition: that of John Dewey. In both Marx and Dewey, he obviously found a sympathetic confirmation of his own disposition toward a completely rationalist, instrumentalist, and materialist approach to life.

It was the emphasis that Dewey placed on the practical application of ideas—his insistence that every philosophical issue be tested in the crucible of experience, and his correlative belief that philosophical issues cannot really be said to exist if they have no immediate application to experience—that exerted an immense appeal for Hook. At a single stroke, all the mysteries of mind and spirit that had occupied Western philosophy from Plato onward were effectively set aside, and what Hook described as "unbridgeable dualisms or supernaturalisms" were no longer to be considered legitimate objects of thought. "What excited me more than anything else," Hook wrote, "was Dewey's revolutionary approach to philosophy that undercut all the assumptions of the classical tradition in philosophy." Henceforth, thinking was to be regarded as "a form of behavior," as a guide to "action in problematic situations." For all practical purposes—and there could be no other—metaphysical reflection was rendered obsolete.

In Hook's case, this species of pragmatism—so firmly anchored in the realm of verification, and so inimical to the idea of transcendence—served as a bulwark against whatever metaphysical or idealist tendencies were to be found in the Marxist philosophy. It is my impression, anyway, that Marxism was never for Hook a surrogate eschatology, but, on the contrary, that under Dewey's influence it became more and more a variety of political pragmatism, and when it failed to meet the requisite tests of verification, he showed himself ready to acknowledge its failure and consider the alternatives. In this respect, at least, Dewey can be said to have served as a salutary influence on his political as well as his philosophical development.

The price of that influence came high, however, for Dewey's is a spiritually arid philosophy. It leaves the soul (as I believe it must be called) defenseless and virtually mute in the face of extreme experience. For the poetry of life it has no way of accounting, and for dealing with the tragedies of history—not to mention the tragic dimension of human experience—its problem-solving mentality has proved to be a feeble instrument. There is a touching moment in Hook's chronicle when he speaks of his discovering the novels of Dostoevsky in his freshman year at City College. "For years I nourished the hopes of writing a book on Dostoevsky . . . on the sweep and significance of his ideas," he writes. And then he adds, surprisingly: "Despite my absorption with political and social affairs, I still believe that the questions of God, freedom, and immortality are the most important of all questions that human beings can face." From an avowed rationalist and atheist, this is an extraordinary admission, but we hear little more about it in the course of his long autobiographical chronicle. Those were not, for the most part, the kind of questions that were given priority on Dewey's philosophical agenda, and it was to Dewey, not to Dostoevsky, that Hook gave his intellectual allegiance.

As a result, Hook's mind was essentially closed to the whole religious dimension of human affairs—even, it must be said, to the religious dimension of the political questions which he so often addressed. In writing about a figure like Whittaker Chambers, for example, his sympathy for and understanding of Chambers's ordeal—which are considerable—grind to a halt when it comes to the religious question. He cannot quite forgive Chambers for the religious crisis he suffered, for such crises are not susceptible to the tests of verification. And this meant, among much else, that Hook could not really fathom the extent to which the appeals of Communism—as well as other totalitarian creeds—have so often in this century been religious in nature.

This does not mean, however, that Hook himself always remained immune to the seductions of faith. Far from it. As resistant as he was to the idea of transcendence, he nonetheless continued to cherish his own notion of the sacred, which he insisted on calling "socialism." Few writers in this century did more than Sidney Hook to discredit the claims that have been advanced in the name of the socialist ideal, and he knew better than most what horrors had been committed in its name. Yet his devotion to that phantom ideal remained an article of faith, a poignant reminder that even the most determined rationalism is not always impervious to a certain kind of mystification.

Religion was not the only realm of the spirit, moreover, to which Hook had turned a blind eye. In the arts he was similarly disinclined to find anything of great human consequence, and in the relations that have obtained between aesthetics and politics in this century—a century in which so many writers and artists have suffered political exile or imprisonment or even death as a result of their artistic pursuits—he does not seem to have taken even a perfunctory interest. In the chapter that Hook devotes to the Congress for Cultural Freedom, he mocks the idea that the high cultural achievements of the West might actually have had an important role to play in serving the interests of political freedom. He gives us a detailed account of the dazzling festival of the arts which the Congress sponsored in Paris in 1952 under the direction of Nicolas Nabokov, but only in order to register his disapproval of the entire project. "The whole premise of the undertaking was oversimplified, if not false," Hook writes. "Since art has flourished even under political tyrannies, there was nothing the festival presented that could not have been offered to the world under the aegis of an enlightened despotism." This statement was not only untrue but was so obtuse in so many ways that it could only have been written by a man for whom the life of art had never really existed either as a personal interest or as a cultural datum. As if, in any case, the problems that the Congress for Cultural Freedom had been created to deal with had anything to do, at that moment in history, with enlightened despotisms. This was still the age of Stalin, who—as Hook must surely have known—took more than a passing interest in such matters. As did every Communist party in the world. On this question, Louis Aragon and Bertolt Brecht and Hanns Eisler were better guides than Sidney Hook.

Something like the same cultural philistinism is also to be regretted in the chapter that Hook devotes to his old associates on *Partisan Review*. In this case, of course, the provocation has been extreme, for Hook did play an important role in the political history of the magazine and there was something shameful in the way its editors attempted to eliminate all trace of his connection with it. (Not that he was the only one to have suffered this treatment—but that is another story.) All the same, Hook's condescending and dismissive account of his former colleagues does him no credit, and could only leave the reader wondering why, if they really had been such a bunch of ignorant dolts and untalented knaves, he ever bothered to get involved with them in the first place. Hook seems not to have understood how much of his own reputation as a writer derived from his association with *Partisan Review* when the magazine was in its intellectual prime. Surely my own case is not untypical: it was in the pages of *Partisan Review* that I first read Hook in the Forties, and what I read there prompted me to look up his earlier books. No matter what the provocation, nothing is to be gained and much to be lost by attempting to repeal that history today.

There are, then, no lack of flaws and failures to be found in *Out of Step* and in the ideas of its author. But on the central question at issue in this book—about the response of the American intellectual community to Communism in general and to Soviet power in particular, from the 1930s to the present day —Hook is not only consistently right, but he gives us the most definitive account we have. He is more thorough in recounting the history of this subject than any other writer, and more tenacious in separating myth from fact. On page after page of this long chronicle, we find accurately described for us a great many episodes that have been willfully and mischievously misrepresented in the political and historical writings of the last twenty years.

This, of course, is the main reason why *Out of Step* and its author have been so harshly treated in the liberal press. Truth-telling of this sort was bound to be damaging to the many reputations it encompassed, and it should have come as no surprise when its victims, or their representatives, attempted to strike back. Yet how rarely were they able to marshal the facts in their own defense. As we have seen in the case of Arthur M. Schlesinger, Jr., what we were offered instead was a wholesale exercise in denial.

It is sobering to look back now to the time—1949–50, say, the period that saw the publication of books like *The Vital Center* and *The Liberal Imagination*—when some of the finest minds of the American intellectual class were vigorously engaged in the effort to free our democratic culture from the noxious illusions about totalitarianism that had cost our country—and the world—so much in the preceding decade, and were gratefully admired for doing so. In 1949, when Arthur Schlesinger looked back on an intellectual class that was disposed to forfeit its defense of free institutions, he spoke without fear of contradiction of a *trahison des clercs*. Today, he—or anyone else—who spoke in such terms would be run out of the academy with cries of McCarthyism! It is because it speaks to this macabre situation with such courage and probity that Sidney Hook's *Out of Step* remains finally such an indispensable text for our time.

August 1987

Irving Howe: "Socialism Is the Name of Our Desire"

"God," said Tolstoy, "is the name of my desire." . . . Without sanctioning the facile identification that is frequently made between religion and socialist politics, we should like to twist Tolstoy's remark to our own ends: socialism is the name of our desire. *And not merely in the sense that it is a vision which, for many people throughout the world, provides moral sustenance, but also in the sense that it is a vision which objectifies and give urgency to their criticism of the human condition in our time.*

—Irving Howe and Lewis Coser, "Images of Socialism," 1954

"APPROACHING threescore and ten," as he wrote in the preface to his *Selected Writings 1950–1990* (Harcourt Brace Jovanovich), Irving Howe assembled a capacious volume of his essays to give us what he describes as "a reasonably fair picture of an intellectual career spanning four decades." Worth noting, perhaps, was the absence of any claim that the "picture" offered to us in this book was to be considered complete. Those of us who began reading Howe in the late 1940s will particularly note the omission of anything from those early years of his intellectual endeavors—a period in which the acrid residue of the old factional fights of the Thirties was very much in evidence, setting the tone and defining the substance of every argument and observation. But if this *Selected Writings* did not give us a complete picture of Howe's work over the years, it nonetheless provided quite a lot—enough, certainly, for us to make a fair assessment of the extraordinary career that the book surveys.

Given the high visibility of that career, it was altogether fitting that we should have such a volume to mark the occasion of Howe's seventieth birthday—and from one of our most prestigious publishing houses, too. For this is one of the ways in which our much maligned bourgeois society has traditionally honored its senior men of letters, and there can be no question that Howe had for many years been a member in good standing of whatever it is that passes for a literary establishment in this country. With his many books, his countless contributions to the mainstream press as well as leading literary and political journals, and the coveted lectureships at Princeton, Harvard, and other elite institutions that have come his way for decades, all capped by his years as a Distinguished Professor at the City University of New York, Howe was indeed a pillar of what is sometimes called the intellectual community and something of a celebrity in the world at large. He once even achieved the distinction—rare among intellectuals of his generation—of being interviewed by the late Charlotte Curtis, then the doyenne of "society news" reporters at *The New York Times*. That was in Miss Curtis's late, "radical chic" phase when radicalism of every stripe had become a social as well as an intellectual and political fashion, and Howe qualified—at least in Miss Curtis's eyes—as one of the respected elders of the radical movement.

In choosing his essays for this volume of *Selected Writings*, Howe duly acknowledged this aspect of his career—really, a kind of sub-career in itself—as a tireless publicist for socialism as a political faith and for radical causes in general, but he did this more as a duty, one felt, than out of any sense of vindication. For even Howe must have heard the news. As the historian Eugene D. Genovese wrote in September, 1990 *Commentary*:

> [S]urely, the Eighties will be remembered as the decade in which socialism met its Waterloo. No amount of blather about the collapse of Communism's having opened the way to "real" and "democratic" socialism will serve. The Communists, for better or worse, introduced the only socialism we have had, whereas the social democrats have everywhere settled for one or another form of state-regulated capitalism. Many things went into the making of the collapse of the Communist regimes, but, as every honest Communist from Gorbachev on admits, the immediate cause has been exposed as state ownership of the means of production—and for reasons that, alas, Ludwig von Mises, among other right-wingers, long ago identified.

Owing to this political development, which Howe allowed to pass without mention in a volume of *Selected Writings* bearing the terminal date of 1990, his unavailing attempts to discover some signs of life in the ashes of the socialist idea were not only dated but also profoundly dispiriting, for we were left with the impression that reality didn't finally count for much in this discussion. For Howe, it seems, the socialist idea was far too precious to be subjected to anything as vulgar as the judgment of history. As a result, the whole "socialist" side of his writing, which over the years has in fact degenerated into a resigned embrace of the kind of facile liberalism he repeatedly denounced in his younger days, was interesting now only as an intellectual datum in the story of his own career. And even in that respect it made curiously distasteful reading, for time has not been kind to the unlovely habit of denouncing in other intellectuals courses of actions and shifts in belief that are not in the end significantly different from those that Howe would in practice, if not always in theory, come to adopt for himself.

Thus, in one of the many piquant avowals of intransigence that pepper his *Selected Writings* with mementos of lost radical causes, Howe had some harsh things to say about literary intellectuals who—in his view at the time—dishonored their vocation by serving as what he called "partisans of bourgeois society." Just imagine! American writers serving as "partisans of bourgeois society." Wow! Would that it had been true, which even in the decade so much despised by Howe—the Fifties—it mostly wasn't. But this was nonetheless one of the grave charges with which Howe belabored his fellow intellectuals in a once-famous essay called "This Age of Conformity," first published in *Partisan Review* in 1954 and reprinted in this volume of *Selected Writings* without comment or amendment. And what had these intellectuals done to deserve such opprobrium? Well, for one thing, they sometimes lent their talents to "middlebrow culture." Remember "middlebrow culture"? Alas, we were all a bit contemptuous of middlebrow culture in those palmy days, but now that we've seen a lot worse—even in some very highbrow circles—I suspect that we would welcome back some of that old middlebrow culture if given the chance. At the time, by the way, Howe was earning at least part of his living reviewing books for *Time* magazine, which wasn't everyone's idea of the best way to resist the temptations of bourgeois society or, for that matter, the snares of middlebrow culture, but it no doubt provided excellent practice in the art of scoring points.

Then there was that other grave charge: that American writers were getting jobs teaching in the universities. Selling out, in other words. And sure enough, before too long, Howe provided us with a vivid example of this particular form of intellectual betrayal by joining the academic ranks himself and proving to be a howling success as a professor in such places as Stanford, Brandeis, and the City University of New York. What was repulsive in all this is not, I hasten to add, that Howe wrote for *Time* or that he entered the ranks of the academy or even that he eventually found a perch that suited him in the bourgeois world (which at last reports was a smart address on the Upper East Side of Manhattan), but that he was so abusive, so hypocritical, and so unforthcoming about himself at the very moment when he was heaping his anathemas upon so many of his contemporaries, some of whom were in fact attempting to deal with the new cultural and political situation in the Fifties a good deal more honestly and intelligently than he was. And who were these miscreants whom Howe was attacking as the vanguard, so to speak, of a benighted movement to conformity in the 1950s? It turned out to have been a rather hilarious cast of villains that Howe assembled for indictment in this essay: Lionel Trilling (who was singled out for special treatment), Arthur Schlesinger, Jr., Mary McCarthy, Daniel Boorstin, David Riesman, Irving Kristol, Nathan Glazer, Sidney Hook, and sundry scholars and graduate students who were not, in the author's view, as stalwart as Irving Howe himself in clinging to the penurious pleasures of the old radical bohemian way of life. Really, "This Age of Conformity" was a shoddy piece of work when it was first published, and it was shameful for it to be reprinted without apology. Its principal interest for us now is purely biographical, for it is a document that marked its author's passage out of the old radical intellectual milieu and into the mainstream of liberal academic culture, in which he has continued to prosper for some three and a half decades. The real relation in which Mr. Howe stood to the issue of intellectual conformity was fully revealed in the next decade. For when one or another writer on his 1954 hit list really did betray his intellectual vocation in the turmoil of the Vietnam War and the counterculture of the late Sixties and early Seventies—Mary McCarthy, for example, in her shameless reports from Hanoi—Howe was no longer inclined to speak about the conformity of intellectuals. The fact is, it was the Sixties that ushered in the real Age of Conformity in the New York intellectual world, and Howe was very much a part of it.

And so he remained, as we can see in the more recent political essays in the *Selected Writings*. Thus, the piece called "Reaganism: The Spirit of the Times," with its ritual obeisances to the pieties of the old radicalism, turned out to be a perfect example of what Genovese was talking about in his contribution to *Commentary*:

> If the dreary remains of the left-wing press may be taken as a guide, the doughty survivors of the radical Left and of Left-liberalism—to the extent that the two can any longer be distinguished—are once again determined to make fools of themselves. Confronted by a victorious worldwide counter-revolution against everything they have stood for, they happily dwell on the evil legacy of Ronald Reagan.

Then there was the attack—by no means the first from Howe—on Aleksandr Solzhenitsyn for failing to take the politically correct position on the Bolshevik Revolution. This, in turn, reminded the reader of the *Selected Writings* that among the many missing items in this volume was anything drawn from the considerable quantity of prose that Howe has devoted over the years to that earlier historian of the Bolshevik Revolution: Leon Trotsky. Considering the role that Trotsky's thought and Trotskyism as a movement have played in the formation of Howe's intellectual life, this was a remarkable omission—more significant, in some respects, than anything that has been included in this volume. I haven't the stomach for the task myself, but I suspect that we would have a better grasp of Howe's understanding—or misunderstanding—of history, including the history of the Bolshevik Revolution and its aftermath, if we were to compare his generally admiring treatment of Trotsky with the harsh judgment he has meted out to Solzhenitsyn. It is not that I believe our perspective on the Revolution must be limited to a choice between Trotsky's view and Solzhenitsyn's—far from it. But these are conspicuous among the figures Howe has chosen to discuss on this subject, and we very much need to have the Trotsky component of the discussion in evidence if we are to form what Howe calls a "fair picture" of his thinking.

From this and much else in and about the *Selected Writings* it was possible to arrive at a basic judgment on Irving Howe's career as a writer and as a figure in our intellectual history: Mine is that wherever the mystique of radical politics in general and the myth of socialism in particular have been allowed to dominate his work, the result is all but worthless. It was precisely what Michael Walzer described, in his introduction to the *Selected Writings*, as the vision of the socialist intellectual that has proven to be most perishable and regrettable in Howe's oeuvre. It is only as a chapter in the history of the political and moral folly of the intellectual Left in this century that this whole aspect of his career—and a sizable aspect it was—remains of any enduring interest. Given the wretched character of that history, Howe's contribution to it is by no means one of its more dishonorable chapters. His anti-Stalinism, for example—very much in evidence in his essay on Lillian Hellman as well as elsewhere in *Selected Writings*—did him credit, even if we must regret his failure to draw the appropriate implications from it. Yet by and large his career in politics was an utter failure—an intellectual failure, that is. In purely careeristic terms, it was the guarantor of his remarkable public success—a ticket to the establishment in a period when his sort of Left-liberal values presided over, and continue to preside over, the precincts of cultural power.

It is solely in his work as a literary critic that Howe now makes an uncompromised claim to our attention, and of this—the most important part of his career—the *Selected Writings* gives us a less satisfactory account than we had reason to expect. The book begins brilliantly with an essay on Louis-Ferdinand Céline that is one of Howe's finest, and there are excellent pieces on, among other writers, Sholom Aleichem, Isaac Babel, and (surprisingly) T. E. Lawrence. Some of the other essays are too fragmentary to be effective; the one on Delmore Schwartz, for example, does not begin to encompass its subject. It is odd, moreover, that Howe should prove to be so disinclined to give more space to his criticism of contemporary writers. The essay on Philip Roth, which once caused something of a stir and prompted a well-known act of literary revenge by Roth himself, is only the most conspicuous of the missing pieces in this category; for in general there is an unexplained silence in this book about the writing of recent decades—a subject on which Howe lavished a good deal of attention. The exceptions to this silence are not always happy ones, however. The essay on James Baldwin, Richard Wright, and Ralph Ellison, called "Black Boys and Native Sons," one of the few to which Howe appends an apologetic postscript in the *Selected Writings*, might better have been left to the oblivion to which Ellison, among others, consigned it when it first appeared in 1963. Howe's claim, moreover, that "by 1990 the 'black aesthetic' movement seems to have faded" is so bizarre that it left one wondering if this critic was any longer paying attention to what was going on.

In two of the longer historical inquiries in the book—"The Idea of the Modern" and "The New York Intellectuals"—there is much that remains cogent even for a reader who found the author's tendency in these essays to mourn the loss of the old radical fire a sentimental and discreditable piety. And it was on this note of sentimental piety for the socialist idea that Howe chose to close this volume. In the essay called "Thinking about Socialism," which dates from 1985, we found Howe invoking what he calls "a liberal socialism, at once pragmatic and idealistic . . . cutting across class lines and appealing to the best in humanity," and so on. Which more or less delivered the reader into the arms of Teddy Kennedy—a denouement to this "intellectual career spanning four decades" that must have been troubling even to Irving Howe in his more reflective moments.

October 1990

Diana Trilling and the Politics of Psychoanalysis

Why can't incompatible things be left incompatible? If you make an omelette out of a hen's egg, a plover's, and an ostrich's, you won't have a grand amalgam or unification of hen and plover and ostrich into something we may call "oviparity." You'll have that formless object, an omelette.

—D. H. Lawrence, *Etruscan Places*, 1932

To the literature of reminiscence that has been devoted to the history of the New York intellectuals from their emergence as anti-Stalinists in the late Thirties to the period of breakup and recrimination in the Sixties, women writers have contributed remarkably little. Mary McCarthy, after writing a savage lampoon of the group in *The Oasis* while it was still ascendant in the Forties, might have been expected to give the subject a full-dress treatment, but she returned to it too late in life to produce anything of significance. The slight, unfinished *Intellectual Memoirs* published after her death added nothing but a self-serving gloss to what she had already written. Hannah Arendt no doubt thought the subject beneath her consideration, though there are bound to be some caustic references to it in her letters—especially in her correspondence with McCarthy. Elizabeth Hardwick has not yet favored us with a candid account of her close involvement with this intellectual circle. It was thus left to Diana Trilling to provide us with the most extensive memoir of this milieu yet written by a woman who was both a witness to and a participant in its literary and political affairs.

Yet the book that Mrs. Trilling wrote in *The Beginning of the Journey: The Marriage of Diana and Lionel Trilling* (Harcourt Brace) is, if not exactly peripheral to the history of this literary circle, only partly an account of its intellectual endeavors. In much larger part, it is a book about the troubled private life of its author. While its subtitle—"The Marriage of Diana and Lionel Trilling"—gives the reader fair warning as to the principal focus of the book, it nonetheless comes as something of a shock to discover that *The Beginning of the Journey* has much more to tell us about Mrs. Trilling's harrowing and protracted immersion in the mystifications of psychoanalysis than about the public role that she and her husband played in the political and cultural life of their time. As intellectual history, *The Beginning of the Journey* adds little to what we already knew about the personal character and political proclivities of the New York intellectuals. It settles a few scores and corrects some minor misconceptions, mainly about the Trillings, and that was about all there was in the way of revising the record. But about another important aspect of New York intellectual life at the time—its fateful attachment to Freudian doctrine and the culture of psychoanalysis—Mrs. Trilling gave us a document of undeniable historical interest. Much of her book is indeed a grim illustration of those lines from W. H. Auden's "In Memory of Sigmund Freud" (1939), which once summarized the spirit of the age:

> If often he was wrong and at times absurd,
> To us he is no more a person
> Now but a whole climate of opinion
>
> Under whom we conduct our different lives.

It is not only in what she wrote about the details of her own horrific experience with psychoanalysis and that of her husband, moreover, that Mrs. Trilling gave a radical priority to Freud over every other means of coming to terms with her life and times. As we follow the course of a narrative that encompasses the many lives that shaped her own, we come to realize that for Mrs. Trilling—and perhaps for Lionel Trilling, too—the Freudian psychoanalytical enterprise constituted a politics as well as a psychology, and even at times a moral system. Its morality was an inverted Puritanism that conferred upon the most extreme varieties of self-revelation and self-vindication the status of an absolute ethical imperative. In the politics of Freudian analysis, villainy was unequivocally identified with the disabling impostures of the bourgeois family. We come to see that it may well have been this view of the bourgeois family that commended Freudian analysis to intellectuals of Mrs. Trilling's generation in the wake of their disenchantment with Marxism. The discovery, in the midst of that disenchantment, that salvation might be accomplished on the couch rather than on the barricades proved to have an irresistible appeal. Now the path to enlightenment and emancipation required not a plunge into the problematic future but a prolonged exhumation of the past, where the primal causes of our present afflictions were believed to lie buried under the disfiguring fictions of a dishonest society suddenly reduced to the dimensions of the family romance. On the couch, Marxian class conflict was transformed into a contest with parents, siblings, and spouses, while the bourgeois enemy remained firmly in place as the obstacle to be surmounted.

To the rigors of this mystical system of trial and redemption Mrs. Trilling gave up a good many years of her life, doggedly pursuing its chimerical promise of transfiguring revelation through the embattled decades of the Depression, the Second World War, and the Cold War. In the course of this long ordeal, which by her own account brought Mrs. Trilling neither happiness nor any sense of having been "cured" of the fears that afflicted her, she was obliged to endure a good deal of ignorant treatment, if not indeed what we should now characterize as medical malpractice. "In my search for cure," she wrote, "I nevertheless went from doctor to doctor, seven in all over the years, and today, at the end of this long road, I still feel that I was never properly analyzed." Three of her doctors died while she was in treatment with them. One, who came highly recommended by the Psychoanalytic Society, turned out to be a drug addict. Another, as she says, was "a Communist fellow-traveler" at a time when both Diana and Lionel Trilling had already become staunch anti-Stalinists. Amazingly, Lionel Trilling also became a patient of the same doctor, with whose family the Trillings even spent a summer holiday lest their psychoanalytical sessions suffer some irreparable interruption. "Today I ask myself," Mrs. Trilling wrote, "whether it was possible that Lionel and I were ever so ignorant of the analytical conventions and of the delicate relation between patient and therapist that we cooperated in such destructive arrangements. The answer is that we were precisely this ignorant, and so was everyone we knew" —including, apparently, the psychoanalysts.

That there was a large element of blind and irrational faith in this surrender to the psychoanalytical enterprise was more or less acknowledged by Mrs. Trilling herself. "Freudian thought excited strong emotions among intellectuals," she wrote, "but not much intellection. Intellectuals tended, indeed, to voice their opinion of analysis in the language of religion: one 'believed' or did not 'believe' in it." Mrs. Trilling, who was in all other respects opposed to the religious outlook on life, remained a true believer in this particular cult. She acknowledged, too, that "a disquieting subtext of my experience of analysis was my failure to trust my own judgment of these people into whose hands I put myself. . . . In fact, I never had entire confidence in any of the therapeutic situations in which I found myself. Yet I never left any of them of my own accord. Instead of looking upon my doctors as technicians whom I hired to perform a necessary service and whom I should dismiss if the service was not satisfactory, I behaved with each one of them as if he or she were indispensable to my well-being."

Mrs. Trilling also had reason to believe that one of the several analysts who treated her husband was actively engaged in demonizing her role in his life and thus attempting to destroy their marriage. One of her own analysts—perhaps the only one she actually admired—made an unwelcome and, for that matter, quite unprofessional attempt to alter the way Mrs. Trilling conducted her career as a critic.

> More than once [Mrs. Trilling wrote], Dr. Kris said of my literary criticism that I must "neutralize" it, by which she meant that in my writing as in my life I must be more accepting, less given to the making of judgments; as a critic, I was to be less critical. . . . But in commenting on my work in these terms, Dr. Kris was not just expressing a biased sexual view; she was moving into an arena in which she had little competence—psychoanalytical training is not a preparation for literary judgment.

Yet in the face of these blatantly moralistic interventions in her life, Mrs. Trilling continued to affirm her interest in, as she puts it, "psychoanalysis as a medical practice." In this regard, she made what she regards as an important distinction between her attitude toward Freud and that of her husband.

> Until the end of his life, Lionel never yielded in his admiration for Freud. But it was Freud the man of ideas, Freud the witness to the tragedy of civilization, whom he esteemed. He was not primarily concerned, as I was and continue to be, with psychoanalysis as a medical practice.

Yet on his deathbed, as Mrs. Trilling duly reported, her husband received the last rites, so to speak, during a final session with *his* psychoanalyst, a woman whom Mrs. Trilling was meeting for the first time. "They saw each other in private," Mrs. Trilling reported, "but when she was ready to leave I took her to the door. I had never before met Dr. Abbate, but at the door she leaned over and kissed me. She said that she wanted me to know how much Lionel had always loved me. It was not something which she had to say, nor was it much to say, but it was enough." Clearly for secular intellectuals of the Trillings' generation, psychoanalysis was something more than "a medical practice."

It was ironic, in any case, for a psychoanalyst to have advised Mrs. Trilling to "neutralize" her penchant for criticism, whether in regard to literature or about life itself, for Freudian analysis is nothing if not a system that compels its acolytes to render the fiercest judgments on those nearest and dearest to them. In this practice, too, Mrs. Trilling exhibited all the unlovely stigmata of the classic analysand. She delivers herself of harsh verdicts and ungenerous characterizations about members of her own family, about members of her husband's family, about many of the people who figured importantly in their professional lives, and even, alas, about her beloved husband himself. It is indeed one of the sadnesses of this book that so much of it is devoted to what may be called a psychoanalytical deconstruction of Lionel Trilling's character.

Armed with the moral authority of the Freudian system, Mrs. Trilling made it one of the tasks of *The Beginning of the Journey* to demystify her husband's reputation—not as a critic, to be sure, but as a man! "I very much disliked the image of Lionel as someone immune to profanation," she wrote. "I felt that it lessened and falsified him. I preferred him in all his vulnerable humanity." Mrs. Trilling held it very much against her husband that, unlike herself, he did not wish to publicize his own need of psychoanalysis or otherwise disclose the problems of his private life to his students, his academic colleagues, or his literary friends. It was clearly beyond her comprehension that such discretion may signify a moral delicacy to be admired. What particularly incensed Mrs. Trilling was that her husband did not disabuse his students of their high opinion of him. Lionel Trilling, she charged, "had a public image to protect, perhaps especially at Columbia," and she could not forgive his reluctance to deface that image through abject public confession.

> At all stages of education [she wrote] there are teachers who become symbolical figures for their students—they have it in common with analysts that certain of their students vest their phantasies in them. While Lionel himself never proposed that literary criticism was an instrument of power and prestige, his work implicitly suggested a significant public role for the teacher-critic. . . . Lionel represented for his gifted students a literary academic whose thought ranged well beyond the academy, linking literature to the wider political and moral life of the nation. The social relevance and moral intensity which in our American mid-century gave criticism its newly important role in society made Lionel himself into a kind of moral exemplar for his students, someone whose life and character might set the pattern for their own public and private choices. Lionel did not create or encourage this image. Consciously he scorned it. Yet unconsciously he conspired in it.

"Obviously I cannot write about Lionel's analytical history with the direct knowledge which I bring to my own," Mrs. Trilling wrote, but this professed disability does nothing to lessen her determination to pursue her project of profanation with a single-minded fervor. She thus offers a peevish and detailed guide to her husband's "vulnerable humanity." This includes, among much else, disparaging descriptions of what are said to be Lionel Trilling's characteristic ways of conducting himself while swimming in the ocean, playing tennis, driving a car, and partnering his wife on the dance floor. Mercifully, we are spared an account of his performance in bed, but we are certainly meant to understand that Lionel Trilling could make little claim to distinction in the realm of masculine prowess. He is even criticized for sleeping less soundly after the birth of their son than when they lived together without parental responsibilities—criticized, that is, for making himself more readily available to respond to the baby's needs in the middle of the night. This must surely be counted as one of the most bizarre indictments in the checkered annals of modern marriage. By the same token, he is criticized for sleeping *too* soundly earlier on in their marriage when, by Mrs. Trilling's own account, her husband was exhausting himself with an overload of teaching and writing in order to support his parents, who were impoverished by the Depression, while his troubled wife frittered away a small legacy from her father on a fruitless pursuit of Freudian nirvana.

On matters small and large Mrs. Trilling compiled her indictment of her husband's offenses quite as if he were the principal malefactor in her life. If Lionel Trilling was disinclined to carry out the garbage, though by no means averse to serving his wife breakfast in bed, this was another matter that had to be subjected to psychoanalytical scrutiny. And if he had the courage to disagree with his wife in describing Whittaker Chambers as "a man of honor," this must be dismissed by Mrs. Trilling as "a careless phrase"—which is a truly preposterous observation considering the gravity of the occasion. Lionel Trilling knew very well what this carefully considered defense of Chambers would cost his reputation, and he was willing to pay the price. It did nothing but trivialize her husband's own honor to treat this matter, as Mrs. Trilling did, as if it were an example of thoughtless composition. The really awful thing about the portrait of Lionel Trilling that emerges from *The Beginning of the Journey* is that Mrs. Trilling's unassailable faith in the ethos and efficacy of the psychoanalytical enterprise shielded her from the least glimmer of understanding the moral violence she has inflicted upon the memory of the man she clearly adored. In this respect, as in others, Mrs. Trilling had indeed performed something of a feat in *The Beginning of the Journey* by incongruously combining an orthodox Freudian reading of her life with the kind of feminist politics that are generally thought to be opposed to Freudian theory.

It was one of the many paradoxes of this book that while its author was very much concerned to exonerate her husband and herself from the charges brought against them by other members of their New York intellectual circle—that they were too square, too bourgeois, too genteel, and insufficiently Jewish in their public identity—Mrs. Trilling herself had provided the public with a far more devastating account of their lives in all of these respects than anything written by Delmore Schwartz, Alfred Kazin, Harold Rosenberg, and the other critics who ridiculed their manners, their politics, their respective literary styles, and the reputations they achieved. About the Trillings' inadequate finances, especially in the 1930s when Lionel Trilling undertook to support his parents, Mrs. Trilling complained a good deal. Never mind that a good deal of cash was flowing into the coffers of a succession of psychoanalysts. Suddenly in this narrative of straitened circumstances in hard times we found the Trillings installed in a garden apartment on the Upper East Side of Manhattan with a housekeeper in attendance in the midst of the Depression. Still, Mrs. Trilling complained that her husband never had a proper study in which to work. (She was not yet a writer herself.) Even in retrospect, she did not seem to understand that by the measures of the time her overworked husband did pretty well in providing her with a respectable standard of living. Yet because she had been brought up in wealthier circumstances—a West End Avenue style of luxury she professed to scorn—nothing that Lionel Trilling earned was ever enough in her view. One can only conclude that with Mrs. Trilling in charge of defending the family name, there was never any need for critics like Alfred Kazin and Delmore Schwartz to call the Trillings to account. Mrs. Trilling had exceeded their indictment on every charge.

Yet for all the criticism of Lionel Trilling that fills the pages of

The Beginning of the Journey, Mrs. Trilling duly acknowledges that she owed her career as a writer to the man she married.

> Before I met Lionel, I never thought of myself as a putative intellectual. I was not even acquainted with the word in this honorific use. Himself an intellectual, Lionel shared the attitudes and tools of the intellectual trade with me. Without him, I would no doubt have remained just another half-educated product of an expensive schooling. From Lionel, I learned not only what to read but also how to think about what I read. He gave me a literary and critical vocabulary and prepared the path to what eventually became my career.

And further:

> With marriage I had entered Lionel's world; it was with his friends that I now chiefly associated. My career as a critic still lay in the future but unconsciously I may have been preparing for it. They were not easy companions, these intellectuals I was now getting to know. They were overbearing and arrogant, excessively competitive; they lacked magnanimity and often they lacked common courtesy. But they were intellectually energetic and—this particularly attracted me—they were proof against cant.

Except for this last point—for both Freudian theory and feminist ideology have engendered whole new realms of cant that were reflected in this book—Mrs. Trilling can be said to have mastered the intellectual style here described. With its arrogance, its fierce competitiveness, its lack of magnanimity, and its utter indifference to questions of moral delicacy, *The Beginning of the Journey* at last qualified its author for full membership in this illustrious intellectual circle. She had learned its lessons well.

October 1993

Saul Bellow, Our Contemporary

THE authors whose books we read when they are new and we are young are bound to occupy a place in our lives that is different from that of other writers. They are our contemporaries. The air they breathe is the same air that we breathe. The history they experience is our history, too, and if their "take" on it differs in some ways from our own, it is nonetheless the same history. We recognize the arguments, the atmosphere, the very texture of events as familiar territory, for the world that is evoked by these writers is in so many respects continuous with our own. The jokes do not have to be explained.

As we—and they—grow older, however, our relation to these writers undergoes a significant change. We come to expect both more and less from them—more, because of the congruence of our joint experience and the sense of identification it engenders; less, because of our growing sense that, like many things in life we did not fully understand when we were young, they will prove in time to be disappointing. It is then that doubt sets in and we come to see such writers as—well, as *writers,* to be judged on their merits like other writers, writers who have now slipped out of the enclosed circle of our experience to become public literary figures. We may still read such writers with keen interest, but we no longer grant them a special place in our lives.

For certain intellectuals of my generation—literary, Jewish, liberal (as we then were) but contemptuous of progressive causes, anti-Communist, skeptical of the academy, indifferent to mass culture, enchanted by the life of art and the life of the mind, yet gloomy about what the modern world held in store for us—Saul Bellow was one of the writers who instantly became part of our conversation with ourselves and with others. The anxieties and aspirations that his fiction expressed, like the breakdown and disarray it depicted and the disabused intelligence and humor it flaunted, had an immense personal appeal.

I missed *Dangling Man* (1944) when it was first published—I was still in high school, reading George Eliot, Nathaniel Hawthorne, and the English Romantic poets for my classes, and novels from the Book-of-the-Month Club for myself—but as an undergraduate I read *The Victim* (1947) with a feeling of great excitement. I had just begun to read the modern classics, and did not doubt for a moment that the author of *The Victim,* who was about the age of my older brother, belonged in their company.

For some years thereafter I read every one of Bellow's subsequent novels as it came out. I gobbled up the advance sections of *The Adventures of Augie March* (1953) as they appeared in magazines, and rejoiced in the success of the book when it was published. The criticisms that book met with—criticisms that I now think cogent and timely—I ascribed to the kind of family quarrels I was just then getting to be familiar with on the New York intellectual scene. Those criticisms did not, in any case, apply to *Seize the Day* (1956), which seemed to me to sum up something essential about the life of the time, the heartbreak side of life in the Fifties.

I found *Henderson the Rain King* (1959) to be something of a detour, an anthropological romance in which the exuberant style that Bellow had forged for *Augie March* fought a losing battle against the abstract character of an arid allegory. *Herzog* (1964) was a triumph, however, a novel from which people I knew read out passages to their friends on the telephone. "Listen to this!" we would say, and recite one of Herzog's wise, crazy letters until we were both convulsed with laughter. (Does anyone do that with novels today?) It was a book that defined our world, and considering what it meant to us, it was a mercy, as Henry James might have said, that it was as good as it was.

Then came *Mr. Sammler's Planet* (1970). Nowadays we tend to forget what a bombshell it was—the first novel to give us a searing account of the moral collapse of the city (New York) and the class (the emancipated Jewish middle class) that were fundamental to our existence. It was also, among much else, a book about the failure of liberalism itself in the wake of the Sixties rebellion, the sexual revolution, and the race war. It had taken the measure of the future of bourgeois urban life in America, and pronounced it doomed. A prophetic book, and still in my opinion the most courageous and sagacious of Bellow's novels.

Mr. Sammler's Planet divided intellectual opinion, or confirmed the divisions that had already occurred as the result of the Sixties uproar. In other words, it took a political stand. Historically, at least for certain intellectuals of my generation, it remains the most important of Bellow's novels. Coming at a moment when so much of the American literary world had joined the "movement," as Sixties radicalism was then called, *Mr. Sammler's Planet* stood out as a high-style novel willing to tell the truth about the disasters that had already befallen us as a result of the emancipatory imperatives of that movement. In its refusal to conform to the left-wing pieties that had already swamped the academy, the media, and the whole cultural scene, it mocked what had swiftly become the conventional wisdom. Which, of course, was why the Left decried it. And why, perhaps, Bellow has never written anything like it again.

It was with *Humboldt's Gift*, published five years later, that I dropped out of the Bellow fan club. This had nothing to do with politics. I had had my own harrowing experiences with Delmore Schwartz, the poet upon whose ruined life the character of Von Humboldt Fleisher was based, and found that I distrusted the fable that Bellow attempted to make of that life. I could not read the novel as anything but an extended exercise in self-exoneration. It had its extraordinary moments, to be sure—bravura scenes in which Schwartz's zany, desperate brilliance was authentically conveyed, along with a vivid sense of the melancholy fate that awaited him (he died in a seedy hotel room after years of dissipation and mental illness)—but I could not abide the way the author had contrived to exempt himself from the moral indictments the book so freely brought against others, indeed against almost everyone.

I continued to read Bellow, but the spell was broken. His later books seemed so intent upon settling old scores and trying out new roles—some of them distinctly too metaphysical for my tastes—that I could no longer read them as autonomous literary works. It seemed to me that Bellow was more and more acquiring the smug and apodictic tone of a writer whose celebrity was now a refuge from experience and a barrier to any direct engagement with the world. His later books made this reader, anyway, long for one of Herzog's letters—irreverent, inspired, combative, and self-mocking—to cut through the fustian and recapture the old magic.

Then came Bellow's first collection of nonfiction pieces—essays, lectures, interviews, eulogies, and so forth—called *It All Adds Up: From the Dim Past to the Uncertain Future* (Viking). Exactly what it did add up to was something of a problem, but this was a book that certainly contained some wonderful things—what might even be called *Herzog*-type things.

There was, for example, the part of his Jefferson Lectures, delivered in 1977, in which Bellow offers his reflections on a little anthology called *The Bitch Goddess Success* (edited by Leslie Katz, 1968). Let me quote:

> I was saying that I had taken to reading daily in *The Bitch Goddess Success* because I found it full of helpful suggestions,

> mantras for meditation. [The composer] Mr. Charles Ives [1874–1954], for instance, in criticizing prize competitions in the arts, says that "a close union between spiritual life and the ordinary business of life is necessary" and that we must keep the balance between ordinary life and spiritual life. Well, this is of course the name of the game. But the maddening fact is that after you have said these obviously true things, you are up against it still. For when Mr. Ives, casting about for an example of the ordinary, says that "a month in the Kansas wheat fields may do more for a young composer than three years in Rome," you ask yourself when he himself last looked at ordinary life in Kansas. Again, he says: "If, for every thousand-dollar prize, a potato field be substituted, so that these candidates of Clio can dig a little in real life . . . art's air might be a little clearer." Then he checks himself slightly by quoting a French moralist: "*On ne donne rien si liberalement que ses conseils*" [One is never so generous as with advice]. But he has not checked himself in time. Digging potatoes? Kansas wheat fields? The last American artist to try those wheat fields was [the poet] Vachel Lindsay when he went forth to preach his Gospel of Beauty in the days before the First World War. The ordinary business of life in the United States and its great cities is what it is because out in Kansas they aren't bringing in the sheaves as they did in 1910.

Now, the rhetorical strategy deployed here may have lost some of its luster since it was first used by Bellow in *Herzog,* but it still holds up, and the point is well made. So are the points he scores against the animadversions of the architect Louis Sullivan (1856-1924), also represented in *The Bitch Goddess Success,* and these have the additional interest of being rooted in Bellow's—and Sullivan's—home ground in Chicago. Indeed, some of the best things in this lecture and the other pieces in *It All Adds Up* are Bellow's evocations of the Chicago he has known most of his life.

Yet there is something going on in his Jefferson Lectures, as there is in most of Bellow's later lectures, essays, and interviews, that remains unacknowledged—something offstage, so to speak, that sparks his indignation without ever being openly confronted and identified. After all, we are not interested in Charles Ives or Louis Sullivan because of their opinions about success. Certainly *The Bitch Goddess Success* is a silly little book, and while Bellow was right to mock it his mockery would have been more persuasive if he had taken his audience into his confidence about the sources of the anger it provoked. (Anger, rarely acknowledged as such, is the pervasive emotion in these later pieces.)

The Jefferson Lectures were delivered a year after Bellow was awarded the Nobel Prize in literature, and he was clearly still smarting over the fact that, as he tells us, "A kind friend, worried about my soul," had sent him that silly book—a gesture clearly regarded as an act of rebuke, which it may well have been. This sets Bellow off on a little tirade about what he dubs the "Goddess of Rebukes." "There was a Goddess of Rebukes, who worked in the shadows behind the Goddess of Success," he writes. "Less prominent, she was perhaps more powerful and enduring. . . . Make no mistake about it: the Rebuke Goddess is stronger than the Bitch Goddess." And further:

> Many of our intellectuals serve as priests of the Goddess of Rebuke, nagging, scolding, and infecting a vulnerable people with gnawing anxiety and remorse. In so doing *they* become successful. They can claim that they do not serve the Bitch Goddess. Personally immune to her, they merely refer to her for purposes of rebuke. This was why my considerate friend sent me the handsomely printed little anthology.

Alas, this sounds less like the sardonic comedy of *Herzog* than like the rage of Von Humboldt Fleisher, which has been (albeit circumspectly) appropriated for a public occasion.

The fact is, moreover, that Bellow is himself no slouch when it comes to serving as a priest of the Goddess of Rebuke, as many of the pages in *It All Adds Up* eloquently attest. Did the editors and writers who produced *Partisan Review* in the late Thirties and early Forties welcome the young Saul Bellow into their circle and help launch his literary career? Yes, indeed, but now the Nobel laureate, secure—or rather, insecure—in his success, feels compelled to treat them with withering condescension.

"Some of the editors," he writes of *Partisan Review*, "had the mentality of Sixth Avenue cigar store proprietors" who just happened to be adept at "importing good things." "Where else," he adds, "would you find Malraux, Silone, Koestler, and Company but in *Partisan Review*?" While acknowledging that the *PR* circle "then had considerable influence with me," he nonetheless still insists in a 1990 interview that "I was never institutionally connected with any of these people."

He also claims that he was a lot smarter about the fallacies of Marxism than the *Partisan Review* crowd, though he seems to have kept remarkably quiet about it at the time. And his novels have remained fairly quiet about the whole subject of Jewish radicalism, too. "I knew all about Lenin and Trotsky," he says of his boyhood, and tells the following story:

> I remember as quite a small kid being in the street with my father. We met a young man called Lyova walking down the street. Lyova told my father he was going back to Russia. Lyova's father was our Hebrew teacher, and his mother, Mary, a fat lady with a huge hat, was my mother's friend. My father said, "That's a foolish thing you are doing. Don't go." He was counseling Lyova not to go, but Lyova must have had some kind of politics. He couldn't have been older than eighteen or nineteen. But things like that happened every day. Lyova went back and vanished.

Lyova and his generation and their progeny vanished from

Bellow's fiction as well, except as background and atmosphere. The American novelist who was better equipped than any other to write the moral history of Lyova's intellectual generation in America could not bring himself to create a novel about the subject he still cannot stop talking about in his 1990–91 interviews. It is only one of the losses we are reminded of in the pages of *It All Adds Up.*

Another is what it has cost Bellow—and us, too, his readers—for him to have become so fixated in recent years on what he calls (after Wyndham Lewis) "the moronic inferno." This miasma of a degraded popular culture, made worse by the media functionaries who serve as its henchmen and beneficiaries, is certainly a subject that cries out for critical analysis and condemnation, and Bellow is undoubtedly correct in describing it—as he did in the Romanes Lecture he delivered at Oxford University in 1990—as "a mental and emotional counterpart to revolution and world crisis, that is probably a by-product of nihilism." Yet it trivializes this huge and malevolent phenomenon to reduce it, as Bellow does again and again in his recent utterances, to the level of a "distraction" that impedes the progress of serious writers like himself and deprives him of the readers he feels are rightly his.

"Writers, poets, painters, musicians, philosophers, political thinkers, to name only a few of the categories affected," Bellow writes, "must woo their readers, viewers, listeners, from distraction." One knows what he means, of course, but it is nonetheless an odd complaint from a writer who now commands a large public. It is the kind of complaint that had a certain cogency when it was made decades ago by Delmore Schwartz in his essays on "The Isolation of Modern Poetry" (1941) and "The Vocation of the Poet in the Modern World" (1951), for Schwartz was lamenting the fate of a literary enterprise that had no hope of winning anything but a minuscule public and a difficult living. But for a Nobel laureate with a huge and admiring public the world over to persist in this complaint in the 1990s smacks, at the least, of a certain disingenuousness.

For the truth is that while the "moronic inferno" has certainly gotten a lot bigger and a lot worse since Delmore Schwartz's day, the status of writers like Bellow—rich, famous, and adored, and showered with literary honors, academic distinctions, and commercial opportunities—has not become endangered. The Romanes Lecture was not, after all, delivered at some obscure provincial seminary.

This is not to say, however, that Bellow does not have real enemies in high places. As I have already indicated, the literary Left long ago inscribed his name on its roster of reputations to be demolished. And from its own political perspective, the Left was right to do so, since virtually everything Bellow has written—or said—is infused by a spirit that is best described as disabused liberalism: a liberalism, now almost extinct, that has stripped itself of precisely the kind of political cant and ideological subterfuge that is still the Left's principal stock-in-trade.

Does this mean, then, that Bellow is some kind of neoconservative? He has repeatedly made a point of refusing to be labeled as such, and whether his insistence in this matter derives from real conviction or is merely a strategy of self-protection, I think he has to be taken at his word. Between the disabused liberalism that Bellow clings to and the neoconservatism he spurns, the political space may be difficult at times to discern; but it is nonetheless real, if only because it remains a place of intellectual refuge for that dwindling remnant of homeless liberals who identify their survival with a refusal of affiliation

That this has now become an illusory position, however, based on a distinction without a difference, has been made plain to Bellow—and to the rest of us—by the hits he has lately taken in the public press. For their effect on Bellow's standing as a writer, these attacks are far more important than the "distractions" caused by the "moronic inferno"—and are not to be confused with them. They represent the kind of political warfare from which no writer in the public eye can now find refuge, and it is part of one's disappointment with Bellow these days that even in the face of these attacks—which are on much more than himself—he seems, whether for reasons of vanity, fatigue, or disgust, unwilling to respond with the full weight of his intellectual gifts. Which means, in practice, that he has ceded the advantage to his adversaries, and left his natural allies to shift for themselves.

The first of the recent blows was struck in *The New York Times* by Brent Staples, a young black journalist who now occupies a highly visible position on that paper's editorial board. Staples has lately established something of a reputation at the *Times* as a militant advocate of political correctness, particularly on the subject of race. (*The New Republic* has dubbed him the paper's "political corrector.") He has even called for the abolition of the term "political correctness"—not, however, because of any disapproval of the thing itself, but in the interests of establishing PC prohibitions as an accepted norm in public speech.

To judge from what he has lately written about Bellow and about the very different work of Eugene Richards, a photographer who has made a career of documenting the wretched lives of the American underclass, Staples would seem to believe, and have us believe, that any unflattering depiction of blacks, either in words or pictures, is incontrovertibly racist if its author is white. In today's incendiary atmosphere, where PC prohibitions and self-censorship have indeed become the norm in the media, the academy, and the culture at large, this is the kind of charge that has the power to incinerate reputations, no matter how exalted, overnight.

Thus, when, in December, the *Times* in its Sunday *Magazine* featured the chapter called "Mr. Bellow's Planet" from Staples's new memoir, *Parallel Time*, and then, a few weeks later, published a promotional review of the book itself on the front page of the paper's *Book Review*, it had the intended effect of branding Bellow a racist. Staples had been a graduate student at the

University of Chicago when Bellow taught there. Though never Bellow's student, he had developed a kind of paranoid fixation on the novelist—an obsession compounded of curiosity, envy, anger, and a remarkable ignorance of the art of fiction. *Humboldt's Gift,* which was published while Staples was a student at the university, "was one of the first novels I'd read on my own," as he writes in *Parallel Time,* and he read it strictly as a guidebook to what he calls "local geography, people included." What sparked his anger was the way the character Rinaldo, an underworld type, talks about blacks in the book. Rinaldo's views, like those of the leading character in *Mr. Sammler's Planet,* are taken by Staples to be nothing but a personal editorial statement by Bellow, and hence an expression of racism.

At no point does Staples seem to have noticed that the white characters in Bellow's novels—and most particularly the Jewish characters, who are far more abundant than blacks—are frequently characterized in even more unflattering terms. Staples reads fiction the way the old literary commissars used to read fiction—and everything else, for that matter—rendering judgments purely on the basis of party-line politics (in this case, of course, racial politics rather than the politics of class).

At the same time, Staples is not above making some politically inspired characterizations of his own, and of an especially nasty sort. His description of the sociologist Edward Shils, another member of the Chicago faculty he did not study with and whose books, as he himself admits, he could not fathom, is amazingly repulsive. And when, after stalking Bellow for months around the campus, he catches up with him on a crowded street, this is the way Staples depicts him: "He moved through the crowd looking downward, hungrily scanning asses, hips, and crotches. . . . The rest of us were a junkyard where he foraged for parts." It seems that once your subject has been branded a racist, everything is permitted.

Then in March came the literary critic Alfred Kazin's ruminations on Jews, Bellow among them—in a piece called, in fact,

"Jews," in *The New Yorker.* For half a century now, Kazin has made a specialty of instructing Jewish intellectuals in America on the correct way to conduct themselves as Jews. I am surprised that some enterprising publisher has not commissioned him to write a book of etiquette on the subject, for it seems to have absorbed him deeply for a long time.

For Kazin, one of the pitfalls of being an educated Jew is the sin of urbane manners. That was, astonishingly enough, the charge he brought against the late Lionel Trilling in *New York Jew* (1978), and he is still advising Jews to avoid a similar fate. But for Kazin the foremost test of authentic Jewishness, especially for descendants of immigrants, has to do not with manners but with politics: under no circumstances must their politics be anything but liberal or radical. In Kazin's moral cosmology, a special kind of damnation awaits any Jewish intellectual who strays from the orthodoxies of the Left-liberal mentality. And if, like Bellow, they happen to be writers, it is a bad sign, too, if they fall into the trap of becoming that hateful phenomenon, "a university intellectual." Worst of all, however, is for such Jews to adopt conservative views. This earns them instant and irreversible opprobrium.

Bellow was indicted in Kazin's piece on all these counts, to which was added, in keeping with the politically correct character of contemporary liberalism, an implied charge of racism. The trouble, Kazin writes,

> is that Bellow is also a university intellectual, loves being in a university, and has moved in the company of the conservative Big Thinkers at the University of Chicago. He has been much involved with the traditionalists Allan Bloom and Edward Shils. Shils even read one of his novels in manuscript. [Heinous charge!] The University of Chicago thrives on absolutes, no doubt because its professors, especially Bellow, think of the city as the last word in philistinism.

This last criticism—about Chicago—is, of course, the sheerest nonsense, and there are many pages in *It All Adds Up,* as well as in Bellow's novels, that poignantly refute it. But reality does not count for much in Kazin's guide to politically correct conduct for Jewish intellectuals. He goes on: "At [a] party, Bellow gave me a turn. I knew that, like many Jewish intellectuals from the immigrant working class who were forced to their knees before the altar of Marxism during the Depression, he had been moving Right." And then comes the zinger, which adds racism to apostasy. "My heart sank," Kazin writes, "when I heard that Bellow once said, 'Who is the Tolstoy of the Zulus? The Proust of the Papuans? I'd be glad to read him.'"

And then, after all this, Kazin pretends to wonder at what he calls "Bellow's vehemence about liberals!"

Alas, my heart sank when I read Bellow's rather feeble response to these assaults in the op-ed piece he wrote for *The New York Times* shortly thereafter. In that piece he speaks of coming "under attack in the press and elsewhere for a remark I was alleged to have made about the Zulus and the Papuans," and insists that "Nowhere in print, under my name, is there a single reference to Papuans or Zulus." And then he goes on to defend the remark he has denied having made by explaining that he "was speaking on the distinction between literate and preliterate societies."

This is such a transparent cop-out—such an egregious attempt to bypass the explosive subject of multiculturalism—that one feels embarrassed on his behalf. Bellow is right, very right, in saying that "Righteousness and rage threaten the independence of our souls." He is right, too, to warn that "We can't open our mouths without being denounced as racists, misogynists, supremacists, imperialists or racists." And he is right again to declare that "As for the media, they stand ready to trash anyone so designated." Yet in his answer to his attackers, he never really engages the central charge that Brent Staples and Alfred Kazin have brought against him, which has little, if anything, to do with distinctions between literate and preliterate societies.

Obviously Bellow is still enough of a liberal, however disabused, to be fearful of the ultimate cultural ostracism that awaits any writer today, no matter how famous, who goes into battle against the radicalization of our culture. In this respect, sadly, he remains very much our contemporary.

June 1994

FROM MODERNISM TO THE "NEW SENSIBILITY"

Clement Greenberg in the Forties

WITH the publication of the first two volumes of Clement Greenberg's *Collected Essays and Criticism,* we are at last on our way to having a comprehensive edition of the most important body of art criticism produced by an American writer in this century.[1] These first two volumes bring together for the first time Greenberg's critical writings from the decade in which he emerged as the most informed and articulate champion of the New York School as well as one of our most trenchant analysts of the modern cultural scene. The two additional volumes promised for the future will presumably bring his remarkable critical oeuvre up to date. John O'Brian, the editor of the series, has so far carried out his duties with an exemplary scholarly tact—both of the new volumes contain useful notes, interesting biographical chronologies, and appropriate bibliographies—and the books have been produced by the University of Chicago Press in a very readable format. Under any circumstances the publication of Greenberg's *Collected Essays and Criticism* would

[1] *Clement Greenberg: The Collected Essays and Criticism*, edited by John O'Brian; University of Chicago; *Volume I: Perceptions and Judgments, 1939–1944*, *Volume II: Arrogant Purpose, 1945–1949*.

have to be considered a capital intellectual event, but in the present climate, when so much that passes for serious criticism is in reality some form of academic twaddle, commercial hype, or political mystification, the appearance of these volumes also has a wonderfully bracing effect. For this is criticism that does not require us to surmount some impenetrable rhetorical barrier in order to discover what it is actually up to. It is plainly written, cogently argued, and admirably precise in the many discriminations and formulations it is concerned to make. For anything remotely comparable in intellectual quality or aesthetic intelligence, one would have to turn to the most illustrious of Greenberg's predecessors—to Julius Meier-Graefe in Germany and Roger Fry in England. In his own generation he stands alone.

It is one of the many virtues of the present edition of Greenberg's writings that it places them firmly in the context of the history which prompted them in the first place. When, some twenty-five years ago, Greenberg published a selection of his essays under the title of *Art and Culture,* he was frank to say that that book was "not intended as a completely faithful record of my activity as a critic." Although drawn from the first twenty years of Greenberg's production, many of the essays in *Art and Culture* had been substantially revised in order to give the reader a clear account of the author's current views. "Not only has much been altered," as Greenberg noted in his preface to *Art and Culture,* "but much more has been left out than put in." *Art and Culture* was certainly a very distinguished book. Indeed, for a quarter of a century it has remained without rival as the premiere work of art criticism in our time. Yet the emphasis which *Art and Culture* placed on the present inevitably had the effect of foreshortening our understanding of the past—both the critic's past, with all of the shifts in emphasis and perspective which any full-scale critical career is bound to encompass, and that of the art which he was attempting to come to grips with in a succession of discrete encounters. It is only with the publication of *The Collected Essays and Criticism* that we have now begun to have placed in our possession a complete account, month by month and year by year, of this crucial critical history.

It is another of the virtues of this edition that it illuminates—and with a fullness and candor that was no doubt inappropriate to the purposes of *Art and Culture*—the broad range of literary, artistic, and political interests that did so much to shape Greenberg's outlook as a writer. The first entry in Volume 1 is a review of Bertolt Brecht's *A Penny for the Poor.* The second is the author's now classic essay, "Avant-Garde and Kitsch," written at the age of thirty and as much concerned with literature as with art. The third is an equally important but not so well known essay, "Towards a Newer Laocoön," which attempted to explain in historical terms how it happened that modern art, in its "revolt against the dominance of literature"—the dominance, that is, of "subject matter at its most oppressive"—came to place "a new and greater emphasis upon form" and upon the physical medium. "Towards a Newer Laocoön" was, as Greenberg acknowledged, "an historical apology for abstract art," and may thus be considered something of a manifesto for the "formalist" view of art which he has steadfastly maintained throughout his subsequent career as a critic.

Interestingly, he was writing in these early years as a Marxist—an anti-Stalinist Marxist of the Trotskyist persuasion, to be sure, but a Marxist all the same. In this phase of his career Greenberg was very much a part of the *Partisan Review* circle that looked to Trotsky as a political guide in attempting to "save" the Revolution from what was looked upon as Stalin's "betrayal" of it. In the fourth entry in Volume 1 of *The Collected Essays*—an essay called "An American View," written for Cyril Connolly's magazine *Horizon* in 1940 and published in London during the Blitz—we are given a clear statement of the political folly which this ideological outlook entailed. "Hitler realizes this much: that in order to keep capitalism there must be fascism," Greenberg wrote; "Trotsky realizes that in order to keep democracy there must be a socialist revolution . . . . We must choose: either capitalism or democracy. One or the other must go. If we insist on keeping capitalism then we cannot fight Hitler. He must win."

Cyril Connolly promptly and correctly responded to this mistaken analysis by writing an article in the same issue of *Horizon* which firmly rejected Greenberg's claims. "It is obvious that this view," Connolly wrote, ". . . rests on an over-simplification of the facts, and if put into practice would lead to disaster." (O'Brian quotes Connolly's response in a footnote.) Before the end of the Forties, however, Greenberg had more or less come to agree with Connolly, describing himself in a *Partisan Review* symposium in 1948 as an "ex- or disabused Marxist." And as an editor of *Commentary* from the late Forties to the end of the Fifties, he was, of course, in the forefront of those ex-radicals who played a role in articulating the case for what came to be characterized as anti-Communist, or Cold War, liberalism—a position from which, I believe, he never thereafter deviated.

What needs to be borne in mind about the role of Marxism in Greenberg's early writings is that (1) it did much to shape his view of history, and (2) it was never allowed to distort his judgment of particular artists. The extent to which a Marxist-influenced teleology came to be subsumed in his reading of art history is another matter. It can be argued—I have argued it myself[2]—that some residue of the Marxist dialectic disposed him to find in art history, and most particularly the history of modern art, something in the realm of aesthetics ("subject matter at its most oppressive") that is more or less akin to the Marxist notion of class struggle as an iron law of historical development. Something of the sort is certainly to be found in such essays as "Avant-Garde and Kitsch" and "Towards a Newer Laocoön," and it persists as a kind of leitmotif in a great many

[2] See "A Critic on the Side of History: Notes on Clement Greenberg," in *The Age of the Avant-Garde* (New York, 1973).

other essays, too. Yet it must be said that Greenberg's response to particular works of art is, more often than not, remarkably free of the ideological strictures to be found in his more theoretical pronouncements. And even in "Towards a Newer Laocoön," he was at some pains to underscore the limit that he placed on his own theoretical imperative:

> My own experience of art has forced me to accept most of the standards of taste from which abstract art has derived, but I do not maintain that they are the only valid standards through eternity. I find them simply the most valid ones at this given moment. I have no doubt that they will be replaced in the future by other standards, which will be perhaps more inclusive than any possible now. And even now they do not exclude all other possible criteria. I am still able to enjoy a Rembrandt more for its expressive qualities than for its achievement of abstract values—as rich as it may be in them.

This is not the observation of a closed mind, and the application of "other possible criteria" occurs more frequently in Greenberg's criticism than one expects from a writer so given to theoretical absolutes.

There is much discussion of poetry as well as of politics in these first two volumes of *The Collected Essays*, and fiction, philosophy, criticism, and, even on one occasion, the ballet—Anthony Tudor's *Dim Lustre*—are likewise given some interesting attention. The Forties was also a period in which Greenberg was much occupied with his translations of Kafka, and Volume II contains the first of his essays on Kafka, written in 1946. There is little question, I think, that Greenberg had both the resources and the sensibility to become a first-rate literary critic. But it was the art rather than the literature of his time that claimed his primary allegiance, and it is, of course, as a chronicle of his art criticism that this new edition of his writings makes its principal claim on us.

During the period under review Greenberg was writing most regularly for *Partisan Review* and for *The Nation*. As O'Brian points out in his introduction to Volume 1, "His longer, justly celebrated essays were written primarily for *Partisan Review*, while his shorter, until now mostly unrecovered articles, appeared mostly in *The Nation*." Read now in sequence, these articles give us an amazingly detailed, close-up view of the art life of the time—not only in their account of the new art that was being shown in New York for the first time, but also in their response to the work of the established masters.

In regard to the former—Greenberg's account of the new art of the Forties—this new edition of his writings amply confirms his reputation as the pre-eminent critic of the New York School. In this first decade of its emergence he seems to have missed very little. As early as 1943, he wrote of David Smith: "Smith is thirty-six. If he is able to maintain the level set in the work he has already done . . . he has a chance of becoming one of the greatest of all American artists." About Jackson Pollock that same year he wrote: "Pollock has gone through the influences of Miró, Picasso, Mexican paintings, and what not, and has come out on the other side at the age of thirty-one, painting mostly with his own brush." About Robert Motherwell's first one-man show in 1944: "he has already done enough to make it no exaggeration to say that the future of American painting depends on what he, Baziotes, Pollock, and only a comparatively few others do from now on." In 1945, on the occasion of Pollock's second one-man show: "the strongest painter of his generation and perhaps the greatest one to appear since Miró." And so on. It isn't at all the case that Greenberg was especially easy on the artists he admired, either. He could be severely critical—as he was, for example, with Arshile Gorky. Yet when Gorky's *The Calendars* was shown in the Whitney Annual in 1948, he did not hesitate to pronounce it "the best painting in the exhibition and one of the best pictures ever done by an American." That same year—"a remarkably good one for American art," as he noted—he spoke of Willem de

Kooning as "one of the four or five most important painters in the country" on the basis of the artist's first one-man show. One could go on quoting from other reviews as well, and we are talking only about the period which ended in 1949—the terminal date of Volume 2.

The figure who looms behind a good many of these judgments—not in the sense of dictating them, for it was never a case of that, but by way of providing a reading of modern art that gave one the essential clues to its further development—is the painter and teacher Hans Hofmann, about whom there are fewer references in Greenberg's writing in this period than we might have expected. Hofmann is first mentioned in a footnote to "Avant-Garde and Kitsch" in 1939, but his own painting is not discussed until 1945, the year of his second one-man show in New York. When, on that occasion, Greenberg spoke of Hofmann as "a force to be reckoned with in the practice as well as in the interpretation of modern art," it was an acknowledgment of an influence that had already played an important role in the critic's thinking—an influence duly celebrated two years later in an essay written for *Horizon* on "The Present Prospects of American Painting and Sculpture."

> Hofmann will in the future, when the accomplishment of American painting in the last five and next twenty years is properly evaluated, be considered the most important figure in American art of the period since 1935 and one of the most influential forces in its entire history, not for his own work, but for the influence, enlightening and uncompromising, he exerts. . . . Hofmann's presence in New York has served to raise up a climate of taste among at least fifty people in America that cannot be matched for rigor and correctness in Paris or London.

Clearly the critic included himself among the beneficiaries of this influence, and so must we. It may even be that much that we still admire in Greenberg's writings about art in this period owes something to the fact that as Trotsky's influence—and the influence of Marxism generally—steadily waned, that of Hofmann's "formalist" reading of modern painting continued to cast its powerful spell.

It would be a mistake, however, to suggest that it is primarily as a sort of retrospective tip-sheet on the emerging eminences of the New York School that this critical chronicle is of interest now. What has kept Greenberg's criticism alive is the quality of the thought which he lavished not only on individual artists as he encountered their work for the first time but also on the larger artistic and historical issues which their work was found to raise. In this collected edition of the criticism one can see more clearly than before how the famous longer essays—"The Decline of Cubism," "The Crisis of the Easel Picture," "The New Sculpture," and "Our Period Style," all written in the years 1948–49—grew out of these individual encounters with specific objects. However generalized Greenberg's observations on individual artists, on art history, and on history itself may sometimes appear to be, they were always firmly anchored in concrete aesthetic experience, and it is another of the strengths of *The Collected Essays* that it makes this internal connection between apodictic judgment and aesthetic actuality far more explicit than it has been hitherto. One may still want to quarrel with the judgment, but one knows better now on exactly what basis it has been arrived at.

Another large interest of these volumes is to be found in Greenberg's writings on European art, and specifically on the School of Paris. The Forties were, of course, the decade in which the decline of Paris as the art capital of the West and the emergence of New York as its successor became an undeniable fact of international cultural life. In Greenberg's critical chronicle of this fateful decade we do not find a celebration of the decline of Paris—and still less any gloating over it—but there is no denial of it, either. If anything, his discussion of it—which, characteristically, takes the form of discussing individual artists—is marked by a tone of deep regret. For the art produced in the great days of the School of Paris remained for him, even in the Forties, a touchstone of aesthetic quality. Again and again in these essays he makes it clear that for him Matisse still loomed as "the greatest master of the twentieth century"—a judgment that was by no means commonplace even in Paris in the Forties—and Cubism remained, as he wrote in 1948, "the only vital style of our time, the one best able to convey contemporary feeling, and the only one capable of supporting a tradition which will survive into the future and form new artists." The intensely serious attention given as a matter of course to Picasso, Bonnard, Chagall, Léger, Braque, Miró, and other luminaries of the School of Paris is itself a reflection of the central place Greenberg continued to accord these artists. The welcome he gave to Dubuffet in the late Forties, moreover, makes nonsense of any notion that his was a criticism in any way governed by chauvinistic bias.

In this respect, it should be said that the campaign lately mounted by certain Marxist historians to suggest that in the 1940s New York somehow contrived to "steal" modern art from Paris by means of a government-sponsored conspiracy will find nothing in *The Collected Essays* to support what is essentially an exercise in political paranoia (if not indeed an attempt to repeal history itself). To Greenberg, as to many others at the time, it came "much to our own surprise," as he wrote in 1948, that "the main premises of Western art have at last migrated to the United States, along with the center of gravity of industrial production and political power." His complaint was that Americans were still so piously attached to the prestige of the School of Paris that they could not bring themselves to recognize what was going on in their own country—but this was an aesthetic judgment, not a political one. And the fact that Paris still loomed so large in the eyes of the New York art world, that art produced in Paris still held such unbroken sway over what dealers showed, critics wrote, collectors bought, and museums acquired—all this, too, makes nonsense of the charge that some secret conspiracy was at work to elevate New York at the expense of Paris. The plain truth is, Paris *did* suffer a decline so irreversible that it has not recovered to this day. It is, in any case, against the background of this abiding piety about art in Paris and its corollary—a general disinclination to believe in the importance of American art—that Greenberg's writings in the Forties about both French and American art need to be read.

Finally, it is worth pointing out that there is much in these volumes on a variety of other subjects that remains of great interest. About the paintings of Arnold Friedman, an American artist only now—forty years after his death—being accorded anything like the recognition he deserves, Greenberg wrote beautifully and repeatedly. His obituary of Mondrian is still a very moving document:

> [Mondrian's] pictures, with their white grounds, straight black lines, and opposed rectangles of pure color, are no longer windows in the wall but islands radiating clarity, harmony, and grandeur—passion mastered and cooled, a difficult struggle resolved, unity imposed on diversity. Space outside them is transformed by their presence.

About Edward Hopper, too, an artist one hardly expected Greenberg to have much interest in, he had some very sharp things to say. Also, about Max Beckmann. Reviewing an exhibition of the paintings Beckmann produced in Holland during the Second World War, Greenberg wrote in 1946 that there were five or six pictures in the show that "warrant calling Beckmann a great artist, even though he may not be a great painter." He then went on to say of Beckmann:

> He is certainly one of the last to handle the human figure and the portrait on the level of ambitious, original art . . . . [T]he power of Beckmann's emotion, the tenacity with which he

> insists on the distortions that correspond most exactly to that emotion, the flattened, painterly vision he has of the world, and the unity this vision imposes—so realizing decorative design in spite of Beckmann's inability to think it through consciously—all this suffices to overcome his lack of technical "feel" and to translate his art to the heights.

On visual art other than painting and sculpture there are likewise some brilliant perceptions. Here is Greenberg on the photographs of Henri Cartier-Bresson:

> The unusual photographs of the French artist, Henri Cartier-Bresson . . . provide an object lesson . . . in how photography can assimilate the discoveries of modern painting to itself without sacrificing its own essential virtues. One thing that painting since Manet has emphasized is that a picture has to have a "back." It cannot simply fade off in depth into nothingness; every square millimeter of picture space, even if it represents only the empty sky, must play a positive role. This, Cartier-Bresson, like his fellow-photographer Walker Evans, has learned preeminently. At the same time, unlike Edward Weston and the later Stieglitz, he has not forgotten that photography's great asset is its capacity to represent depth and volume, and that this capacity's primary function is to describe, convey, and make vivid the emotional "use-value" of beings and objects. It is to anecdotal content that Cartier-Bresson, rightly, subordinates design and technical finish.

Notwithstanding the great variety of subjects that are dealt with in this critical chronicle, we are seldom in any doubt that it is one subject, above all—the emergence of abstract art, which Greenberg described in 1944 as "one of the most epochal transformations in the history of art"—that lies at the center of *The Collected Essays.* In these first two volumes Greenberg's response to this "epochal" event, while generally positive and welcoming, remains fluid and analytical. He is fully aware of the aesthetic costs entailed in the triumph of abstraction, and not reluctant to talk about them. If he can already be said to be writing here as a "formalist" critic, he also shows himself to be open to, and even enthusiastic about, a good deal that the formalist criticism of a later generation has shut its eyes to. What the first two volumes of *The Collected Essays* make abundantly evident, moreover, is that he is a bigger and more various writer than he has generally been thought to be. This being the case, the future volumes in this series will be keenly awaited.

January 1987

Clement Greenberg and the Cold War

No art critic of our time has been the subject of more discussion than Clement Greenberg, who was born in 1909 and published the bulk of his critical writings between 1939 and 1969. Yet the nature of that discussion has at times been so contentious, not to say acrimonious, that the effect has been to obscure the virtues that made this criticism loom so large—and for so long a time—in the minds of both his admirers and his adversaries. It seems to me unlikely that the publication of two further volumes of Greenberg's *Collected Essays and Criticism* will do much to alter this situation.[1] The academy, the museums, the media, the art journals, and a good deal of the intellectual press, not to mention foundations, corporate sponsors, and the cultural agencies of government, are now in the hands of apparatchiks who have a vested interest in defending both the kind of art and the kind of writing about art that Greenberg has famously deplored, and it is not to be expected that they will surrender their animus on the present occasion.

On the contrary, opposition is likely to be intensified, for the discussion of the issues raised in Greenberg's criticism is even

[1] *Clement Greenberg: The Collected Essays and Criticism*, edited by John O'Brian; University of Chicago; *Volume III: Affirmations and Refusals, 1950–1956*, *Volume IV: Modernism with a Vengeance, 1957–1969*.

more adamantly politicized today than it was in the days when he was still a regular contributor to critical opinion. In a culture now so largely dominated by ideologies of race, class, and gender, where the doctrines of multiculturalism and political correctness have consigned the concept of quality in art to the netherworld of invidious discrimination and all criticism tends to be judged according to its conformity to current political orthodoxies, even to suggest—as Greenberg's writings invariably do—that aesthetic considerations be given priority in the evaluation of art is to invite the most categorical disapprobation.

So rapidly has the radicalization of critical opinion accelerated in the past decade that in the years that have elapsed since the publication of the first two volumes of *The Collected Essays and Criticism*, the editor in charge of this otherwise exemplary edition of Greenberg's writings—John O'Brian, now professor of art history at the University of British Columbia—has clearly felt obliged to abandon the politically neutral tone he brought to the presentation of the earlier volumes and to adopt a more belligerent voice for the later volumes. No doubt this is due, in part, to the shift that occurred in Greenberg's own political views over the course of his critical career, and in even larger part to O'Brian's disapproval of that shift.

In his early years as a critic, Greenberg was a Trotskyist—which is to say, an anti-Stalinist Marxist—yet by the end of the Forties he had already described himself as an "ex- or disabused Marxist," and by the Fifties he had joined the ranks of the anti-Communist liberals. (O'Brian prefers to call the position of the latter "Kantian anti-Communism.") From the perspective of the academic Marxists who came out of the Sixties, this put Greenberg on the wrong side of the Cold War, making him politically suspect if not actually retrograde, and it is more or less from that perspective that O'Brian has written his introduction to the last two volumes of *The Collected Essays and Criticism.*

Hence the tremendous emphasis that O'Brian places on the

Cold War as the principal influence on Greenberg's criticism in the Fifties and Sixties. The main charge is that an "acquiescence to the *Pax Americana* and its policies was accompanied by a corresponding shift in [Greenberg's] stance as a cultural critic." To support this charge, O'Brian dwells at some length on the long essay that Greenberg published in *Commentary* in 1953 under the title "The Plight of Our Culture," which is now reprinted in Volume III. This is indeed an important essay that ought to be better known. It is not only the best response to T. S. Eliot's *Notes Towards the Definition of Culture* that I know of, but also one of the most cogent analyses of the problem of democratic culture any critic has given us in the last forty years. Unfortunately, it is one of the odd features of this new edition of Greenberg's writings that O'Brian has allowed his own political animus to distort its meaning. My guess is that he was so concerned to bring his reading of Greenberg's later criticism into line with the political views of his friend and colleague Serge Guilbaut, the author of *How New York Stole the Idea of Modern Art*, that he scarcely noticed the degree of misrepresentation that such an effort required.

"In 'The Plight of Our Culture,'" O'Brian writes, Greenberg "revoked his earlier criticism of mass-circulation magazines and their blurring of distinctions between high and low culture." It is also claimed that "Greenberg deduced that the newly dominant culture of the middle classes had the capacity to resist dilution and adulteration by mass culture as well as produce what he still most desired: . . . 'formal culture with its infinity of aspects, its luxuriance, its large comprehension.'" For O'Brian, then, "the transformation in Greenberg's thinking was an about-face," and "in the space of a couple of years, pessimism about the culture of modernity had given way to optimism" for purely political reasons. "Thus Greenberg's Cold War politics and cultural optimism merged," he writes, and this "ex- or disabused Marxist" is now said to have joined other New York intellectuals in believing that "democracy and capitalism . . . already were demonstrating what might be accomplished in the realm of middlebrow culture."

All of this suggests, of course, that "The Plight of Our Culture" is a rousing, politically inspired apology for middlebrow culture, and hence a retreat from Greenberg's vigorous defense of high culture in his classic essay "Avant-Garde and Kitsch," first published in 1939 and reprinted in Volume 1 of *The Collected Essays and Criticism*. Yet, in fact, "The Plight of Our Culture" is one of the most thoughtful and categorical indictments of middlebrow culture any American has ever given us. Far from representing an "about-face" on the imperatives of high culture, this very dour analysis of its fate under the pressures of democracy and capitalism puts a good deal of the blame for its problematic condition on the corrupting force of middlebrow culture. What does make "The Plight of Our Culture" different from "Avant-Garde and Kitsch" is its refusal to formulate its subject in orthodox Marxist terms (though Marxist thought still exerts a considerable influence on its analysis of culture) and its acknowledgment of the changes that had lately occurred in the relation of middlebrow culture to high art.[2] Yet to characterize this examination of middlebrow culture as "optimistic" requires a suspension of attention to its most salient points, if not indeed a flight of ideological fancy.

[2] Still, there was much in "Avant-Garde and Kitsch" that did not belong to Marxism, and much, too, that is perfectly consistent with the view of high art to be found in "The Plight of Our Culture" and all the later criticism. For example:

> [I]t is true that once the avant-garde had succeded in "detaching" itself from society, it proceeded to turn around and repudiate revolutionary as well as bourgeois politics. The revolution was left inside society, a part of that welter of ideological struggle which art and poetry find so unpropitious as soon as it begins to involve those "precious" axiomatic beliefs upon which culture thus far has had to rest. Hence it developed that the true and most important function of the avant-garde was not to

"The Plight of Our Culture" occupies some thirty pages in the new edition of Greenberg's writings, and cannot therefore be summarized in its totality. But here, anyway, are some of the relevant passages from Greenberg's analysis of middlebrow culture:

> The liberal and fine arts of tradition, as well as its scholarship, have been "democratized"—simplified, streamlined, purged of whatever cannot be made easily accessible, and this in large measure by the same rationalizing, "processing," and "packaging" methods by which industrialism has already made lowbrow culture a distinctive product of itself. Almost all types of knowledge and almost all forms of art are stripped, digested, synopsized, "surveyed," or abridged. The result achieved in those who patronize this kind of capsulated culture is, perhaps, a respect for culture as such, and a kind of knowingness, but it has very little to do with higher culture as something lived.
>
> The middlebrow in us wants the treasures of civilization for

---

"experiment," but to find a path along which it would be possible to keep culture *moving* in the midst of ideological confusion and violence. Retiring from public altogether, the avant-garde poet or artist sought to maintain the high level of his art by both narrowing and raising it to the expression of an absolute in which all relativities and contradictions would be either resolved or beside the point. "Art for art's sake" and "pure poetry" appear, and subject matter or content becomes something to be avoided like a plague.

It has been in search of the absolute that the avant-garde has arrived at "abstract" or "nonobjective" art—and poetry, too. The avant-garde poet or artist tries in effect to imitate God by creating something valid solely in its own terms, in the way nature itself is valid, in the way a landscape—not its picture—is aesthetically valid; something *given*, increate, independent of meanings, similars or originals. Content is to be dissolved so completely into form that the work of art or literature cannot be reduced in whole or in part to anything not itself.

> himself, but the desire is without appetite. . . . A sense of continuity with the past, a continuity at least of truth, of enduring relevance, belongs to a genuine culture almost by definition, but this is precisely what the middlebrow does not acquire. . . . He might be able to do so, eventually, by exerting humility and patience, but these he is somehow never able to muster in the face of culture. In his reading, no matter how much he wants to edify himself, he will balk at anything that sends him to the dictionary or a reference book more than once. (Curiosity without energy or tenacity is a middlebrow trait wherever and in whomever it appears.) Towards his entertainment, no matter how much he wants it to be "significant" and "worthwhile," he will become recalcitrant if the "significance" is not labeled immediately and obviously, and if too many conditioned reflexes are left without appropriate stimuli. What the middlebrow, even more conspicuously than the lowbrow, wants most is to have his expectations filled exactly as he expects to have them filled.
>
> Middlebrow culture, because of the way in which it is produced, consumed, and transmitted, reinforces everything else in our present civilization that promotes standardization and inhibits idiosyncrasy, temperament, and strong-mindedness; it functions as order and organization but without ordering or organizing. In principle, it cannot master and preserve fresh experience or express and form that which has not already been expressed and formed. Thus it fails, like lowbrow culture, to accomplish what is, perhaps, the most important task of culture for people who live in a changing, *historical* society: it cannot maintain continuity in the face of novelty, but must always forget and replace its own products.

As for the relation that obtains between high culture and middlebrow "standardization," Greenberg can hardly be said to take an optimistic view. "High culture, however—authentic, disinterested culture—has so far suffered more than it has gained in the process," he writes. And his characterization of popular culture doesn't offer much of a basis for optimism, either:

> At the same time lowbrow, "machine," commercial culture is there everywhere to offer its relief to all those who find any sort of higher culture too much of an effort—lowbrow culture being powerful not only because it is "easy" and still suits the majority, but also because it has replaced folk culture as the culture of *all* childhood, and thereby become our "natural," "autochthonous" culture. (And, unlike folk culture, lowbrow culture neither contributes—at least not fundamentally—to high culture nor effaces itself in its social presence.)

You may, if you like, call this optimism or an "about-face" or—what is really implied by the charge—Cold War propaganda, but it sounds both pretty grim and pretty accurate to me, and not exactly a cheerleader's view of either capitalism or democracy.

It is also true that Greenberg acknowledges that "like lowbrow culture, middlebrow culture is not all of a piece," that "the good and the bad are mixed," and that middlebrow art "is not wholly adulteration and dilution." This, too, strikes me as true, at least for the time in which it was written, but not to offer much solace. Really, the only thing that Greenberg found to admire in "the middlebrow's respect for culture" was, as he wrote, that "it has worked to save the traditional facilities of culture—the printed word, the concert, lecture, museum, etc.—from that complete debauching which the movies, radio, and television have suffered under lowbrow and advertising culture." Yet anyone reading this passage in the 1990s must be aware of how much more has been surrendered by these "traditional facilities of culture" to the demands of lowbrow, popular culture over the last forty years. But even forty years ago, when our institutions of high culture had not yet sunk to their present levels, Greenberg's view of even this development was anything but rosy:

> But doesn't the damage still outweigh the gains [he asked], and can any amount of improvement at the lower levels compensate for deterioration at the highest, where the most authentic manifestations still have their being, where the forms and values of every other level originate—no matter how perverted subsequently—and where our experience is still most significantly and enduringly preserved?

As the passages I have quoted from "The Plight of Our Culture" attest, this is an essay that raises fundamental questions about the fate of high art in our society. They are the kind of questions, moreover, that have acquired an even greater urgency today when the middlebrow culture described by Greenberg in 1953 has been largely gutted of whatever virtues that could once be claimed for it and, for both political and commercial reasons, is now effectively supplanted by something much worse. (See, for an egregious example, Tina Brown's *New Yorker*.) For O'Brian to reduce these questions to a highly simplified scenario of Cold War politics not only misrepresents the content of "The Plight of Our Culture" but renders it irrelevant to our current cultural concerns—which is, to say the least, a curious policy for the editor of these books to pursue.

What O'Brian clearly cannot forgive is that Greenberg had taken the anti-Communist side in the early stages of the Cold War, and, as he writes, "remained committed to the Cold War agenda of the U.S. government." This is the "original sin" that for O'Brian has left an ineradicable taint upon everything that has been gathered in Volumes III and IV of this *Collected Essays and Criticism*, right down to its last pages. For "in 1969," he writes, of what turns out to be the closing item in Volume IV, Greenberg "conducted a lengthy interview with Lily Leino for dissemination by the U.S. Information Agency, the umbrella organization for the Voice of America." I frankly rejoice that someone in the USIA bureaucracy had the brains to ask a writer of Greenberg's distinction to speak on the Voice of America broadcasts, but for O'Brian it remains a mark of the writer's contract with the Devil.

And what sort of thing was Greenberg broadcasting for the Voice of America in 1969? Recalling a period twenty-five years before "when everybody was so sure that Americans couldn't produce art of any consequence—and that included Americans themselves," Greenberg was, among other things, complaining that

> a lot of inferior art is taken seriously all over the world. It's a paradoxical situation when someone like Rauschenberg—who's nowhere nearly as good as Eakins, Homer, Ryder, or the early John Sloan, or Milton Avery, not to mention Marin—is viewed as a major figure because of the credit American art in general now enjoys in the world.

He also had some praise for Andrew Wyeth! But it was probably this sort of thing that O'Brian found particularly offensive:

> I've seen some contemporary Soviet art, and as far as I can tell, art in the Soviet Union is controlled by Philistines. The same appears to be true in China and in every other place where Bolsheviks are in power. I call them Bolsheviks instead of Communists because I feel that that's more accurate, more specific. "Socialism" in backward countries means Bolshevism—Stalinism, if you want—and that means something barbaric, because "socialism" in a backward environment becomes, among other things, an aggressive expression of backwardness.

Some of us knew that all this was perfectly true when Greenberg made his broadcast in 1969, and now all the world knows it was true. Yet because he spoke the truth under U.S. government auspices, Mr. O'Brian apparently finds it tainted. That is indeed the triumph of ideology over veracity.

There is no question but that the Cold War played a significant role in shaping American cultural life in the decade and a half that followed the end of World War II, and that ex-radical intellectuals of Greenberg's generation made an important contribution to the formulation of that role. I said as much more than thirty years ago when Greenberg's first book of essays, *Art and Culture*, was published, and O'Brian accurately quotes me to that effect. "To understand *Art and Culture* is to understand a great deal about the artistic values that came out of the war and the Cold War years," I wrote in *Arts Magazine* in October 1962; "to question it is to question some of the salient achievements and aesthetic beliefs of those years."

What is so curious and distorting about O'Brian's characterization of Greenberg's role in this intellectual history is that he leaves the "salient achievements" of the Cold War period—which mean, in this context, the Abstract Expressionist movement—unquestioned while at the same time endeavoring to reduce the "aesthetic beliefs of those years" to a purely political scenario. It is in this respect as well as others that he reveals his loyalty to the radical politics of the Sixties, with its anti-American paranoia, its sentimentalization of Marxist ideology, and its adamant refusal to acknowledge the moral superiority of American democracy over Soviet tyranny.

For what, after all, was the Cold War about if not the conflict between American (and Western) democracy and Soviet tyranny? O'Brian is not, to be sure, one of those nut cases who attempt to demonstrate that the fame and influence of Jackson Pollock was the creation of Nelson Rockefeller and John Foster Dulles and that Harry Truman had somehow contrived to promote the interests of American abstract painting even while going through the motions of condemning it. He leaves the ideological dirty work to Serge Guilbaut and the cadres of radical art historians who have now succeeded in portraying the achievements of the New York School as nothing but a tainted product of America's role in the Cold War. Yet what he has given us in a large part of his introduction to Volumes III and IV of Greenberg's *Collected Essays and Criticism* is a somewhat more respectable and respectful version of the same ideological narrative.

There is no way to understand what in 1962 I spoke of as "the salient achievements and aesthetic beliefs" of the war and the Cold War period without some acknowledgment of the lethal effects that Stalinist influence had on American art and culture in the 1930s. The Stalinist-inspired Popular Front culture of the Thirties was, in all its essentials, an irredeemably philistine and middlebrow culture, and it laid upon the arts in this country a curse of mediocrity and sentimentality from which it did not begin to recover until the 1940s. (That is the reason why William Faulkner and Wallace Stevens were dismissed as reactionary eccentrics in the 1930s while Grant Wood and Thomas Hart Benton were acclaimed as geniuses.) If there is a serious criticism to be made of Greenberg's essay "The Plight of Our Culture," it would have to do with his failure to acknowledge the extent to which the middlebrow culture of the 1940s and early 1950s had been fashioned in the Popular Front culture of the 1930s.

In its artistic and cultural interests, this was one of the things that Trotskyism set out to combat in the Thirties, and it was out of that conflict that Greenberg wrote his essay "Avant-Garde and Kitsch" in 1939. But even stripped of its Stalinist distortions, the Marxism of the Thirties proved to be a poor guide to what was actually happening in American art in the Forties, and it is much to Greenberg's credit that he recognized the change for what it was. (By the same token, it is much to O'Brian's discredit that he still doesn't.) This was the political drama that was made manifest in virtually every area of postwar American cultural life. Whereas in the early plays of Arthur Miller, for example, you see the middlebrow sentimentalism of the Popular Front mind reenacted with a vengeance, in the criticism of Lionel Trilling you see the attempt to liberate literary and social thought from its corrupting influence. It is in that context that Clement Greenberg's criticism of the Fifties and Sixties needs to be understood, and it is a sad commentary on the intellectual life of the 1990s that the editor of this fine edition of *The Collected Essays and Criticism* still doesn't get it. Hence his determination to reduce every aesthetic idea, if not aesthetics itself, to a suspect political datum.

March 1993

Lincoln Kirstein and the "Aesthetic" Generation

LINCOLN Kirstein (1907–1996) is one of the most remarkable figures in the cultural history of the modern era, not only in the United States but anywhere, and the collection of his writings, *By With To & From: A Lincoln Kirstein Reader* (Farrar, Straus & Giroux) edited by Nicholas Jenkins, is therefore certain to be of great interest in many respects. If only for his role in bringing George Balanchine to America and founding the New York City Ballet, Kirstein would be guaranteed a place of high distinction in the annals of twentieth-century cultural life, but the scope of his achievements in the arts is far more extensive than that, of course. As a poet, as an editor, and as a writer in many fields—not only literature and dance but virtually all the visual and performing arts—he made important and sometimes crucial contributions. He was much involved, too, in the creation of institutions, in the codification of taste, and in the support of the artists he believed in. He was a patron and administrator as well as a critic, historian, and creator, and it is one of the virtues of this new *Lincoln Kirstein Reader* that it brings together a sizable sampling of Kirstein's essays in the various fields that interested him as well as some of the autobiographical writings that illuminate the place these subjects occupied in his own life. If the book does not finally tell us everything about Kirstein's extraordinary career—it omits, for example, his once famous attack on Alfred H. Barr, Jr., and the Museum of Modern Art, an institution that Kirstein himself helped to shape in its early days—it does nonetheless give us a rich account of his many-sided talents and accomplishments. No doubt there will sooner or later be other books to complete the complex story of this unusual life.

On the occasion of this excellent *Reader*, however, I think it may be important to recall that Kirstein belonged to a generation and a period that are nowadays but dimly understood by a good many of the people in the arts, including a good many critics and curators, who are their principal beneficiaries. In the title I have given these remarks on Kirstein and his period, I have called his the "aesthetic" generation, and I know very well that the word "aesthetic" is bound to cause dismay and distaste—even, alas, among some who have lived by it—for the aesthetic conception of art is now much under attack in discussions of art and culture. To its former association with a febrile aestheticism and the overcultivation of sensibility—in an essay on the photographs of Walker Evans in this book, Kirstein himself observes that "the development of sensibility for its own sake damned the 'nineties' as well as the 'twenties'"—has lately been added a virulent political campaign that has sought to discredit the concept of the aesthetic in the name of "diversity," equality, and democracy. Yet, though the word "aesthetic" is now so battered by ideological assault and so disparaged by the orthodoxies that have supplanted it, there is finally no other way to describe the kind of vital interest that Kirstein and certain of his contemporaries brought to their endeavors in the arts. To surrender the word in the discussion of those endeavors is tantamount, in my view, to surrendering art itself to sheer demagoguery. Thus, if I have enclosed the word in quotation marks, it is as much to underscore its importance as it is to acknowledge the opprobrium that it has acquired in the current debate.

The figures I have in mind among Kirstein's contemporaries are a diverse lot, and they often differed a good deal about almost everything but their loyalty to an aesthetic standard of judgment in art, whether they used the word or not. Among them I would include Alfred Barr, Clement Greenberg, Virgil Thomson, R. P. Blackmur, A. Hyatt Mayer, B. H. Haggin, Edwin Denby, James Thrall Soby, Stark Young, Katherine Dreier, Carl Van Vechten, and Walker Evans—hardly an exhaustive list, but the first names that come to mind. Some were older than Kirstein. Blackmur and Van Vechten are acknowledged as mentors in this book. Some were younger. And behind all of them was a still older American generation that included Bernard Berenson, Albert C. Barnes, James G. Huneker, Duncan Phillips, Willard Huntington Wright, Montgomery Schuyler, Walter Pach, and Henry McBride. Some of these figures came to reject modernist painting, as Kirstein eventually would. Some were its most ardent champions. But it was nonetheless over *aesthetic* issues that they differed, just as it was over an aesthetic issue—in this case, the aesthetic legitimacy of modernist painting—that Kirstein broke with the Museum of Modern Art in 1948. The arguments did not invoke political criteria as tests for the art to meet. There were plenty of others to do that, of course—especially in the 1930s when the champions of Midwestern regionalism, on the one hand, and the followers of the Communist Party line, on the other, joined in denouncing modernist art on political grounds—but this was not the kind of argument that emanated from the debates of the "aesthetic" generation itself. Theirs were essentially aesthetic disagreements that turned on the thorny issue of pictorial innovation and its relation to tradition. These disagreements were not finally susceptible to amicable resolution, yet even in the heat of controversy they had the effect of illuminating real artistic issues and did not, as a rule, take refuge in the kind of counterfeit debate that nowadays swamps almost all discussion of the arts.

I think Jenkins's *Reader* would have been even more interesting than it is—and a shade less pious, too—if he had confronted this issue directly by reprinting "The State of Modern Painting," which Kirstein published in *Harper's Magazine* in 1948. This article caused an immense sensation at the time, for its dismissal of modernist painting was total and absolute—a declaration of what Mr. Kirstein himself identified as "a new opposition [which was] not conservative . . . [but] reactionary," and which especially denounced "improvisation as a method, deformation as a formula, and painting (which is a serious matter) as an amusement manipulated by interior decorators and high pressure salesmen." As Irving Sandler wrote in a reprise of this controversy:

> One would suppose that Kirstein meant Pollock or Rothko, but no, he had Léger and Matisse in mind—Matisse, "a decorator in the French taste, the Boucher of his epoch, whose sources in the miniatures and ceramics of Islam are, inch for inch, his superior.[1]

Among the painters Kirstein preferred to Matisse were David Alfaro Siqueiros, Pavel Tchelitchev, and Paul Cadmus—all subjects of hagiographic essays reprinted in this *Reader*. Kirstein was also beating the drum in those days for a revival of nineteenth-century Salon painting. He was right, in other words, to characterize his taste in painting as "reactionary," and I think Jenkins would have done the readers of this *Reader* a service by giving them the details of this controversy.

It is mainly in his writings on photography and sculpture that Kirstein has excelled as a critic and historian of the visual arts. The essays on Walker Evans and Henri Cartier-Bresson, which are reprinted in the *Reader*, are rightly regarded as classics of the literature, and the monograph he devoted to Elie Nadelman, of which there is no trace here, is, in my view, a critical masterpiece.

[1] See Irving Sandler's introduction to *Defining Modern Art: Selected Writings of Alfred H. Barr, Jr.* (Abrams, 1986), pages 31–32.

(As the original edition was small and expensive and is now unobtainable, it should be reprinted in a cheaper edition.)

Some of the best things in the *Reader* are, not surprisingly, Kirstein's writings on the ballet and on Balanchine in particular. Yet for some of us, anyway, his championship of the Balanchine ballet aesthetic involves a paradox. For Balanchine, with his faith in "the logic of movement" and his unquestioned belief, as he said, "in the dance as an independent category, as something that really exists in itself and by itself," was, in his own sphere of aesthetic endeavor, as much of a modernist as Matisse and a good deal of his achievement was as "pure" and "abstract" as the painting of Mondrian or Rothko. That Kirstein has never been able to appreciate this aesthetic resemblance, which is so obvious to a great many other people, must remain one of the mysteries of his career. It is as if he were determined to reserve for the art of painting all of the "literary" materials that Balanchine had eliminated from the art of ballet. Whatever the reason, where dance is concerned, Kirstein has remained an ardent modernist—whether he calls himself that or not—whereas in painting he is right to call himself a reactionary, and this paradox is writ large in Jenkins's *Reader*.

For anyone with a keen interest in modern literary history, the most interesting pages of the *Reader* are those devoted to *Hound & Horn*, the splendid magazine that Kirstein founded while still at Harvard in the late Twenties. As he now acknowledges, T. S. Eliot was the inspiration—"*The Criterion*, later *The Dial*, were models of what magazines might be," he writes, and "Eliot seemed to me, at the time, the most important authority in the world for anything and everything that could occupy me." Yet, he now confesses that

> at a time when burgeoning "modernism" was a mandatory stance, my idiosyncratic models were Balzac's *Lucien de Rubempré*, Bulwer-Lytton's *Pelham*, and Benjamin Disraeli's *Coningsby*.

So the conflicted attitude toward modernism was there at the beginning, though it remained remarkably well concealed in the pages of *Hound & Horn*, and this may account for the slight air of condescension that colors Kirstein's memoir of the magazine, written nearly half a century later.

> I abandoned the magazine after seven years [he writes], not entirely because my interests had altered and I was otherwise magnetized (by the ballet). The real reason I did not fight to continue *Hound & Horn* . . . was that I didn't give a damn for politico-philosophical tendencies which I felt were devouring the magazine's space, and I was neither equipped to deal nor interested in dealing with them.

In the end, he writes, "The single piece prompted by myself which I feel does me most credit was a translation of some of the great *sura* of the Koran"—a strange epitaph, to say the least, to a great literary journal.

Some of the other pieces gathered in this *Reader* are now dated and even slightly embarrassing—the valentine to James Cagney, for example, and the really mawkish tribute to Marilyn Monroe ("She was a criterion of the comic in a rather sad world," etc.), which is as awful in its own way as the Andy Warhol "Marilyn" portraits.

But this is only to say that what I have called the "aesthetic" generation had its weaknesses as well as its strengths, and it was its strengths that gave us entrée to much of what we now understand to have been the real achievement of the arts in this century. The errors of judgment, the eccentric detours, the logrolling for friends and loved ones, even what Kirstein calls the "silliness," are easily forgiven—though they should not be forgotten—in the larger perspective of history. Compared to the cynical and destructive—or should one say deconstructive?—forces that have now commandeered the arts and their institutions in this last decade of the century, both the "aesthetic" generation and their immediate predecessors leave behind a clean smell and a proud record, and the best pages of this *Lincoln Kirstein Reader* are an important part of that record.

December 1991

The "Apples" of Meyer Schapiro

It is the fate of certain intellectual figures to achieve a position of such unassailable eminence that their actual writings—the basis upon which less exalted laborers at intellectual tasks are routinely judged—come somehow to be regarded as *hors concours*. If these writings are mainly papers for learned journals and special occasions, and are thus likely for long periods to remain scattered, out of print, or otherwise difficult to obtain, so much the better. Compared to the aura that attaches itself to figures of this sort, whose writings acquire in time a kind of archival status, the scribbling of books—especially on a regular basis—comes to seem an almost vulgar enterprise, something best left to the second-rate minds that produce the great majority of them in any case. If, in addition, there is a reputation for unusual eloquence in the classroom and spectacular virtuosity on the lecture platform and for a range of learning and experience all but universal in scope, then the legend of the genius-scholar-intellectual is likely to remain immune to serious inquiry. The sheer splendor of such renown has the effect of discouraging the critical instinct.

Therefore, when the writings of such figures are at last gathered into books, they tend to be treated less as objects of analysis than as reliquaries containing the remains of a sacred substance. To criticize or to question such writings seems, under the circumstances, a little gross—an act of impiety if not of impertinence—when what is clearly called for is a kind of obeisance. And so, little or nothing of the content of the writing is seriously challenged. Reverence serves not to clarify but to quarantine whatever concrete contributions to learning or criticism may be found in it.

Meyer Schapiro has long been a legendary figure of this sort, and something like this odd, nullifying process of uncritical homage has been very much in evidence in the reception of his *Selected Papers*. Three volumes of these have now appeared: *Romanesque Art* (1977), *Modern Art: 19th and 20th Centuries* (1978), and *Late Antique, Early Christian and Mediaeval Art* (1979), all under the imprint of George Braziller, Inc. The fourth and final volume, *The Theory and Philosophy of Art*, is being prepared for publication. Even as we await this final volume, however, there can be little doubt that these *Selected Papers* represent an unusual achievement. The range of learning to be found in them is both wide and deep, and the sheer passion for the art that informs their every detail is itself exemplary, and at times exhilarating. Yet what sort of thinking *about* art lies at the heart of these voluminous writings? Schapiro's scholarly prowess certainly fulfills—and on occasion may even be said to overfulfill—our expectations. The encyclopedic knowledge of many different fields of learning is amply demonstrated. In this respect, at least, the legend of the scholar and polymath long associated with the name Meyer Schapiro is easily confirmed. But what, in the end, does the richness and variety of all this learning actually tell us about art itself?

This is the question that has yet to be asked about Meyer Schapiro's work as a writer on the visual arts, and I think we pay him a dubious sort of homage by avoiding it. An intellectual enterprise on this scale calls for scrutiny, yet scrutiny is precisely what these *Selected Papers* have not received. It is almost as if the quality of thought to be found in the more than one thousand pages already published is somehow to be regarded as incidental to their importance.

At the risk, then, of appearing to dishonor so prodigious an accomplishment, let us examine what I believe there is good reason to consider the central contradiction of Schapiro's thought in these papers. Briefly—and no doubt too simply—put, this contradiction may be stated as follows: Whereas the author of these papers is consistently concerned to find in works of art conceived in circumstances of total religious belief a "free," even secular, and purely *aesthetic* component more or less akin to the artistic autonomy we have come to associate with the art of the modern period, he is just as consistently determined to deny to the art of the modern period precisely the kind of autonomous aesthetic interest that has long been thought to be its most distinctive characteristic. Or, to state this contradiction in the form of a question: Why is so much importance attached to what Schapiro calls the "strong current of aestheticism in the culture of the twelfth century" while the stronger and far more explicit current of aestheticism in late nineteenth- and twentieth-century art remains relegated to a place of almost marginal significance?

Surely one of the most beautiful of Schapiro's essays—as well as one of the most revealing of his own outlook on art and culture—is "On the Aesthetic Attitude in Romanesque Art" (1947), which he has placed at the opening of Volume I of his *Selected Papers*, and to which he refers the reader again in a prefatory note to Volume III. Schapiro has devoted a large part of his academic career to the study of the Christian art of the Middle Ages, and this essay may therefore be taken as a credo, even perhaps as a manifesto. In it, Schapiro is concerned to celebrate the vitality of that "strong current of aestheticism in the culture of the twelfth century" I have already mentioned, and thus to combat "the common view," as he calls it, "that mediaeval art was strictly religious and symbolical, submitted to collective aims, and wholly free from the aestheticism and individualism of our age." In this endeavor he goes so far as to speak of a "new art" emerging in Western Europe in the eleventh and twelfth centuries—"a new sphere of artistic creation without religious content and imbued with values of spontaneity, individual fantasy, delight in color and movement, and expression of feeling." Accompanying this new art, he argues, was "a conscious taste of the spectators for the beauty of workmanship, materials, and artistic devices, apart from the religious meanings." Much of the content of "On the Aesthetic Attitude in Romanesque Art" consists, in fact, of quotations from "random texts" (as Schapiro calls them)—"passages in chronicles, biographies, letters, and sermons"—that are felt to define this "conscious taste" for "ornament, artistic skill, and imagination." A taste, in other words, for all those attributes of form, shape, texture, and the processes of execution that are so central to modern aesthetic criticism. These texts, Schapiro avers, "surprise us by their resemblance to the more developed critical awareness of later periods when art criticism and the theory and history of art have emerged as distinct fields."

Exactly how seriously Schapiro intends us to take this revisionist view of Romanesque art is difficult to say, however. He certainly states the matter forcefully, and it is only upon rereading this essay that we are likely to be struck by the author's somewhat cavalier acknowledgment—made in passing, as it were—that this "new art" exists "on the margins of the religious work" that forms the central body of medieval art. Only then, perhaps, are we left wondering why so much is being made of something so admittedly marginal to the subject. Is it because this marginal aesthetic current is somehow to be preferred to the dominant religious attitude? Does its elevation not make even medieval art conform to the standards of our own modernist culture, and thus make the Christian art of the Middle Ages in some curious way consistent with our own?

The questions raised by this revisionist view are only compounded—and indeed confounded—when we turn our attention to Volume II of the *Selected Papers* and notice that something very odd happens to this same current of aestheticism—so vividly apparent to Schapiro on the margins of medieval art—when he takes up the study of the modernist art in which it might be expected to manifest itself with an even greater clarity and force. It is there, of course, but it no longer appears to be of very compelling interest to him. In any case, it is swamped by all sorts of extra-aesthetic interests, and its vaunted autonomy is made to shrink into insignificance under the burden of the many other meanings it is made to bear. Specifically, the central place that is denied to symbolism in medieval art is somewhat too readily—I should even say somewhat too promiscuously—granted to modernist art through the agency of certain disciplines (notably psychoanalysis) that tend to obscure rather than to illuminate this purely aesthetic factor. Cézanne—to cite the outstanding example in these pages—turns out, strange as it may seem, to have been a lot less free in his pursuit of a purely aesthetic realization in his art than were those anonymous carvers and painters of the twelfth century that Schapiro has been so eager to acquit of anything but an aesthetic intention.

The crucial text here is Schapiro's essay, in Volume II, "The Apples of Cézanne: An Essay on the Meaning of Still-Life" (1968). This is a virtuoso performance of a sort that will be familiar to anyone who has ever listened to Schapiro on the lecture platform. The polymath with an ardent command of many disciplines surrounds the art objects under analysis with a range of reference that has the appearance of significantly deepening our understanding of the mind that produced them. Yet the appearance proves to be deceiving, for in the course of the analysis—which, in this case, proves only to be a psychoanalysis, and a pretty crude one at that—the mind of the *painter* all but disappears from view as our attention is fastened upon the troubled history of his libido. Writers either quoted or alluded to in this essay include Horace, Virgil, Propertius, Philostratus, Tasso, Jacob Boehme, Andrew Marvell, Flaubert, Baudelaire,

Hervey de St. Denys—author of a study of dreams, *Les Rêves et les moyens de les diriger* published in 1867—and the American philosopher George H. Mead; but as the references accumulate and the texture of the prose thickens, their relevance to an understanding of Cézanne's still-life painting grows ever more distant. In the end, though we have been taken on a grand tour of the place occupied by nudity and apples in Western art and folklore, Cézanne's own exquisitely painted apples are seen to be little more than hostages to the miserable sexual timidities of his youth.

The apples in a Cézanne still life are said by Schapiro to represent "a displaced erotic interest." This, finally, is the "meaning" we are promised in the title of the essay. And if the painter chose on occasion to place his apples in juxtaposition with some onions, this is naturally assumed to suggest—what else?—"the polarity of the sexes." These apples, you may be sure, are really female breasts in disguise, for "in Cézanne's habitual representation of the apples as a theme by itself," writes Schapiro, "there is a latent erotic sense, an unconscious symbolizing of a repressed desire."

But there is even more to this curious scenario than that, of course. The analysis of Cézanne's "frustrated . . . repressed," and "shameful" desires—to cite only a few of the terms employed by Schapiro to describe the animating impulse at work in the still-life paintings—inevitably leads us back to the disturbances of the painter's childhood. "It may be," writes Schapiro, "that Cézanne's interest in still-life goes back to unknown early fixations in the home." He then offers us a conjecture that "in Cézanne's intense concern with still-life there was an effort of reconciliation, of restoration of order to the family table, the scene of conflicts with the father and of anxiety about his own shameful desires." Why those rumpled tablecloths in the still-lifes are not found to be rumpled bedsheets in disguise, I cannot imagine. What an opportunity has been overlooked in this detail! But it comes as a surprise, in any case, to be told that "Cézanne's pictures of the nude show that he could not convey his feeling for women without anxiety." That Cézanne's pictures of mountains, houses, rocks, trees, and the light and landscape of Provence also show a certain anxiety—that this "anxiety" is, indeed, central to his style and his vision as a painter—seems to have been forgotten in the quest for a higher (or is it a lower?) meaning.

Quite apart from the crudity of the method employed in the analysis—and, in my opinion, its application in this facile manner brings discredit upon the whole Freudian enterprise—what are we to make of the way Schapiro strips the aesthetic impulse, so far as Cézanne is concerned, of the least semblance of that prized autonomy which was so enthusiastically discovered on the margins of Romanesque art? Surely we are confronted here with a sizable contradiction, for the repressions of the bourgeois family are accorded a reality—indeed, a domination and priority—in Cézanne's art that Christian belief and "religious content" are denied to the same degree in a significant portion of Romanesque art. How was it that Cézanne failed to achieve a freedom of artistic expression so emphatically won by the artists of the twelfth century?

This is but one—I think it is the central one—of the many questions raised by Schapiro's writings on the visual arts, and the answer, I suspect, will be found to lie beyond the disciplines of art history. It is more likely to be found in the realm of biography and ideology. When the biography of Meyer Schapiro comes to be written, it will have to be explained, for example, how the outlook of a secular Jew of radical political sympathies shaped his interpretation of a profoundly religious Christian art. Approached from this perspective, the aesthetic autonomy that is made so much of in "On the Aesthetic Attitude in Romanesque Art" acquires another order of significance. It looks more and more like a reflection of the scholar's yearnings in the presence of a body of art that, in its very essence, upholds a religious attitude that is so profoundly opposed to his own most cherished convictions. Similarly, the radical socialist in Schapiro could scarcely be expected to allow an artist like Cézanne—no matter how sincerely admired—a freedom from the depredations and deformities of bourgeois life that his own ideological cast of mind regards as an iron law of history. At the heart of these voluminous *Selected Papers* there thus remains an unresolved conflict—the conflict between the aesthete and the ideologue—that sooner or later will have to be faced if their author is to be taken seriously as a significant analyst of our artistic heritage.

Winter 1980-81

Susan Sontag: The Pasionaria of Style

It is now just over twenty years—by traditional calculation, a generation—since Susan Sontag burst upon the New York literary scene with a series of essays and reviews that had everybody talking. It is worth recalling, however, that the talk was by no means universally favorable. Yet the disfavor these critical studies met with was of a special kind, and did nothing to impede the fame they rapidly brought to their author. Whether she wrote about *Flaming Creatures* or Albert Camus, about "Camp" taste or Claude Lévi-Strauss or the movies of Godard and Bresson, Sontag seemed to have an unfailing faculty for dividing intellectual opinion and inspiring a sense of outrage, consternation, and betrayal among the many readers—especially older readers—who disagreed with her. And it was just this faculty for offending respectable opinion that, from the outset, was an important part of her appeal for those who welcomed her pronouncements. She was admired not only for what she said but for the pain, shock, and disarray she caused in saying it.

Sontag thus succeeded in doing something that it is given to very few critics to achieve. She made criticism a medium of intellectual scandal, and this won her instant celebrity in the world where ideas are absorbed into fashions and fashions combine to create a new cultural atmosphere. In 1966, when her early essays were collected in *Against Interpretation*—the book's very title was a provocation—she was hailed as a contemporary classic. Scarcely five years had passed since she had made her literary debut. So far-reaching was her renown that it quickly found its way even into the distant literary underground behind the Iron Curtain. On a visit to Leningrad only a year after the appearance of *Against Interpretation*, I met young writers and university students who had already read her work and were full of eager questions about it.

As is usually the case with careers of this sort, the element of timing was crucial. Criticism was unquestionably in the doldrums in the early 1960s. The literary culture that had long nourished it—the culture of modernism, with its "difficult" texts requiring lengthy and laborious study—was already in decline. Literature itself, of the high, serious, complex kind, had begun to look a little stuffy and calcified—an academic rather than a creative or a vital interest. The attention that had formerly been concentrated on literary analysis was now turning with greater enthusiasm and a more evident sense of pleasure to movies, dance, the visual arts, and certain modes of popular culture. The whole ethos of moral earnestness and finical discrimination that had dominated cultural life in the 1950s, uniting such otherwise disparate endeavors as Abstract Expressionism in painting and the New Criticism in literature, had clearly collapsed. Exactly what was in store to take its place was not yet obvious or defined, but the appetite for change and release was sharp and accelerating.

In retrospect, it now appears that 1959 was the pivotal year in this development. That was the year the first Happenings were staged in the New York art world. That was the year, too, of Godard's *Breathless*, Truffaut's *The Four Hundred Blows,* and Fellini's *La dolce vita.* And with the publication that same year of Robert Lowell's *Life Studies*, William Burroughs's *Naked Lunch*, and Norman O. Brown's *Life Against Death,* literature, too, joined in the movement to disembarrass itself of its old constraints and stake out a territory similarly devoid of inhibition, formality, and other impediments to the unfettered expression of the self.

What gave Sontag's early essays their aura of daring and controversy was the remarkable air of confidence she brought to the task of defending and codifying the values implicit in this movement to strip the arts of what she herself described as "moral sentiments." Bidding a not-so-fond farewell to art that was conceived, as she put it, as "a species of moral journalism," she hailed the advent of a "new sensibility," whose most distinctive feature was said to be that "it does not demand that pleasure in art necessarily be associated with edification." Fundamental to the new sensibility—as she wrote in her manifesto-like essay "One Culture and the New Sensibility" in 1965—was "a new attitude toward pleasure." And it was as the Pasionaria of this new, pleasure-seeking revolution in sensibility that Sontag emerged as a critical spokesman of the Sixties.

She was nothing if not explicit in spelling out what this revolution in sensibility entailed. The first thing to be discarded was what she called "the Matthew Arnold idea of culture," which was now judged to be "historically and humanly obsolescent." "The Matthew Arnold notion of culture," she wrote, "defines art as the criticism of life—this being understood as the propounding of moral, social, and political ideas." This was deemed abhorrent on several grounds. It took literature, with "its heavy burden of 'content,' both reportage and moral judgment," as a model, and this would no longer do. "The primary feature of the new sensibility," Sontag insisted, "is that its model product is not the literary work." It looked instead to the "new non-literary culture" as a creative and spiritual paradigm, and there the "basic unit," she noted, "is not the idea, but the analysis of and extension of sensations."

Then, too, the Matthew Arnold idea of culture insisted on "the distinction between 'high' and 'low'" culture, which Sontag now found to be "less and less meaningful." The new sensibility was alleged to have liberated itself from this fussy, outmoded distinction between high culture and popular culture. "If art is understood as a form of discipline of the feelings and a programming of sensations," Sontag wrote, "then the feeling (or sensation) given off by a Rauschenberg painting might be like that of a song by the Supremes." With this and many similar pronouncements, we were certainly a very long way from the Matthew Arnold idea of culture, which Arnold himself defined, in the preface to *Culture and Anarchy*, as "a pursuit of our total perfection by means of getting to know, on all the matters which most concern us, the best which has been thought and said in the world."

The first criticism to be made of *A Susan Sontag Reader* (1982) is that it omits the essay "One Culture and the New Sensibility," from which I have been quoting here and which formed the concluding chapter of *Against Interpretation*, serving, in effect, to summarize its entire spirit. Without this essay, the account given us in the *Reader* of the ideas promulgated by Sontag in the Sixties remains incomplete and more than a little blurred. Despite what Sontag said about "the idea" no longer functioning as the "basic unit" in the new cultural outlook that she favored, it was above all as an audacious champion of ideas that Sontag herself commanded attention and cast a spell. Hers was but one case among many in the Sixties—a particularly distinguished one, of course—of intellectuals engaging in strenuous flights of cerebration on behalf of ideas that promised deliverance from the tyranny of cerebration.

Foremost among the ideas vigorously espoused in *Against Interpretation* was a refurbished and scrupulously up-to-date version of the radical aestheticism that had long been associated with the "decadent" movement of the 1890s. This meant, amid much else, replacing the Matthew Arnold idea of culture with the Oscar Wilde idea of culture. What was now to be exalted was "form," "style," and "the sensory experience of the work of art," as Sontag proclaimed again and again in *Against Interpretation*.

(See especially the essays "Against Interpretation," "On Style," and "Notes on 'Camp,'" which are all included in the *Reader*.)

Acquiring appropriate access to "the sensory experience of the work of art" was no easy task, however. The obstacles strewn by our wretched culture on the road to the desired aesthetic paradise were many and formidable. There was, for example, the dreaded notion of "content"—yet another hateful, life-denying legacy of the Matthew Arnold idea of culture.

"Whatever it may have been in the past," Sontag wrote in 1964, "the idea of content is today mainly a hindrance, a nuisance, a subtle or not so subtle philistinism." The philistinism in question was no ordinary philistinism, however. It was "thoroughly ingrained among most people who take any of the arts seriously," and the worst perpetrators of this brand of philistinism, by far, were the critics who had the temerity to look for "meaning" in art. For it was they who committed the crime of "interpretation," which in our culture was said to be, among other things, "reactionary, impertinent, cowardly, stifling."

"What the overemphasis on the idea of content entails," Sontag wrote, "is the perennial, never consummated project of *interpretation*. And, conversely, it is the habit of approaching works of art in order to *interpret* them that sustains the fancy that there really is such a thing as the content of a work of art." (The emphasis is Sontag's.) "In place of a hermeneutics," Sontag wrote in a celebrated declaration, "we need an erotics of art."

It was in the interest of liberating our responses from the tyranny of "interpretation" that Sontag offered us, in her essay "On Style" (1965), instruction in what the "erotics of art" might be. What was involved, it turned out, was a programmatic abandonment of "the old antithesis of style versus content." "Everyone is quick to avow that style and content are indissoluble," she wrote. But this avowal she judged to be worthless. "In the *practice* of criticism, though, the old antithesis lives on, virtually unassailed," Sontag wrote, and she set about assailing it with considerable energy and animus.

There was something a little odd about this attack on the style-versus-content antithesis, however. For one thing, the argument advanced in the essay never really resolved the issue it ostensibly addressed. "On Style" contains a great many diverse observations about its subject—some keenly intelligent, some very tendentious, some merely commonplace—but in the end it simply comes down on the side of style, belittles the notion of content, but does not really destroy it, and thus leaves "the old antithesis" more or less intact. For another, the argument on behalf of style is conducted in a cultural void. Reading "On Style" in 1965, one was dismayed to discover that it showed not the slightest awareness of the fact that many of the best modern critics of the arts—Julius Meier-Graefe, Roger Fry, and Clement Greenberg on painting, Adrian Stokes and Edwin Denby on dance, Paul Rosenfeld and Virgil Thomson on music, Stark Young and Francis Fergusson on drama, R. P. Blackmur and others on poetry—had written, and written at length, on matters of "form," "style," and "the sensuous experience of the work of art" with an attention to detail and a sense of complexity that far exceeded anything Sontag was attempting, or was even aware of. Rereading "On Style" in the *Reader*, one wonders if its author was really equipped in 1965 to deal with its subject. So much that was central to it had been either omitted or overlooked.

Perhaps it was not to be expected, however, that the Oscar Wilde idea of culture would yield much in the way of illuminating the problem of the relation of form in art to content. Aestheticism, after all, is not primarily a philosophy of art. It is a philosophy of life. It differs from formalism—with which, alas, it is often confused—in being less interested in the perfection of objects than in "a programming of sensations" and in cultivating a certain taste. Whereas formalism attempts to sever the connection between art and life in order to uphold the autonomy of art, aestheticism affirms their ineluctable attachment while at the same time making experience the principal *raison d'être* of all aesthetic endeavor. No formalist, for example, would ever have boasted, as Wilde did, that he had put his genius into his life and only his talent into his art. From the formalist perspective, this is an abject confession of artistic failure.

Sontag sometimes sounds as if she were espousing the formalist view, especially when she is inveighing against "moral sentiments" in art. But when, in the last paragraph of "On Style," she observes that "it remains to be said that style is a notion that applies to any experience (whenever we talk about its form or qualities)," we are made vividly aware that it is something other than the integrity or autonomy of the work of art that is primarily at issue in this essay.

It is not, in any case, in the essay "On Style" but in the notorious "Notes on 'Camp'" that we were given our clearest view of the implications of Sontag's aestheticism. It was "Notes on 'Camp'" —published in *Partisan Review*, in 1964—that made Susan Sontag a famous and controversial figure. For this essay caused a considerable uproar in New York intellectual circles when it first appeared, and it instantly won the attention of the media in a way that critical essays seldom do. It remains today, nearly two decades after its appearance, a classic text in the literature of aestheticism.

The uproar that greeted it, it must be said, was deserved. For "Notes" achieved something radical and incendiary in offering its readers—the readers of *Partisan Review*, with its long-standing commitment to a Marxist variant of "the Matthew Arnold idea of cultures"—a moral holiday. "Notes" spoke for fun, for frivolity, for a wholesale release from the burdens of seriousness. It made the very idea of moral discrimination seem stale and distinctly un-chic.

The essay was not without its evasions. On the one aspect of Camp sensibility that everyone acquainted with the phenomenon was most acutely aware of, for example—its roots in the subculture of homosexuality—"Notes" was extremely coy. But this, too, contributed to its success in offering a rousing description and defense of Camp's cultural appeal. "Camp is a certain mode of aestheticism," Sontag declared, and this declaration had the effect of de-parochializing its special qualities. Of these, clearly the most important for Sontag was that the Camp sensibility, "among other things, converts the serious into the frivolous." What she called its "essence" was "its love of the unnatural."

Camp was thus hailed as "the sensibility of failed seriousness," and it was precisely for the praise the essay lavished on "failed seriousness"—and on the consequences that would follow from it—that "Notes on 'Camp'" both caused a scandal and won a following. "Camp is the consistently aesthetic experience of the world," Sontag wrote. "It incarnates a victory of 'style' over 'content,' 'aesthetics' over 'morality,' of irony over tragedy." "The whole point of Camp is to dethrone the serious," she insisted, and it naturally followed that Camp would also serve as "a solvent of morality." Sontag said—as if we needed to be told!—that "These notes are for Oscar Wilde."

Yet despite her eloquent avowal of this radical position, it is part of the pathos of Sontag's career that she has never been entirely at ease with the aestheticism she has so vigorously espoused. Even in "Notes on 'Camp,'" she spoke of a "conflict in my own sensibility." "I am strongly drawn to Camp," she wrote, "and almost as strongly offended by it." This hint of a disclaimer, if that is what it was, was not very persuasive when "Notes" was first published, for in the Sixties Sontag's defense of aestheticism was conducted with an air of stridency and militancy that brooked no possibility of contradiction. Although this *sotto voce* suggestion of a dissent from her own position is not very persuasive even now, it did, after all, turn out to signify something important. It was not that Sontag was ever prepared to abandon her stand on aestheticism and all its implications. It was only that she did not want it to cost her anything.

It is this desire to have it both ways, I think, that accounts for the very real split that has afflicted Sontag's work more and more openly since the publication of *Against Interpretation*, and at times has rendered it, at the very least, morally incoherent. This split would be easier to grasp if Sontag had not excised from the *Reader* nearly all trace of her political writings. The longest single essay in *Styles of Radical Will* (1969), after all, was her unforgettable account of her trip to Hanoi during the Vietnam War—an essay that can justly be called a classic of its kind. Another important contribution to that book was the essay "What's Happening in America," with its famous declaration that "[t]he white race *is* the cancer of human history." Afterward, of course, she more or less retracted this statement, but only because she came to feel that it represented an insult—to *cancer!* With such a writer, it is sometimes difficult to give credence to protests against "the propounding of moral, social, and political ideas." The notion of "content" may have become "a hindrance," but it is, apparently, not one that is easily expunged from the literary mind.

Sontag is nothing if not acutely conscious of every turn her mind has taken, and it is one of the purposes of the *Reader* to set the record straight—if that is the word—on the history of its author's contradictory course (except for explicitly political contradictions: there is no hint in the *Reader* of Sontag's Town Hall speech, in 1982, denouncing Communism). It will be recalled by readers of "On Style" that Sontag insisted on a complete separation of "form" and "content" when it came to judging two of the films, *The Triumph of the Will* and *Olympia*, that Leni Riefenstahl made in Nazi Germany under Hitler's personal sponsorship. The passage is worth quoting. "Because they project the complex movements of intelligence and grace and sensuousness, these two films of Riefenstahl (unique among works of Nazi artists) transcend the categories of propaganda or even reportage. And we find ourselves—to be sure, rather uncomfortably—seeing 'Hitler' and not Hitler, the '1936 Olympics' and not the 1936 Olympics. Through Riefenstahl's genius as a filmmaker, the 'content' has—let us assume, against her intentions—come to play a purely formal role." Which, incidentally, reminds us of Sontag's statement in "Notes on 'Camp'" that "Camp sees everything in quotation marks."

Yet in the essay called "Fascinating Fascism" (1974), reprinted in the *Reader*, Sontag registers a loud protest against the movement to purify "Leni Riefenstahl's reputation of its Nazi dross." "The line taken by Riefenstahl's defenders, who now include the most influential voices in the avant-garde film establishment," Sontag writes in this essay, "is that she was always concerned with beauty." The line, in other words, that Sontag herself took in "On Style." But in "Fascinating Fascism" she writes as if she had only just discovered the Nazi content of these films.

Now, what is extraordinary about the presentation of these contradictory views in the *Reader* is not that the critic has changed her mind on a significant subject. It is entirely to Sontag's credit that she did change her mind, especially on this subject. No, what is extraordinary is that Sontag denies that any significant change occurred. Following "Fascinating Fascism" in the *Reader* is a lengthy interview with Sontag that was originally published in *Salmagundi* in 1976, and the very first question addresses precisely this issue. (That, I suppose, is the main reason the interview is reprinted in the *Reader*.) After quoting from Sontag's comments on Riefenstahl in both "On Style" and "Fascinating Fascism," the friendly interviewer says: "At the very least, these two statements contrast with each other. Is there also a continuity between the two essays?" And this is Sontag's reply:

> A continuity, it seems to me, in that both statements illustrate the richness of the form-content distinction, as long as one is careful always to use it against itself. My point in 1965 was about the formal implications of content, while the recent essay examines the content implicit in certain ideas of form. One of the main assertions of 'On Style' is that the formalist and the historicist approaches are not in competition with each other, but are complementary—and equally indispensable.

I am not at all certain that criticism concerned with the content of a work of art can best be described as "historicist," but whatever it is called, there is nothing in "On Style" that suggests that it is indispensable to anything but a certain philistinism.

Sontag says in this interview that she is now—or was it then?—convinced "of the perils of overgeneralizing the aesthetic view of the world." Yet it is precisely upon this tendency that her writings are based. There are more and more hints in her work that she yearns to transcend it and make contact with something more substantial. In the last essay in the *Reader*, on Roland Barthes, she remarks that "Barthes harbored spiritual strivings that could not be supported by his aesthete's position," and this statement seems to describe Sontag's position as much as Barthes's. Yet the *Reader* gives us little reason to believe that these strivings can be realized until the spiritual vacuity of aestheticism—and its moral smugness, too—are rigorously confronted. But this would oblige Sontag to reconsider, among much else, the Matthew Arnold idea of culture, and of this there is no serious sign in *The Susan Sontag Reader.*

September 1982

“CLOSING TIME IN THE GARDENS OF THE WEST”

Cyril Connolly's Horizon

Nineteen-eighty-nine marked the fiftieth anniversary of the birth of *Horizon*, the literary monthly which Cyril Connolly founded in London in the early months of the Second World War. That year also marked the fortieth anniversary of the magazine's demise. Calling itself "A Review of Literature & Art," *Horizon* was published for exactly a decade—and what a decade it was! The first issue went to press barely three months after Britain, still a world power but woefully ill-prepared to fight a major war, found itself locked in lonely combat against the Nazis, who were very shortly in control of most of Europe. The last issue, with its unforgettable dirge—"it is closing time in the gardens of the West," etc.—emerged from a weaker and even bleaker, now "socialist" England, which was so impoverished and dispirited that it looked more and more like a casualty of the war in which it had been victorious. Through the darkest days of the Blitz and the V-1 ("doodlebug") bombings, with British losses steadily mounting abroad and what remained of cultural life—the life of the mind—under attack at home from the philistine press as frivolous and escapist, Connolly went right on producing, month after month, an unabashedly highbrow literary journal of extraordinary quality and vivacity. It was an amazing feat, and all the more amazing because Connolly had already pronounced himself a failure—"a lazy, irresolute person, over-vain and over-modest, unsure in my judgments and unable to finish what I have begun." But then, as David Pryce-Jones has written, "the depiction of himself as some sort of royal failure was the foundation of [Connolly's] success." My own view is that *Horizon* was Connolly's greatest achievement—greater, certainly, than any of his own books. It was also one of the most remarkable intellectual achievements of its period, a triumph of spirit over circumstance.

Announcing in the first number that "the aim of *Horizon* is to give the writers a place to express themselves, and to readers the best writing we can obtain," Connolly also emphasized that "our standards are aesthetic, and our politics are in abeyance." The first point, about aesthetic standards, was valiantly adhered to. The point about politics was more complicated. The very number in which the claim was made contained political articles by J. B. Priestley and Herbert Read—"vague political ramblings," as *Horizon*'s patron Peter Watson correctly observed—and others were expected to follow, as Connolly himself promptly acknowledged. Yet there is an important sense in which Connolly meant what he said about a suspension of what he called "our" politics. He was clearly referring to the kind of Marxism that had exerted so powerful an influence on his generation of British writers in the 1930s.

In his "Comment" for *Horizon*'s inaugural issue, he noted that "the impetus given by Left Wing politics is for the time exhausted." (For Connolly, the departure of Auden and Isherwood for America marked the end of the movement.) So, too, in Connolly's view, was the age of literary experiment drawing to a close. (He was right about that, too.) Thus, as he also wrote in *Horizon*'s first number, "however much we should like to have a paper that was revolutionary in opinions and original in technique," he did not believe that the customary amalgam of Marxism and modernism was any longer possible or appropriate to the task at hand. "At the moment," he wrote in one of those lapidary statements for which he was already celebrated, "civilization is on the operating table and we sit in the waiting room."

As Connolly conceived of it, *Horizon* was to be one of the instruments for securing the patient's survival. He supported the war—there was no mistaking his, or *Horizon*'s, position on that question—but he was adamant about keeping the journal's pages free of the canting propaganda that the war inevitably engendered. *Horizon* was to be a kind of literary sanctuary—"The Ivory Shelter," he called it—a demilitarized zone of the mind in which the creative and critical intelligence might prosper even at a time when so many lethal forces were arrayed against it. If an important part of *Horizon*'s task was to keep alive the memory of past artistic achievements (Mozart and Mallarmé, French classical drama and Henry James), and thus provide a sense of continuity and kinship with the very civilization that was now threatened with extinction, it was also the magazine's function to find and publish the writers who would carry on the work of that civilization into whatever future there might be. Connolly found them, too, most notably his old school friend George Orwell, so opposed in so many ways to Connolly's own literary outlook but many of whose now famous essays on politics and popular culture nonetheless made their first appearance in *Horizon*'s pages during the war.

The editorial policy Connolly adopted for *Horizon* was avowedly eclectic, and he knew very well that this was bound to incur the wrath of both radicals and conservatives, who were alike in preferring a more homogeneous "party" line. The first objective, as Connolly saw it, was to repair the damage that a decade of Marxist aesthetics had wrought: "it is our duty," he wrote in February 1940, "gradually to re-educate the peppery palates of our detractors to an appreciation of delicate poetry and fine prose."

> If literature is an art [he wrote in the same issue], then a literary magazine should encourage the artists, whether they

> are Left or Right, known or unknown, old or young, and *Horizon* therefore makes no more apology for Priestley's admirable essay, or Sir Hugh Walpole's revealing glimpse of Henry James, than it does for Orwell's analysis of Boy's papers or Auden's Elegy on Freud which will appear in the next number. Names mean nothing. *Horizon* is not to be judged by its names but by the quality of its contents and we hope eventually that the presence of the most detested best-seller or the most obscure young poet on the cover of *Horizon* will be enough to indicate that they have written something remarkably good. As to discovering a Joyce or an Eliot in one number, all we can do is bait the trap, to provide a medium where the future Rimbaud *will* find payment, good company and a sympathetic public. But it is possible that there are no Rimbauds, and that we must fall back on being the publishers of [Stephen Spender's] September Journal.

That last line was a characteristic example of Connolly's mordant candor, for Stephen Spender, although unnamed on the masthead, was at this time one of Connolly's closest collaborators on *Horizon*, and an excerpt from his "September Journal" was featured in the issue in which this not very flattering comparison was made.

The story of how Connolly accomplished what he did in *Horizon*, of the other people who made that accomplishment possible, and of Connolly's own life during the *Horizon* period, has now been told for the first time in a splendid new book—Michael Shelden's *Friends of Promise: Cyril Connolly and the World of "Horizon"* (Harper & Row). Shelden, an American academic who was born in Oklahoma and now teaches at Indiana State University, is himself a first-rate writer, and the book he has given us in *Friends of Promise*—his first, by the way—is the kind of literary history, replete with vivid biographical portraits and shrewd critical judgments, that one had quite given up expecting from our professors of literature. One would like to think that

Shelden represents a new turn in the fortunes of academic literary study—a return, that is, to a tradition that has been largely lost—but that is probably too much to hope for. Talent of this sort rarely represents anything but itself

In any event, the account of Connolly in this book is the best I have read, its only serious rival being David Pryce-Jones's *Cyril Connolly: Journal and Memoir* (1984), an excellent book of much smaller compass. For its absorbing picture of literary life in wartime London, moreover, *Friends of Promise* is likewise exemplary, and not least because of the fine sense of proportion it exhibits in dealing with a subject which, given its large cast of characters and the drama of the war itself, could so easily have been distended into one of those inert, outsize chronicles that exhaust our patience and defeat their own purposes. Shelden is clearly a master researcher, and he has been obliged to ferret out a good deal of elusive detail both in the archives and from surviving witnesses. Yet the result is scholarship that has been completely assimilated into a shapely and unflagging narrative. One would be tempted to say that *Friends of Promise* reads at times like a good novel, if only there were still novels that gave us as many well-drawn characters as this book does.

Besides Connolly himself, these characters include his first wife, Jean Bakewell, a wealthy American girl from Baltimore whom Connolly met in Paris; Peter Watson, art collector, aesthete, and heir to a British margarine fortune, who put up all the money for *Horizon* and served as its art editor; three of Watson's homosexual lovers, Denham Fouts, Waldemar Hansen, and Norman Fowler, who were Americans; Stephen Spender, *Horizon*'s associate editor during its first year; Sonia Brownell, Connolly's young assistant, who married *Horizon*'s most celebrated contributor, George Orwell, on his deathbed; and Lys Lubbock, Connolly's beautiful mistress and *Horizon*'s business manager, who eventually moved to New York and married an American. Among the minor characters in the narrative, playing walk-on roles, are such figures as Logan Pearsall Smith, Evelyn

Waugh, Dylan Thomas, T. S. Eliot, Clement Greenberg, Lucian Freud, Arthur Koestler, Elizabeth Bowen, and, not least, Connolly's father, a retired army major, who enters the story as a somewhat farcical character but makes his exit as a very poignant figure.

Except for Peter Watson, whose portrait—the first candid account I have seen of this troubled but sympathetic figure—is one of the best things in the book, none of the other characters is given the attention that is lavished on Connolly, who dominates the story as ringmaster and presiding genius. Shelden is anything but a starry-eyed admirer of Connolly's every foible. While the gifts that made Connolly such an exceptional figure are fully acknowledged and brilliantly described in *Friends of Promise*, Shelden misses nothing of the restless, egotistical, spoiled-child aspect of the man, all those elements of Connolly's character that were so egregiously in evidence in his relations with women and, for that matter, with his other benefactors as well. Connolly spent much of his adult life living—and usually living well—off of other people's money. He envied the rich and was in the habit of condescending to them—unless he could obtain something from them, in which case he was inclined to court them until the prize had been won and then criticize them to their friends. At school he had learned to make himself amusing to his social superiors, and he turned that gift, too, into an instrument of advantage and preferment. He perfected a posture of charm, talent, mischief, and brilliance that proved to be very appealing, and then enclosed it in the pre-emptive claim to failure that absolved him from having to fulfill his talents.

It was only with *Horizon* that, for the first and last time, he delivered what he grandly promised. Otherwise, his well-rehearsed justification for his career as a shameless sponger was his much-vaunted ambition to write a literary masterpiece. In the earlier stages of this fantasy ambition, the great book was to be a novel. Then, in the *Horizon* period, though novels were from time to time worked on, the talk shifted to a study of Flaubert, one of Connolly's idols; then it was to be a book about France, which had early on claimed his loyalty as a model of civilization. None of these books was ever written, of course. He became an expert, however, at persuading people that he would write them, no doubt because in some part of his mind he believed it himself. Yet somehow there were always more engaging things to occupy his time and give him pleasure. He signed contracts and collected advances, and was remarkably adept at getting people to pay up. On this whole aspect of Connolly's literary career, the American publisher Cass Canfield made the definitive comment when he finally realized that Connolly was never going to write the books he had contracted for. "I give Connolly full credit," Canfield said, "for being one of the most charmingly devious literary gentlemen not actually behind bars."

Something similar might be said about his relations with women, who pampered him, often paid his bills, flattered his ego, served his pleasures, and otherwise went along with his every scheme, sometimes under threat of suicide and always under the spell of his charm and his need, only to find that the promises were usually broken in affairs of the heart, too, and there was always another candidate in the wings, if not already in bed, to supplant them. Shelden isn't given to moralizing but he is a keen judge of character, and his account of Connolly's, while for the most part sympathetic, is unblinking. He knows very well where the virtues of his protagonist are to be found, and is sharp about separating the glamour of Connolly's life from the sometimes unlovely reality. None of this, I hasten to add, has the effect of diminishing our interest in Connolly. On the contrary, the more we learn about him, the more he comes to resemble a character in a novel—the novel of his life, as it were, which he couldn't write but which he never tired of performing for all who knew him.

Yet it is finally because of his performance as the editor of *Horizon* that Connolly's claim on our attention remains more than that of an interesting character. *Enemies of Promise* (1938), though parts of it can still be read with interest, is now more likely to survive as a literary document of the 1930s than as a living classic. *The Unquiet Grave* (1944), though it has always had its admirers, among them, oddly enough, Ernest Hemingway, looks more and more like a period piece, and its famous opening line—"The more books we read, the clearer it becomes that the true function of a writer is to produce a masterpiece and that no other task is of any importance"—looks, in retrospect, like the plea-bargaining of a guilty talent. As for the various collections of essays and parodies—*The Condemned Playground* (1945), *Ideas and Places* (1953), *Previous Convictions* (1963), and *The Evening Colonnade* (1963)—all of them contain some good things, especially *Ideas and Places*, which includes material from *Horizon*, but no one would describe them as great criticism. *Horizon* itself is Connolly's monument. Which is another reason why the focus of Shelden's book is exactly right.

Even with *Horizon*, however, a distinction must be made between the first half of the decade in which it was published—in other words, the war years—and the second. With exceptions to be noted, the magazine's real achievement lies in those first five years. The poetry—much of it written by W. H. Auden and Dylan Thomas—was better, and so was most of the prose. And the attention to art, though no match for what *Horizon* was able to bring its readers after the war, was nonetheless more important because the life of art had suffered even more restrictions during the war than literature had. Moreover, the momentum sustained in those first five years had a fervor—a sense of mission—that was lost in the drab, spiritually constricted period which followed.

> During the war [Shelden writes] *Horizon*'s purpose had been clear. Every issue had been a reaffirmation of the importance of culture in wartime; and the enemies of culture had been easy to spot and to criticize. But in the post-war period those enemies were more difficult to define, the battle lines were

> more loosely drawn, and the purpose of the struggle was much less certain. *Horizon*'s historical moment had come and gone; never again would one small independent magazine assume such an important place in the cultural life of the nation, attracting so many important writers without cash, political interest or a new literary movement as bait. Watson and Connolly had seized the moment and made the most of it; the decline of their extraordinary partnership was unavoidable.

It was a measure of Connolly's sense of the historical moment that he so eagerly welcomed writers whose literary purposes were so different from his own.

> In December 1939 George Orwell told him that he had just finished a book called *Inside the Whale*, which contained three long essays. Connolly asked whether he could publish part of it in *Horizon*. At that point the book had no publisher, and Orwell was not sure that he would find one. He was also uncertain that the essays were suitable for *Horizon*. The shortest of the three, "Boys' Weeklies," was still rather long for magazine publication, and its subject hardly seemed appropriate for *Horizon*'s "highbrow" readership. . . . Serious essays on popular culture are common today, but "Boys' Weeklies" was the first important essay of its kind written in England. Much to his credit, Connolly had the foresight to accept it, even though it took up nearly a third of the magazine. . . . Over the next ten years many writers would benefit from this policy, but no one used it to better advantage than Orwell, who wrote half a dozen important essays for the magazine.

As Shelden correctly observes, "Connolly's decision to publish 'Boys' Weeklies' demonstrated that *Horizon* was not going to be a simple caretaker for literature during wartime. It would take risks and do the unpredictable, without much regard for what was happening in the war."

Connolly did much the same thing for Arthur Koestler, who was in England as a refugee and just beginning his career as an English-language writer.

> When Koestler arrived in London, Connolly took it upon himself to provide him with a place to stay, and shortly afterwards helped him to become an established writer in London. In turn, Koestler gave *Horizon* three important articles: "The Yogi and the Commissar" in 1942, "The Birth of a Myth" in 1943, and "The Intelligentsia" in 1944. The second essay, which was about the death of Richard Hillary, was chosen by readers as the most popular work in the magazine for 1943. . . . Koestler remained forever grateful for Connolly's support, saying many years later: "Cyril took me under his wing. I want to emphasize very warmly my indebtedness to Cyril. Instead of spending my time in loneliness and isolation like so many exiles, or confined to an emigré clique, I was welcomed into the *Horizon* crowd."

The postwar period was inevitably different. Connolly made an important discovery in Angus Wilson, who was then working at the British Museum and had written about a dozen short stories which had never been published. A friend showed a few of these to Connolly in 1947, and he promptly accepted two for *Horizon.* Years later Wilson wrote Connolly that "If I had not been chosen by you for publication in *Horizon* it is almost certain that my writing would have petered out as the unfertilized hobby of a man who was looking for some means of expression but never found it."

For the most part, however, Connolly looked abroad for new stimulation—first to his beloved Paris, of course, and then more and more to the United States. The many articles he published by or about Sartre, Camus, Gide, and other French writers cannot have for us today the kind of excitement they undoubtedly had for Connolly and his readers at the time—our whole relation to the postwar French literary scene has so drastically changed—but it was nonetheless a sign of his editorial acumen that Connolly immediately grasped what was new and important in Paris and gave it full play in the magazine. At times this enthusiastic interest in "abroad" led him astray—most conspicuously in a special number of *Horizon* devoted to Switzerland which today is all but unreadable. But even this misfired effort has to be understood as part of Connolly's attempt to re-establish a sense of cultural connection between a diminished Britain and whatever remnants of a shattered Europe showed some evidence of intellectual vitality.

If, about the many pages devoted to France in these postwar issues of *Horizon*, there is a sense of piety—of worshiping at a familiar shrine in the hope of recapturing a lost emotion, if not indeed a lost youth, there is about the attention paid to the United States a more vivid sense of genuine discovery. From the outset Connolly had taken an uncommon interest in American writing and painting, reprinting Clement Greenberg's classic essay on "Avant-Garde and Kitsch" shortly after its initial appearance in *Partisan Review* and publishing an essay on "Painting in America," by John Rothenstein, as early as 1941. But it was in the postwar period that this interest flowered. The special double number devoted to "Art on the American Horizon" in October 1947 gave its readers a better account of American cultural life at that moment than any single thing published in the United States. It included, among much else, the first publication of an excerpt from Ralph Ellison's *Invisible Man*; Clement Greenberg's important essay "The Present Prospects of American Painting and Sculpture," in which Jackson Pollock was named as "the most powerful painter in contemporary America" and David Smith was described as "the only other American artist of our time who produces art capable of withstanding the test of international scrutiny"; a report on American architecture written by

Philip Johnson and Edgar Kaufmann, Jr.; an essay on American advertising by Marshall McLuhan; "The Higher Learning in America" by Jacques Barzun; "American Foreign Policy" by Joseph Alsop; fiction by John Berryman; poems by Marianne Moore, Wallace Stevens, E. E. Cummings, and W. H. Auden, and an account of Los Angeles from Christopher Isherwood.

One of the best things in that issue, moreover, was Connolly's lengthy introduction, a chronicle and commentary based on his own visit to the U.S.

> At a time [Connolly wrote] when the American way, backed by American resources, has made the country into the greatest power the world has known, there has never been more doubting and questioning of the purpose of the American process; the higher up one goes the more searching becomes this self-criticism, the deeper the thirst for a valid mystique of humanity. Those who rule America, who formulate its foreign policy and form its opinion, are enormously conscious of their responsibility and of the total inadequacy of the crude material philosophy of life in which they grew up. The bloody-minded, the smug, the imperialist, the fascist, are in a minority. Seldom, in fact, has an unwilling world been forced to tolerate, through its own folly, a more unwilling master.

Connolly was by no means an uncritical admirer of what he found in America, but as this passage attests, he never succumbed to the kind of vulgar and uninformed anti-Americanism that was already rampant in Britain and in Europe. And about the literary scene he was, not surprisingly, particularly sharp. In 1947, for example, he appears to have divined the fate of Truman Capote with an almost preternatural foresight.

> The hunt for young authors who, while maintaining a prestige value . . . may yet somehow win the coveted jack-pot, is feverish and incessant . . . "Get Capote"—at this minute the

> words are resounding on many a sixtieth floor, and "get him" of course means make him and break him, smother him with laurels and then vent on him the obscure hatred which is inherent in the notion of another's superiority. . . . America is the one country (greatly to its credit) where an author can still make a fortune for life from one book, it is also the country where everyone is obsessed with the idea, where publishers live like stockbrokers, and where authors, like film-stars, are condemned to meditate from minute to minute last year's income tax, next week's publicity.

About many things, indeed, Connolly had a very clear understanding. For an American reader some forty years later, this issue on "Art on the American Horizon" marks the high point of *Horizon's* postwar period, and it remains an invaluable guide to the onset of our own postwar era.

Early on in the war Connolly had foreseen the shape of things to come for both Britain and America.

> Whatever happens in the war [he wrote in his "Comment" for the February 1940 issue], America will be the gainer. It will gain enormously in wealth, and enormously (through the refugees) in culture. England will be poverty stricken, even in victory, and will have either to be a poor reactionary state, a Victorian museum piece, like Hungary or Austria, or a poor progressive country, like Denmark or Scandinavia.

He was a remarkable man, despite his flaws and his failures, and *Horizon* was his most remarkable accomplishment. Michael Shelden is to be congratulated for having written a book that does him—and *Horizon*—justice in every respect.

September 1989

An Orwell for the Nineties

A modern literary intellectual lives and writes in constant dread —not, indeed, of public opinion in the wider sense, but of public opinion within his own group. As a rule, luckily, there is more than one group, but also at any given moment there is a dominant orthodoxy, to offend against which needs a thick skin and sometimes means cutting one's income in half for years on end. Obviously, for about fifteen years past, the dominant orthodoxy, especially among the young, has been "left."

—George Orwell, "Writers and Leviathan," 1948

IT was inevitable, I suppose, that the collapse of Communism and the waning of the Cold War would sooner or later bring in their wake a revaluation of the writers most explicitly identified with the anti-Communist cause. It was not to be expected, however, that this process of revaluation would redound to the favor of the writers in question. History may have proved them to have been right about Communism and the Soviet system all along, but it is precisely their having been right—right, it will no doubt be said, for the wrong reasons—that will be held against them. In this country, anyway, the imperatives of cultural life remain as unforgiving as ever about assaults on Left-liberal orthodoxy, which is as dominant today—in the academy, in the media, and in literature and the arts—as it was in George Orwell's day. The truth is, smart literary opinion has always looked with disfavor on the forthright expression of anti-Communist views, and never hesitated to castigate even the mightiest figures for going "too far" in their critique of the Communist system. Somehow, despite all the acknowledged enormities—never mind the unacknowledged ones—the system had to be absolved and the facts mitigated in the name of an unquestioned ideal.

One recalls now with a certain interest, for example, George Steiner's blistering attack on Aleksandr Solzhenitsyn for daring to remind us that it was Lenin, rather than Stalin or Hitler, who created the model for the most hateful of modern political institutions—the slave-labor camp—and that the dimensions of the Soviet terror were no less horrific than those of the Nazi era. "To infer that the Soviet terror is as hideous as Hitlerism," Steiner wrote in his review of *The Gulag Archipelago* in *The New Yorker* of August 5, 1974, "is not only a brutal oversimplification but a moral indecency." I daresay that Steiner's sense of moral indecency, or at least his expression of it, has probably been modified by recent events in Russia and Eastern Europe. The noise of all those Lenin monuments being toppled must have reached even his reclusive ears. Yet it is important to recall attacks of this kind, which always had less to do with the realities of Communism and the Soviet system than with the need to uphold the pieties of Left-liberal orthodoxy, if we are to understand the assaults still to come on the writers who insisted on telling the truth about the longest reigning tyranny of the twentieth century.

In the case of George Orwell, the attempt to soften, re-interpret, and otherwise misrepresent his criticism of Communism and the Soviet system was already well established long before there was any clear sign that the collapse of Communism was imminent in the Soviet Union. It was given a renewed impetus by the Vietnam War that brought us, among much else, Mary McCarthy's furious attack on Orwell in *The New York Review of Books*.[1] Again, this had less to do with the realities of Communism—in either the Soviet Union or Vietnam—than with the need to defend the Left-liberal position on the war, which was pro-Communist and anti-American. What made Mary McCarthy's attempted demolition of Orwell's reputation especially significant at the time, of course, was that it came from a writer whose own reputation had been made in the anti-Communist left-wing milieu of *Partisan Review*, where Orwell had been a revered figure. It thus marked a new willingness, which was then widespread on the liberal Left, to disavow the criticism of Communism in the name of an anti-war movement that identified Washington, rather than Moscow or Hanoi, as the primary enemy of peace and democracy. Mary McCarthy understood very well what Orwell would have made of her pusillanimous apologia for the Communist system in Hanoi, not to mention her accompanying vilification of the United States, and so the whole edifice of his anti-Communist critique—which included a devastating description of the kind of fellow-traveler she had now become–had to be discredited if her own sense of superior virtue and that of the anti-war movement were to be sustained.

This assault on Orwell's anti-Communist views reached a new climax in 1984 with the debate over the meaning of *Nineteen Eighty-Four*. There was, for example, the Signet edition of *Nineteen Eighty-Four* that, in both Walter Cronkite's introduction and Erich Fromm's afterword, attempted to deflect the book's criticism of Communism in Russia and make it seem as if those political strictures were actually directed against a society like our own. As Robert Conquest wrote in a splendid essay at the time,

> to apply Orwell's highly specific totalitarian terror–falsifica-

[1] See the title essay of Mary McCarthy's *The Writing on the Wall* (Harcourt Brace & World).

> tion concepts to assorted Western notions is to dilute, indeed to stultify, Orwell's point. . . . Above all, this sort of thing distorts Orwell's view of the totalist terror state as something distinct and different from our own imperfect societies—indeed, something to be resisted at all costs.

Conquest's analysis of this point is worth looking at in some detail, for it is quite the best response we have seen to this shameless attempt to turn *Nineteen Eighty-Four* into a political allegory of Western capitalist society. As Mr. Conquest wrote in *Tyrants and Typewriters: Communiqués from the Struggle for Truth*:

> The foundation of *Nineteen Eighty-Four* is, in fact, Stalin's Russia. In his *George Orwell*, Raymond Williams (writing from a left-wing viewpoint) criticizes him for this. Williams rightly argues that he could have gone beyond "a single political tendency" and sought models all over; and in effect censures him for *not* seeing a potential totalitarianism in the Western system.
>
> Had Orwell indeed thought that the *Nineteen Eighty-Four* regime could have arisen from the corruption of conservatives, capitalists, Labourites, or whatever, he had a particularly good opportunity of developing it—with a neo-capitalist-conservative totalitarianism in Oceania to balance "neo-Bolshevism" in Eurasia. He did nothing of the kind, and those who argue that every political culture, with its imperfect politicians, insensitive bureaucrats, occasional abuses of power, sporadic euphemisms and falsifications, is seen by Orwell as equally liable to breed totalitarianism, are simply not reading the book (or, come to that, Orwell's other explicatory writings of the same period).
>
> He did not do so, because he did not in fact see the West as seriously tending in that direction. Much as he detested Conservatives and Catholics, press lords and movie moguls, he did not envisage them as precursors of the terror state. And he saw

> Western culture, on which they were the warts, as nevertheless the hope of the world. . . . The Soviet Union, on the other hand, was his model of a frightful local present and a possible frightful world future.

It speaks volumes, of course, about the compulsion of the orthodox Left to blunt and distort Orwell's criticism of Communism in *Nineteen Eighty-Four* that this fundamental truth about his work should even need to be defended in this way.

Now, with the publication of Michael Shelden's *Orwell: The Authorized Biography* (HarperCollins), we may well be entering a new phase in the history of Orwell's reputation, for there is much about this book to suggest that this is the way Orwell is likely to be perceived by liberal opinion in the future. Indeed, it is almost enough to make one believe in the impersonal imperatives of the *Zeitgeist* that such a benign, politically defanged portrait of Orwell should make its appearance at the very moment when we are embarking upon the first years of the post-Communist, post-Cold War era.

As readers of his excellent earlier book—*Friends of Promise: Cyril Connolly and the World of "Horizon"* (1989)—will already know, Shelden does not write from any very special political position. He is, I suppose, a sort of liberal with no very pronounced ideological convictions about any of the issues that were so central to Orwell's life and work. Because of this political detachment, his biography was bound to be a vast improvement on Bernard Crick's *George Orwell: A Life* (1980), and it is. Crick's *Life*, which was foolishly authorized by Orwell's widow (who subsequently, to her credit, repudiated it), was clearly animated by a determination to undercut Orwell's political vision in *Nineteen Eighty-Four* and many of his other writings. (In the final chapter of the book, the politics of *Nineteen Eighty-Four* are characterized by Crick as "at best incautious, at worst foolish.") In other words, Crick was writing from the stronghold of the "dominant orthodoxy" that Orwell had spent much of his mature life vigorously opposing.

Shelden's approach is very different, much more in the vein of conventional literary biography. He has turned up a good many letters heretofore unknown and tracked down old friends of Orwell—including old girl friends—who were never before interviewed. On at least one subject—Saint Cyprian's, the boarding school where Orwell spent much of his boyhood and which he wrote about in "Such, Such Were the Joys" (1947)—Shelden's account is so exhaustive that it leaves one hoping that we shall never have to read about it ever again. Most absorbing of all as sheer biographical narrative is the story of Orwell's last years on the remote Scottish island of Jura—a story which, if Orwell had been able to write it, would have made a better novel than most of the conventional novels he wrote.

Yet, as fine as much of Shelden's book is, it leaves one doubting that biography is finally the most effective means of getting at Orwell's importance as a writer. For the net effect of this book is to shift attention away from Orwell's intense absorption in the politics of totalitarianism and make politics itself seem, if not exactly marginal to Orwell's interests, then at least subordinate to the personal and literary concerns that are Shelden's own primary interest. This does not so much ignore Orwell's political philosophy as render it vaguely innocuous, overly personal, and possibly even eccentric—more a matter of the man's psychology than of the writer's moral vision. As a result, what might be called the crank element in Orwell, which is certainly not to be denied in any complete account of his life and work, is constantly underscored while his abiding political preoccupations are made to seem more the attribute of an odd personality than the single most significant aspect of his life's work.

This is not to say that Shelden in any way neglects the details of Orwell's intense involvement in political questions. His account of the writing of *The Road to Wigan Pier* (1937) is excellent, and so is his summary of the ambivalent attitude toward socialism that went into the writing of that book.

> Like everything else in his book, Orwell's approach to socialism is individualistic [he writes]. He wants to be part of a collective effort, but he also wants to be free to speak his mind, to disagree with colleagues, to read what he wants, to go where he wants to go. He does not want to be a statistic in someone else's master plan. He advocates a classless society, yet he fears losing his own distinct identity as a son of the middle class. . . . Almost all his doubts about established socialist thinking are related to what he perceived to be its tendency to encourage conformity and its preoccupation with centralized planning.

It was precisely this attitude that won for Orwell a reputation as what he himself called "a right-wing deviationist" among the stalwarts of the orthodox Left, and this in turn caused him immense trouble when it came to getting his work published.

About the difficulties that Orwell faced in dealing with editors and publishers in thrall to the pieties of the Left, both in the late Thirties and well into the Forties, Shelden also gives us a detailed account. The story that he tells about the writing and publication of *Homage to Catalonia* (1938), Orwell's account of his experience in the Spanish Civil War, is one of the best things in the book. It is startling to discover that at least one reviewer —Desmond Flower writing in *The Observer*—declared that "Mr. Orwell is a great writer" on the basis of *Homage to Catalonia*, but otherwise the fate of this book was appalling. It sold scarcely seven hundred copies, and did not find a publisher in the United States until 1952, by which time, of course, Orwell was a best-selling author the world over because of *Animal Farm* and *Nineteen Eighty-Four*. Shelden is too honest a writer to neglect either Orwell's political involvements or his ambivalent attitudes toward socialism and orthodoxies of the Left. It is what he makes of them in this book, especially when it comes to the writing of *Animal Farm* and *Nineteen Eighty-Four*, that raises doubts about his critical understanding of Orwell's most important work and about the ability of a liberal biographer to do justice to the substance of Orwell's achievement. There are times, indeed, when Shelden is so intent upon "saving" Orwell from his Cold War reputation that he significantly distorts the meaning of his work.

About *Animal Farm* (1945), for example, he writes as follows:

> As a clever satire on Stalin's betrayal of the Russian Revolution, *Animal Farm* caught the popular imagination just when the Cold War was beginning to make itself felt. For many years "anticommunists" enjoyed using it as a propaganda weapon in that war, but this was a gross misrepresentation of the book and a violation of the spirit in which Orwell wrote it. He was not a fanatical opponent of the Soviet Union. Indeed, given the fact that Stalin's agents had almost managed to imprison him in Spain, his view of the Soviet system was most enlightened.

From the use of the word "clever" to the placing of "anticommunists" in quotation marks to the astounding assertion that Orwell was not a "fanatical opponent of the Soviet Union"—was he then an *un*fanatical opponent?—to the notion that it was "most enlightened" to take a more benign view of the Soviet system, this entire passage is a complete betrayal of what Orwell achieved in *Animal Farm* and what he stood for as a writer. Orwell may still have harbored the wish—or, rather, the illusion—that "the existence of democratic Socialism in the West [might] exert a regenerative influence upon Russia," as he wrote to Dwight Macdonald at the time, but there can be no question that he was a staunch anti-Communist when he wrote *Animal Farm*, and remained so for the few remaining years of his life.

And when he comes to writing about *Nineteen Eighty-Four* (1949), Shelden takes refuge from the book's politics in what can only be called the fallacy of biographical reduction.

> It is Orwell's most compelling work, and its enormous success over the years is well deserved, but it is also his most misunderstood work. Endless theories have been put forward to explain its vision of the future, but not many critics have been willing to see how firmly rooted it is in Orwell's past. Almost every aspect of Orwell's life is in some way represented in the book. Winston Smith's yearning for the green wilderness of the "Golden Country" is very much connected to Orwell's long-standing affection for the lost Edwardian world of his childhood in Henley.

And so on. We are hardly surprised to find Shelden assuring us that "Orwell's experience of bullying at St. Cyprian's cannot be discounted as an influence on *Nineteen Eighty-Four*." It is in passages like this that one comes to despair of the entire genre of literary biography.

Consider, as a contrast—the contrast between literary fallacy and political reality—the following passage in "From the Underworld: The Will to Power and the Socialist Order," a more recent essay by Robert Conquest from *The Times Literary Supplement* (September 20, 1991), a review of a biography of Lenin.

> Many in the West had become accustomed to the existence of the Soviet Union, treating it as though it were a normal component of the world scene . . . while in fact it was a ghastly aberration, which distorted history for most of our century. In Russia, one quite often hears the complaint, "How is it that Orwell understood our system, and so many Soviet experts in the West did not?" The answer is that for Westerners a considerable effort of the imagination was needed to understand an essentially alien political movement and the correspond-

> ingly alien political and social order it created. Orwell had the imagination; the experts did not. And, in many cases, still do not.

Shelden doesn't, either. Hence his eagerness to save Orwell from what he clearly regards as the embarrassment of his Cold War reputation.

Orwell was always a complicated figure for the Left to deal with. He remained an avowed socialist to the end of his life, yet he was not the kind of socialist the orthodox Left could accommodate. Though in no sense a conservative, he *was* something of a "right-wing deviationist" when it came to Communism and the Soviet system. He may have hated capitalism, but it was Communist totalitarianism that he made the target of his most ambitious writings. This was the hard truth that the Left found so difficult to swallow, and still finds difficult to swallow. When it could no longer prevent Orwell from winning a wide readership, it commenced to re-interpret the meaning of his work in order to blunt its effect. The saddest thing about Michael Shelden's *Orwell* is that, despite its many fine details, it belongs in the end to this campaign to misrepresent the nature of Orwell's achievement. It reminds us that the vaunted political "center" that academic liberalism sometimes claims for itself—and to which Mr. Shelden can, I think, be said to belong—remains tethered to the agenda of the orthodox Left that Orwell so much despised. This Orwell for the Nineties is, in other words, very like the Orwell that the Left has been insisting on since the heyday of Stalinism in the Thirties—an ideological fiction.

November 1991

Bloomsbury Idols

[I]t was exciting, exhilarating, the beginning of a renaissance, the opening of a new heaven on a new earth, we were the forerunners of a new dispensation.

—John Maynard Keynes, "My Early Beliefs," 1938

Bloomsbury, like Clapham was a coterie. It was exclusive and clannish. It regarded outsiders as unconverted. . . . Remarks which did not show that grace had descended upon the utterer were met with killing silence. . . . Like Clapham, Bloomsbury had discovered a new creed: the same exhilaration filled the air, the same conviction that a new truth had been disclosed, a new Kingdom conquered.

—Noel Annan, *Leslie Stephen*, 1952

IT is startling now to be reminded that as recently as 1968—a year that saw a great many changes in our cultural life —Bloomsbury could still be described, without fear of contradiction, as "unfashionable." In fact it was so described by Michael Holroyd in the mammoth biography of Lytton Strachey which he published that year. Yet no sooner was the pronouncement made but Bloomsbury was suddenly all the rage again, and it was no doubt Mr. Holroyd's biography which set this great reversal in motion. There is no reason, however, to suppose that Holroyd deliberately set out to achieve so large a goal. According to his own testimony, anyway, his original intention was far more modest. Yet the consequences of his immense biographical enterprise proved to be fateful indeed. Bloomsbury was triumphantly restored to literary fashion, and a not inconsiderable revolution in taste was launched on a course which shows no sign of abatement. The time for a revival of the Bloomsbury ethos was riper, perhaps, than even Holroyd had quite understood at the time.

It tells us much, I think, that Holroyd set out to write one kind of book and ended by writing a book of a very different kind. For in the changes that overtook his task in the course of its realization we are given a key to the larger revival which his book was crucial in inaugurating. His original plan, he tells us, was to write "a revaluation of Strachey's place as a serious historian." This, not surprisingly, proved to be a futile endeavor. By no tenable standard, either then or now, could a case be made for Lytton Strachey as "a serious historian." He had never been that kind of writer, and any attempt to portray him as such was therefore doomed from the outset. Bertrand Russell—not exactly an unfriendly witness—was only stating the obvious when he observed that Strachey was "indifferent to historical truth."[1] This did not mean that Strachey was a figure without interest, however. Far from it. Only that the focus of interest, at this distance in time, would lie less in what Strachey wrote than in what he was. It was precisely this discovery which, when he finally made it, opened up Holroyd's subject for him. Thenceforth his project followed an unimpeded course. "I had come to the conclusion," he writes, "that Strachey was one of those historians

[1] "He is indifferent to historical truth," Russell wrote, "and will always touch up the picture to make the lights and shades more glaring and the folly or wickedness of famous people more obvious. These are grave charges, but I make them in all seriousness." *The Autobiography of Bertrand Russell: 1872–1914* (Atlantic Monthly Press, 1967), page 99.

whose work was so personal that it could only be illuminated by some biographical commentary." This was the crucial turn, not only in the writing of *Lytton Strachey: A Critical Biography* but in the revival of Bloomsbury itself. Not criticism but *biography* was to be the foundation on which this revival would be based.

This is in itself a development worth pondering. Literary and artistic revivals, while always answering to some need or desire of the historical moment in which they are brought forth, vary greatly in the purposes they are destined to serve. They are by no means uniform either in their appeal or in their function. The great revival of seventeenth-century Metaphysical poetry initiated by T. S. Eliot in the early decades of this century, for example, had virtually nothing to do with a biographical interest in the poets themselves. It was strictly critical and creative—the work of a poet seeking to recover a tradition that would nourish and support the artistic aims of his own poetry. Eliot took an entire generation of poets and critics with him in his revisionist view of the English poetic tradition, and decisively changed the history as well as the historiography of literature in the process. When new biographical studies of the Metaphysical poets came to be written, they were produced as a result of this literary revival—they were not its cause.

Precisely the opposite has been the case with the Bloomsbury revival. It is biography which has set the pace of this revival and provided its principal texts and pretexts. The large body of criticism inspired by the revival—to the extent, that is, that it may be regarded as criticism at all—has remained, for the most part, closely tethered to the biographical mode, taking its cues from the lives rather than from the works of the group's major and minor figures. In part, of course, this turnabout is yet another reflection of the precipitous decline of criticism that began to make itself felt in the Sixties at the very moment, in fact, when the fortunes of Bloomsbury were beginning to be revived. Looking back, it can now be seen that the one development was a necessary prerequisite to the other. Criticism, after all, addresses itself to achievement, whereas biography is chiefly concerned with character and circumstance. Criticism creates standards; biography—as it is currently practiced, anyway—creates idols (or else topples them). Criticism deals with the accomplishments of mind, biography with the affairs of the heart. Can there be any doubt as to which of these the champions of Bloomsbury are primarily interested in? We all know (or we should) that there are great biographies that transcend these distinctions—biographies which are governed by a clear critical intelligence. But they have been remarkable for their rarity in every generation since Dr. Johnson wrote his *Lives of the Poets*, and few indeed can be found in the proliferating biographical literature on Bloomsbury. The latter, on the contrary, has tended to specialize in the creation of idols and to avoid the kind of disinterested judgment which it is one of the essential tasks of criticism to perform.

Lytton Strachey is far from being the only member of the Bloomsbury group to benefit from this changed relation of criticism to biography—though in his case it proved to be indispensable to the rehabilitation of his reputation, for it is unlikely that he would any longer be read at all if not for the biographical luster conferred upon him by Holroyd's *Strachey* and the succession of Bloomsbury biographies which have followed in its wake. No less a figure than Virginia Woolf, surely the best writer (though not, I think, the finest mind) in the group, has enjoyed an even more spectacular benefit from this drastically altered perspective. For it is not Woolf's novels which are primarily responsible for the radical elevation of her reputation in recent years, but the many volumes of *Diaries* and *Letters* and memoirs that have been added to Quentin Bell's avowedly uncritical biography to form a literary edifice which so overshadows the fiction that the latter is now largely read (and admired!) as a gloss on the life of its author. Prior to this outpouring of biographical revelation, Woolf's novels could claim a certain following, to be sure, but they cannot be said to have won anything remotely approaching the acclaim and adulation which are nowadays routinely lavished upon even the least of them. Nor was it (as it is sometimes claimed) only the contributors to *Scrutiny* who found Virginia Woolf seriously deficient as a novelist. This tended to be the judgment of the best critics writing on both sides of the Atlantic for decades prior to the present revival. There may be reason to quarrel with certain aspects of this critical consensus, but it must be recognized that it was a consensus and that it represented a considered judgment of the *novels*. It did not duck the task of critical judgment by taking refuge in factitious interpretations of the troubled life of the woman who wrote them.

Where biography is given such radical priority over criticism, the actual accomplishments of a writer or artist are inevitably placed at an intellectual discount, if indeed they are not rendered altogether superfluous. And it follows from this practice that a lack of significant accomplishment will not in itself be deemed a serious obstacle to the writing of a full-scale biographical study. The absence of an *oeuvre* demanding to be taken seriously may even facilitate the writing of such biographies. Where accomplishment is seen to be negligible the biographer is at liberty to devote uninterrupted attention to the life, and will feel under no obligation to provide the kind of overweight analyses of literary or artistic trifles which so encumbered Holroyd's *Strachey* and made its "critical" interludes something of a chore to read. (My guess is that most readers simply skipped them.) This, in any case, is the stage we seem to have arrived at in the biographical literature on Bloomsbury: there is no longer even a pretense that it is the subject's literary, artistic, or intellectual distinction that causes a new biography to be written. All interest now focuses on the life itself. And yet this is not quite correct either. For much that is crucial and contradictory in life must, perforce, be left out—or else made to seem marginal—in the interests of erecting an idol. It is not so much the real life of these failed writers and artists that is expected to command our interest as it is their so-called "lifestyle," which in the case of Bloomsbury means, above all, that peculiar combination of sex, snobbery, aestheticism, ambition, and what Keynes characterized as "immoralism" which served the group as an ethical model in its own day and which functions as a standard for its admirers today. "Lifestyle" is what the biographer is left with as his subject when the work is relegated to the background.

In this respect, the lives of Vanessa Bell and Vita Sackville-West are ideally suited to the new biographical mode. As artists in their respective fields—Bell as a painter, Sackville-West as a writer—they scarcely count as anything more than minor episodes in the history of English taste. Both were heaped with praise, honors, and commissions in their lifetimes, as minor talents often are, yet almost nothing in their work survives today as living art. Nor, interestingly, do we find any serious critical claim made for their work in the books which have now been written about their lives. This refusal to make a critical case cannot, in the present instances, be ascribed to intellectual incompetence. Both Frances Spalding, the author of *Vanessa Bell* (Ticknor & Fields), and Victoria Glendinning, the author of *Vita: The Life of V. Sackville-West* (Knopf), have elsewhere shown themselves to be in possession of real critical gifts. Spalding gave us an excellent critical biography of Roger Fry in 1980. *Roger Fry: Art and Life* was anything but a flawless book, but it was written, all the same, on the assumption that Fry's accomplishments as a critic, painter, and connoisseur constituted the principal reason for our interest in him. Spalding recognized, moreover, that Fry's ideas had exerted an immense influence on subsequent critical thought, and still served as a touchstone wherever the formalist criticism of art continued to be practiced or debated. She therefore made a sustained attempt to trace the development of those ideas and elucidate their meaning. It was this intellectual focus, rather than its account of Fry's amatory history, that gave *Roger Fry: Art and Life* its special distinction.

Victoria Glendinning's practice is somewhat different. In her critical journalism she has not hesitated to render some sharp and intelligent judgments of her own contemporaries, but she seems to regard the art of biography as an essentially noncritical literary genre. In her biographies of Elizabeth Bowen and Edith Sitwell she dropped many hints as to where the problems for criticism might lie in the respective *oeuvres* of these writers, but she avoided the tasks of criticism herself. Now in *Vita* even these hints are kept to a minimum—and with good reason, I suppose. For surely a writer of Glendinning's gifts must know that Sackville-West's work would not be likely to survive even the most cursory sort of critical inquiry. Yet what does it mean to write the life of a writer whose work one cannot take seriously? It means that the biographer must find something exemplary in the life—something so important that it transcends the failure of the work. As to exactly what this is in the case of Vita Sackville-West—well, that is a question which takes us back to Bloomsbury and the spirit of its current revival.

Vanessa Bell and Vita Sackville-West occupy very different places, of course, in the historical hierarchy of Bloomsbury personalities. Vanessa Bell, the sister of Virginia Woolf, the wife of Clive Bell, and the lover, successively, of Roger Fry and Duncan Grant, stands—as Sackville-West does not—at the very center of the group as one of its animating and indispensable spirits. It was Vanessa Bell who established the principal households, first in London and then in the countryside, where the social, intellectual, and sexual attitudes promulgated by Lytton Strachey and his friends at Cambridge came to be transformed into a new bohemian code. She thus served Bloomsbury as both its housemother and its earth mother, initiating nothing in the realm of art or ideas but bringing enormous reserves of energy, audacity, confidence, and practical management to the creation and re-enforcement of the "new dispensation," as Keynes called it, which governed the lives of the group as an ideal alternative to the standards it was hell-bent on rejecting.

Vanessa Bell was central, in other words, in helping to set and maintain the moral tone of Bloomsbury. That she was also an artist was absolutely essential to her position and the authority it exerted, yet it hardly seemed to matter that her artistic accomplishments were so slim. It was the fact of her being an artist—and an artist of a certain type: a modernist—rather than the quality of her art that was necessary for the moral role she played. But it was morals (of a certain kind), not art, that paradoxically gave to Bloomsbury aestheticism its special quality. It is for this reason, by the way, that an art historian like Frances Spalding may not be the best sort of biographer for a figure like Vanessa Bell. Art history is finally peripheral to the subject, which is moral rebellion.

This being the case, it is especially important that we understand the nature of the Bloomsbury rebellion. What in fact were the standards that Bloomsbury sought to demolish? Following the conventional wisdom on this subject, Spalding characterizes these as "the Victorian intellectual and moral pressures that had, to a greater or lesser extent, weighed on [the] youth" of Vanessa Bell and her friends. Yet the biography which Spalding has now given us does not really support this view. Certainly no orthodox Victorian paterfamilias would have given his daughter the complete freedom of his large and unexpurgated library from the age of fifteen onward, as in fact Sir Leslie Stephen did in the case of his daughter Virginia. Nor would this Victorian ogre of legend have permitted a daughter to enroll in an art school, with all of its attendant moral risks, at the first sign of her artistic interests, as in fact Stephen did in the case of his daughter Vanessa. This, in turn, reminds us that in the entire literature on Bloomsbury there is a curious and telling tendency to telescope the history of its antecedents in order to establish a more direct link with the high Victorian age than Bloomsbury actually had. And it is not just any view of the Victorian age which is called upon to serve this purpose, but a specifically Stracheyesque view of Victorian repression and hypocrisy.

The truth seems to have been a little more complicated, however. For it was not so much a Victorian as an Edwardian upbringing that Vanessa Stephen and her sister were given. And while the Edwardian code unquestionably contained certain elements of the Victorian ethos, these were already being undermined (where they were not completely effaced) by the more liberal and even radical impulses which found expression in such diverse movements and events as the aestheticism of the Nineties, the Fabian Society, the clamor for women's suffrage and education, realism in fiction and the theater, and the debate over imperialism which caused such fierce divisions at the time of the Boer War and deeply affected the literary imagination of the generation immediately preceding that of Virginia Woolf. Almost nothing in the whole Bloomsbury phenomenon—neither its feminism, its homosexuality, its pacifism, its anti-imperialism, its aestheticism, nor its quarrel with realism—is wholly intelligible, in fact, without reference to the concatenation of changes which erupted with such far-reaching force in the Edwardian period. Even the vaunted anti-Victorianism of Bloomsbury represented the codification of an attitude already ascendant in the Edwardian age. Yet Bloomsbury continues to be discussed as if it sprang up—by virgin birth, as it were—as a simple rebellion against the cartoon characters who populate the pages of *Eminent Victorians.*

The writer who best understood this matter was Bertrand Russell, who was in a position to observe the development of Bloomsbury from the perspective of a contemporary belonging to an older generation. Writing in his *Autobiography* about the Cambridge Conversazione Society, where so many Bloomsbury attitudes were first adumbrated, Russell made a point of isolating this Edwardian element as a key to understanding these attitudes. "Some things became considerably different in the Society after my time," Russell wrote.

The tone of the generation some ten years junior to my own

> was set mainly by Lytton Strachey and Keynes. It is surprising how great a change in mental climate those ten years had brought. We were still Victorian; they were Edwardian. We believed in ordered progress by means of politics and free discussion. The more self-confident among us may have hoped to be leaders of the multitude, but none of us wished to be divorced from it. The generation of Keynes and Lytton did not seek to preserve any kinship with the Philistine. They aimed rather at a life of retirement among fine shades and nice feelings, and conceived of the good as consisting in the passionate mutual admirations of a clique of the elite.

And further:

> After my time the Society changed in one respect. There was a long drawn-out battle between George Trevelyan and Lytton Strachey, both members, in which Lytton Strachey was on the whole victorious. Since his time, homosexual relations among the members were for a time common, but in my day they were unknown.

It is sad to see a writer as intelligent as Frances Spalding succumb to a sort of historical amnesia about all this. She certainly knows the whole period well enough to have gotten it right. For what was the life of Vanessa Bell if not an attempt—and a failed attempt at that—to live "a life of retirement among fine shades and nice feelings"? She, too, seems to have "conceived of the good as consisting in the passionate mutual admirations of a clique of the elite," and to have lived much of her adult life in accordance with this brittle standard. In this, as in so much else in the Bloomsbury story, we see the legacy of Edwardian aestheticism transmuted into the even narrower ethos of coterie bohemianism, with inherited social snobberies now inverted to reject the respectable and the conventional in favor of the perverse and the esoteric.

Had Spalding been writing the life of a more important artist, I think it likely that the work would have obliged her to re-examine the many received assumptions which have been allowed to pass into *Vanessa Bell* like so much unopened baggage. But there is nothing in Vanessa Bell's work that requires a critic to rethink anything in the art of the period Spalding is writing about—except, perhaps, the way artistic reputations were sometimes made. The work simply registers a succession of passive and mildly talented responses to the artistic ideas which gained currency in Bell's circle of friends and lovers, and what reputation it acquired in the artist's lifetime had much to do with the promotional efforts of this same circle.[2]

Not surprisingly, Spalding is on much firmer ground when she turns away from the art of Vanessa Bell (which she does as often as possible in this book) to recount the bizarre history of her subject's personal affairs. Yet there, too, while nothing if not candid in disclosing a great many unpleasant facts—especially regarding Vanessa Bell's protracted liaison with the homosexual Duncan Grant—Spalding can never quite bring herself to align

[2] The charge that Bloomsbury reputations were often the result of the group's own efforts at self-promotion is nowadays commonly dismissed as just another example of the kind of paranoia endemic to *Scrutiny* and the Leavis circle. It is therefore instructive to read the following passages from an article written by Clive Bell in November 1917 about an exhibition organized by Roger Fry: "Only one Englishman holds his own with the French painters, and he, of course, is Duncan Grant. . . . Grant is . . . blessed with adorable gifts and a powerful intellect, he should . . . become what we have been awaiting so long, an English painter in the front rank of European art." And further in the same article: "Of the remaining British artists, the most interesting, to my mind, is Vanessa Bell. . . . Today there are at least three women artists who hold their own with their male counterparts—Marie Laurencin, Goncharova, and Vanessa Bell—whose claim to take rank amongst the best of their generation will have to be answered very carefully by those who wish to disallow it." See *Pot-Boilers* by Clive Bell (Chatto and Windus, 1918).

these facts, which have much to do with concealment and a kind of emotional martyrdom, with the values that Bloomsbury prided itself on living by. Foremost among these values —according to the Bloomsbury myth, anyway—was what Virginia Woolf called "the old Cambridge ideal of truth and free speaking." This has been said again and again to have been the moral cornerstone of the Bloomsbury ethic. Yet the truth is, this "ideal of truth and free speaking" was rarely, if ever, the governing principle of Vanessa Bell's adult life. For one thing, she could never speak openly of her true feelings about the homosexual attachments which remained central to Duncan Grant's existence during all the years they lived together. On the contrary, she was obliged to extend hospitality and even a show of affection to his many male lovers as a condition for being allowed to have a place in his life. She always knew that Grant had never loved her in the way that she had come to love him, and she accepted the humiliations of the situation in silence. But by then, of course, remaining silent about the way she lived was already a habit with Vanessa Bell. When she rejected her husband and took other lovers, and he took up with a succession of mistresses, to whom she was also obliged to extend hospitality throughout her life, this too had to be concealed—most notably, from Clive Bell's wealthy and eminently respectable parents, whose tastes and interests Vanessa Bell loathed but upon whose financial generosity the Bells were largely dependent for their "free" way of life. (Neither Vanessa nor Clive Bell ever had to work for a living.) The "life of retirement among fine shades and nice feelings" wasn't cheap, and it was the benighted parents of her husband—the very archetypes of the philistine squirearchy which Bloomsbury held in such contempt—who were expected to pay the bills. Reading *Vanessa Bell*, one quickly comes to realize that the Victorians had nothing to teach Bloomsbury when it came to self-interested concealment and hypocrisy.

The most egregious example of the Bloomsbury double standard—for that is what it always came down to—is to be found in the appalling tale of Vanessa Bell's daughter, whose father was known to virtually all members of the inner circle to be Duncan Grant but who was nonetheless brought up to believe that she was the child of Clive Bell. Again, the principal reason for this deception seems to have been the need to conceal the truth from Clive Bell's parents, who, being the sort of dodoes they were, could not be expected to react to the actual situation with the requisite sympathy and understanding. And no wonder—for there was quite a lot to the situation that required some understanding. At the time of the child's birth, Vanessa Bell found herself presiding over a difficult *ménage à trois*, with David Garnett more or less in residence as Duncan Grant's favorite of the moment. As it turned out, the man who proved to be the most passionately devoted to the newborn child was neither its actual father nor its official one but Garnett, the child's father's lover, who promptly announced his intention of marrying the girl—which, to the horror of Vanessa Bell and Duncan Grant, he actually succeeded in doing some twenty-odd years later. About that, interestingly, these pillars of Bloomsbury liberation acted as if they were performing a charade of outraged Victorian parenthood.

Meanwhile, Bloomsbury's celebrated candor in matters having to do with sexual behavior—all the much-quoted talk about "buggers" and "semen" and such—was totally suspended in the girl's upbringing. Not only was she kept in perfect ignorance about the fact that the man whom she and her mother lived with was her real father, but she was also kept in the dark about the most elementary facts of life. So complete was the daughter's innocence in this respect that at the age of seventeen she had to be sent to a physician to be instructed in the mysteries of sex. Even this proved to be futile, alas, for the physician (a woman) was so stunned by the girl's ignorance that she could not bring herself to explain anything. Clearly, the ideal of "truth and free speaking" had its limitations even for Bloomsbury. So too, by the way, did the application of Bloomsbury's feminist standards.

Thus, while the Bells' two sons were brought up in the expected atmosphere of sexual candor and as young adults were encouraged to disclose the details of their sexual affairs to their mother, Vanessa Bell's daughter was allowed no such freedom of action or expression. She seems to have been raised in a moral void, denied the advantages (such as they were) of Bloomsbury's "new dispensation," yet denied as well whatever comfort, security, or guidance might have been provided by the conventions it was designed to displace.

About all this, too, Spalding gives us a very frank and unsparing account. Yet for all of its frankness, there is finally something just a bit obtuse about this book. It is as if the glamour and prestige of its dramatis personae have had the effect of stripping its author of her capacity to form a judgment of either the actions or the characters she so meticulously describes. Just as every aesthetic allowance must be made, implicitly or otherwise, for Vanessa Bell's limited artistic accomplishment, so must every moral allowance be made for the way she lived her life. The result is a biography which substitutes psychological understanding for moral insight—which is now the standard formula for Bloomsbury biography.

One has the feeling in reading *Vita: The Life of V. Sackville-West* that Victoria Glendinning, too, might have preferred to write a biography similarly devoid of moral intelligence. But in this case it just wasn't possible. The protagonist of the book is herself such a monster of moral insensibility and so much of her story entails a description of the human wreckage left in the wake of her sometimes casual, sometimes insidious depredations, that, try as Glendinning does to avoid it, she cannot help showing her distaste from time to time and even registering a note of censure. Perhaps to compensate for this tendency, she offers a handsome array of exonerating factors to explain some of Sackville-West's more outrageous actions—the crazy mother, the weak husband, the laws and customs governing primogeniture, etc.—but they avail her not. In the end she cannot bring herself to duck the problem of Sackville-West's atrocious character, and she wins our enduring gratitude for refusing to swallow the preposterous notion put forward by Nigel Nicolson in *Portrait of a Marriage* —one of the really remarkable literary farces of the Seventies—that Sackville-West's marriage to Harold Nicolson somehow constituted a model of modern marital bliss.

But that whole story in most of its details lies well outside the history of Bloomsbury and its revival. Sackville-West was an outsider who entered Bloomsbury as Virginia Woolf's lover, and she remains a permanent part of its history solely as the character who inspired Woolf to write *Orlando*, the most original work of fiction that Bloomsbury produced and the only work of the imagination in which so many of its abiding values—particularly its social and sexual snobbery, its hermaphroditic ideal, its compulsion to aestheticize all experience, and its Camp attitude toward history and morals—are openly stated and definitively embodied. Yet it is precisely because of Sackville-West's importance in this one regard that *Vita* proves to be inadequate. Almost any biography of this sort would be. For once the basic facts have been established—and in the case of *Orlando* they have never been in doubt since the day of its publication—this is a problem not in biography but in criticism, and in *Vita*, of course, there is no criticism.

The more one looks into the Bloomsbury revival, the more convinced one is that Bloomsbury, despite the immense number of books, articles, and reviews already devoted to it, is a subject which has not yet found its writer, and that the writer it calls for is unlikely to be a specialist in biography. Bloomsbury can be said to have produced only four figures of enduring intellectual interest: Virginia Woolf, E. M. Forster, John Maynard Keynes, and Roger Fry. Of these, only Keynes and Fry can be claimed as major figures in the intellectual disciplines they pursued. Forster looks smaller with every passing day, and Woolf was never the major novelist she is nowadays assumed to be (usually for a variety of extraliterary reasons). In the realm of high culture Bloomsbury's achievements are actually remarkably small. But the Bloomsbury revival is not really concerned with high achievements of mind or art. It was not in art or literature but in the realm of moral rebellion that Bloomsbury achieved its most significant and enduring influence, and it is precisely *that* which has been recalled and embellished and newly propagated in the current revival. It is therefore to this moral rebellion—in which, incidentally, Bloomsbury's aestheticism will be seen to be a symptom rather than a cause—that criticism will be obliged to address itself.

And the best place for criticism to begin its inquiry into the Bloomsbury rebellion is with that remarkable confession of categorical error which Keynes delivered to the Memoir Club in 1938 under the title, "My Early Beliefs." "We repudiated entirely customary morals, conventions and traditional wisdom," Keynes wrote.

> We were, that is to say, in the strict sense of the term, immoralists. The consequences of being found out had, of course, to be considered for what they were worth. But we recognized no moral obligation on us, no inner sanction, to conform or to obey. Before heaven we claimed to be our own judge in our own case. . . . It resulted in a general, widespread, though partly covert, suspicion affecting ourselves, our motives and our behavior. This suspicion still persists to a certain extent and it always will. It has deeply colored the course of our lives in relation to the outside world. It is, I now think, a justifiable suspicion.

Keynes was not announcing his conversion to a new faith, to be sure. "Yet so far as I am concerned, it is too late to change," he observed. "I remain, and always will remain, an immoralist." Yet he had come to understand very clearly the implications of the moral rebellion that he had helped to set on its course.

> [W]e repudiated [he continued] all versions of the doctrine of original sin, of there being insane and irrational springs of wickedness in most men. We were not aware that civilization was a thin and precarious crust erected by the personality and the will of a very few, and only maintained by rules and conventions skillfully put across and guilefully preserved. We had no respect for traditional wisdom or the restraints of custom. We lacked reverence, as [D. H.] Lawrence observed and as Ludwig [Wittgenstein] with justice also used to say—for everything and everyone. It did not occur to us to respect the extraordinary accomplishment of our predecessors in the ordering of life (as it now seems to me to have been) or the elaborate framework which they had devised to protect this order. . . . As cause and consequence of our general state of mind we completely misunderstood human nature, including our own. The rationality which we attributed to it led to a superficiality, not only of judgment, but also of feeling. . . . I fancy we used in the old days to get around the rich variety of experience by expanding illegitimately the field of aesthetic appreciation (we would deal, for example, with all branches of the tragic emotion under this head), classifying as aesthetic experience what is really human experience and somehow sterilizing it by this mis-classification.

It is only when criticism can bring itself to take up the issues which Keynes so cogently defined some forty-five years ago that we shall come to a true understanding of the Bloomsbury phenomenon. Until then the biographers will continue to ply their wares, concentrating on ever more minor and peripheral figures, and the making of idols will go on unabated.

January 1984

The Tynan Phenomenon

One of my unarguable postulates about aesthetics is that life mimics art, not art life.

—Kenneth Tynan, *He That Plays the King*, 1950

Occupation: *Opinion-monger, observer of artistic phenomena, amateur ideologue.*

—Kenneth Tynan, Foreword, *Tynan Right & Left*, 1967

The word "art" is now really no use to me at all. . . . When I hear the word "art" now, I begin to yawn; to me, it's somehow a cop-out word, a word to dodge and hedge with, a word that means something different in everyone's mouth. . . . I've tried, in everything I've written over the last five years or so, to avoid using the word. . . .

—Kenneth Tynan, *The Sound of Two Hands Clapping*, 1975

FROM time to time a critic emerges who may truly be said to personify a period—to embody in his person as well as in his writings the spirit of a certain historical moment. The late Kenneth Tynan (1927–1980), who is now the subject of a "candid" biography written by his widow Kathleen, was certainly a critic of this sort.[1] In no other writer of his generation in England were the special aspirations and the sometimes crippling contradictions of the post-World War II cultural scene in Britain so conspicuously or so entertainingly displayed. In none were the peculiar gyrations of the Zeitgeist so graphically traced. Kingsley Amis is no doubt funnier and greater, John Wain graver, Doris Lessing more knowledgeable—even if not always wiser—about politics, and Philip Larkin altogether a weightier figure. Yet Tynan had something that even the most gifted of his literary contemporaries generally lacked: he described it, in speaking of the theater, as "star quality," and there can be no question but that he was in possession of a large measure of this mysterious attribute from an early age. Even his many enemies were disinclined to deny it, however much they resented his success and envied his celebrity. Driving ambition, demonic energy, literary talent, journalistic flair, critical acumen, and a ferocious appetite for work: to all of these was added, in Tynan's case, an indispensable gift for making himself as much of a personality as the great performers he wrote about with so much ardor and admiration. Tynan was a writer who cast a spell—the kind of spell that belongs as much to the realm of show business, which was one of his specialties, as to the world of arts and letters. In this respect at least, though he has had many imitators, he has had no real successor. The role expired with his own demise. Indeed, considering the awful disarray of his last years, it seems even to have predeceased him

That much of what he wrote has proved to be ephemeral ought not to come as any surprise. Permanence is not the province of either journalism or celebrity—the two realms in which Tynan scored his greatest successes—and he was more adept at describing the effect of an immediate theatrical event than at assessing its permanent significance. He was not what

[1] *The Life of Kenneth Tynan,* by Kathleen Tynan (William Morrow & Company, 1987).

you would call a thinker. He appropriated ideas as they served his purpose, and he was not given to fussing over inconsistencies. As a critic, Tynan worked very much as certain high style actors do, always ready, with the rhetorical flourish or the *coup de théâtre* that disarms complacency and causes both shock and applause. He was richly endowed with the histrionic instinct and knew a great deal about winning—and keeping—the attention of his audience. He understood very well that it isn't necessarily by means of reasoned argument that the critic—especially the critic of theatrical performance—sways his readers, that intensely held convictions, persuasively stated, often accomplish far more—and far more quickly—than pious praise or respectful analysis or, for that matter, clever disparagement.

Not that he ever hesitated to dispense the latter in large and lethal doses: Vivien Leigh's performance as Blanche in Laurence Olivier's production of *A Streetcar Named Desire*, for example, he characterized as that of "a posturing butterfly, with no depth, no sorrow, no room for development, and above all, no trace of Blanche's crushed ideals." And this was a valentine compared to his account of the same actress's attempt to play Shakespeare's Cleopatra. Clearly he was deeply in love—and was seen to be in love—with the magic of the theatrical event, and eager to serve as its impassioned acolyte. His quarrels with actors, playwrights, theater companies, and the stage itself were always lover's quarrels, and a large part of his appeal lay in his ability to kindle in his readers, if only for as long as it took them to read his reviews, a kindred emotion.

It helped, of course, that in writing about the theater, he knew what he was talking about, and very early on, too. His first volume of dramatic criticism, *He That Plays the King*, was published in 1950 when Tynan was twenty-three. It is a remarkable book, without a dull page or a dead sentence, and its many paragraphs devoted to what Tynan called "heroic" acting—Laurence Olivier as Richard III, Ralph Richardson as Peer Gynt,

John Gielgud as Hamlet—are as fine as anything he ever wrote about the actor's art, which was always to be his best subject. On Gielgud as Hamlet:

> His voice is all soul, injured and struggling: but the body is curiously ineffectual, with the result, for me, that his acting lacks stomach and heart. He prances fluently enough, but with the grace of ballet rather than of animals and men. One thinks of Olivier in terms of other species, of panthers and lions: one thinks of Gielgud in terms of other arts, of ballet and portrait painting.

Again and again in that first book Tynan identified with an astonishing aesthetic precision the qualities and the defects that would continue to distinguish a generation of great actors for many years to come.

He described *He That Plays the King*, quite accurately, as "a book of enthusiasms, written by an *aficionado*, out of an almost limitless capacity for admiration." Given this penchant for hero worship, it was a mercy that the British stage offered the young Tynan so much that truly merited the praise and concentration he was so eager to lavish upon it. Later, in the Fifties, when he brought this almost limitless capacity for admiration to the political arena, he wasn't so lucky.

In political matters Tynan, to be blunt about it, was an ignoramus, and the theater—however fine it might be artistically—proved, not surprisingly, not to be the place in which to acquire the rudiments of a political education. When, in the biography that Kathleen Tynan has now devoted to her late husband, we read that "through Arthur Miller's work Ken received an education in social responsibility," we hardly know whether to laugh or cry—and not because Mrs. Tynan has in any way misrepresented the facts of the case, but precisely because she has given us an altogether fair account of the level on which Tynan's political thought, if indeed it can be called that, generally operated.

From the moment of his political conversion in the Fifties, Tynan spouted nothing but the standard left-wing clichés whenever he turned his attention, as he increasingly did, to political causes. From his youth in provincial Birmingham he had been a dandy and an aesthete. Even the Second World War, which in England, as elsewhere, was not easily ignored, somehow failed—as Mrs. Tynan acknowledges—to make much of an impression on Tynan. The point is, when he turned Left, announcing in 1955 that "I have seen *Mother Courage* and I am a Marxist," he remained a dandy and an aesthete, judging every political issue as a matter of style and taste. In an almost literal sense, politics became another branch of theater for him.

In the short term, this political turn did much to increase Tynan's popularity and influence. (I am not suggesting that popularity was his motive; more likely, his political turn was only another example of his talent for spotting a trend.) Yet in the end it was one of the things that ruined him for criticism. In *He That Plays the King* he had written that "the study of actors should be a full-time task, involving endless research and intense concentration," and he complained that "it is a sad truth that nearly all our dramatic critics are, in the last analysis, dilettantes." In my opinion Tynan *was* a great critic of acting, but he was incapable of according to politics the kind of research and concentration he brought to the art of the actor, and thus remained in political matters what he despised in his own field—a sentimental dilettante. In a lengthy interview conducted in 1970—it was published for the first time in *The Sound of Two Hands Clapping* five years later—he blithely described Fidel Castro as "a high definition performer," comparing him in this respect to Winston Churchill and Johnny Carson! Sadly, he didn't seem to grasp that such utterances were guaranteed to render him ridiculous. But by then he had given up being a critic, and had thus abandoned the only vocation that had ever really suited his talents. In writing *The Life of Kenneth Tynan*, Mrs. Tynan—who is herself a professional writer: this is her third book—had an interesting, if melancholy, tale to tell, and for the most part she tells it well. But she has not entirely solved the problem of dealing with herself as a character in the story. As we might expect from a widow's book that is at once a biography and a memoir, this *Life* is written with a good deal of sympathy and affection. It is also, however, a biography in the new mode. Which means that we are spared little or nothing about the more sordid and reprehensible aspects of Kenneth Tynan's private life. Exactly why Mrs. Tynan has chosen to go into these matters in such excruciating detail is not altogether clear. Certainly they illuminate nothing essential about his work as a critic—and it is in his work as a critic, after all, that Tynan makes his primary claim on our attention. Perhaps she felt it would have been inappropriate to withhold such details in writing the biography of the man who achieved a certain fame—at least in Britain—for being the very first to use the word "fuck" in a London Sunday paper *and* in a BBC broadcast, and who was also, of course, the man who gave the world *Oh! Calcutta*.

But if so, that would only explain the sexual revelations, and not the detailed account of Tynan's snobbery, his careerism, his drinking, his tantrums, his political muddles, his outrageous treatment of family and friends, and his relentless pursuit of fame and the famous. It is a wicked thought, but sooner or later in reading this dolorous chronicle of Kenneth Tynan's life one cannot help wondering if there is not a large element of sexual revenge at the very heart of the book Mrs. Tynan has given us. From its own account, to be sure, there can be little question but that Tynan gave both his wives—and plenty of other women besides—ample reason to seek such revenge. But the spectacle of its enactment in the form of a posthumous biography by his widow is nonetheless not a very pretty one, and it is all the more dismaying in a book that finally seems to miss the point of Tynan's significance as a writer.

For a reader of my generation, which was also Tynan's, it comes as something of a shock to be made to realize how quickly he has become an historical figure representing a distant era. In my view, anyway, he remains essentially a figure of the Forties and the Fifties when he did his best work—an essentially English figure whose American career, which ended in a shambles of physical ruin, financial debt, and psychological turmoil in (where else?) the alien environs of Southern California, now reads like a grotesque and protracted epilogue out of Evelyn Waugh. From his school days in Birmingham, Tynan had been enamored with *The New Yorker*, with Hollywood movies (and movie stars), and American show business, yet when his ardent wish to become an eminence in that world—a star among the stars—came to be abundantly fulfilled, it turned out to mark the beginning of an irreversible decline. One of the last notes he made to himself when he was dying was a reminder to ask Gore Vidal for a loan of twenty-five thousand dollars: an epitaph that even Waugh might have hesitated to invent.

Like so many of the aesthetic rebels of his generation, he had been born into a prosperous middle-class family that provided him with the means of rejecting it. In Tynan's case, however, the family was a little unusual, for his parents were never married. His father, who had a separate wife and family, was known in public life as Sir Peter Peacock, the mayor of Warrington, who was a wealthy businessman and had once stood for Parliament. In Birmingham, where he lived half the week, commuting in his chauffeur-driven Daimler, with Tynan's mother, a former postal clerk, he was simply Mr. Tynan.

Kenneth Tynan claimed never to have known about his father's double life until the day of his death, which occurred when Tynan was about to leave Oxford. He was outraged that he had never been told about his illegitimacy. But Kathleen Tynan clearly doesn't believe he didn't know, and it does strain credulity when everyone else in the story seems to have been fully aware of the situation, and Sir Peter Peacock was hardly an obscure figure. Feigned or not, his outrage provided the young Tynan with the grounds for rejecting his mother while availing himself of the money with which she generously supported his extravagant tastes—a practice that continued even after Tynan's first marriage to an American girl with an income of her own.

Amazingly, he appears to have developed the disciplined habits of a professional critic even before he went to Oxford. Equally important is the fact that even in wartime the theater in Birmingham was a flourishing artistic enterprise. By the time he entered Oxford after the war, Tynan not only knew that he was destined for a career in the theater—whether as critic, actor, or director was not yet clear—but also had already seen enough high-level work to have become something of an expert.

It was at Oxford that he first emerged—very much by his own design—as a star. His clothes were expensive and outrageous, his antics legendary, his intellectual precocity already a source of fame, and, not incidentally, his allowance from Sir Peter Peacock extremely generous. Most important of all, however, is the fact that he was already an accomplished writer. "His tutor C. S. Lewis," Mrs. Tynan writes, "said of Ken's early essays in English literature that if Lamb and Gibbon had been the same person, Ken's were the kind of essays they would have produced at prep school." Much that he wrote about the theater while he was at Oxford went straight into *He That Plays the King*. There can hardly have been another critic of his generation who was so well prepared to take up the role.

The key to the immense impression that Tynan made as a dramatic critic, first at Oxford and then when he took London by storm, was his special gift for outfitting a serious critical intelligence in the habiliment of cosmopolitan glamour. In a society that had emerged from the war with reduced expectations and a sense of lost glory and now lived in an atmosphere of austerity and gloom, this alliance of glamour and intellect exerted an electrifying appeal, especially for the young—and all the more so because unlike the reigning cosmopolitan critics of the older generation, such as Cyril Connolly, Raymond Mortimer, and Harold Nicolson, Tynan's critical outlook was untouched by any lachrymose nostalgia for a lost golden age. It was firmly anchored in the present and impatient to create a future.

If there was always a certain element of rhetorical tinsel in Tynan's writing, there was something still more important—his deep attachment to the great classics of the English stage. Just to read through the amazing number of pieces Tynan devoted to ambitious productions of Shakespeare's plays in the Forties and Fifties is to be reminded of how deep that attachment always was in the period of his finest achievements as a critic. The American theater never provided its critics, or of course its audience, with anything like a comparable range of artistic experience. When Tynan left *The Observer* for *The New Yorker* in the late Fifties, he uprooted himself from the native artistic soil that had nourished his finest achievements. He was never again a writer of the same quality or spirit. In New York, the glamour component swamped the critical intelligence it had once served so well.

By that time, too, the sense of building an artistic future, which had always been so important in Tynan's critical writing—and so important to his readers—had been overtaken by politics and become inseparable from it. In the London theater there had still been a sufficient number of artistic occasions that recalled Tynan to his original vocation. It was in America that he was finally and irrevocably transformed into an archetype of radical chic—the high-living, celebrity-seeking exponent of socialist causes, assiduously cultivating his dream of sexual liberation while running up enormous debts and systematically destroying his own health. The last pages of Mrs. Tynan's *Life* are terrible to read, for they trace the course of a tormented mind on a suicidal path. For anyone old enough to remember what it was like to read Tynan in *The Observer* in the Fifties—to recall the excitement and fun and sense of high artistic adventure that those weekly Sunday articles delivered with such unfailing regularity—*The Life of Kenneth Tynan* is a poignant reminder of how much the world, and not only the world of criticism and the theater, has changed, and changed for the worse, since the days when his star was so spectacularly in the ascendant.

October 1987

The Flowers on Sartre's Grave

In one of the reports that Jane Kramer used to send to *The New Yorker* from Paris in the 1980s, there is a brief account of the way the grave of Jean-Paul Sartre in the Montparnasse cemetery had become an object of piety for a new generation of French students:

> Thousands of students marched in his funeral cortege through Montparnasse, and got to know the place, and a lot of them come back now to visit. They come when the weather is good, to read and walk around with a *pain au chocolate* and enter into a kind of custodial communion with their hero. There is always a flower on Sartre's grave; Simone de Beauvoir left a rose on the day of the funeral, and afterward the students took over.

Because Kramer no doubt shared this reverence for the man who had presided for so long as the leader of French intellectual life, there was no speculation in her piece, which was written in 1985, as to exactly what the students might have wished to commune with their "hero" about. Was their communion an expression of solidarity with his beliefs, or was it only an act of *hommage* to the kind of intellectual imperium over which Sartre and his circle had once ruled with an iron hand? It would be interesting to know what was in the minds of those students as they made their pilgrimage to lay flowers on Sartre's grave, for elsewhere in Europe history had already inflicted some devastating blows upon the immense edifice of ideological falsehood which Sartre and his contemporaries on the French intellectual Left had devoted decades to creating, and even in Paris their political legacy was in ruins.

At the height of Sartre's dominion over French intellectual life, it clearly lay beyond the power of American criticism to modify the malevolent influence of that dominion in even the smallest degree. America, after all, was the principal target of Sartre's wrath. Being the sole military power capable of resisting the victory of Soviet socialism, which in Sartre's mind was never clearly differentiated from the triumph of Stalinism, the United States was demonized as the enemy of mankind. That it was also the stronghold of capitalism and a bastion of bourgeois democracy only added to the crimes for which it was held accountable. It hardly mattered that in the real world, the monumental crimes of the era were committed by Stalin and then Mao against their own populations and those that fell under their control. Through the special alchemy of the Sartrean dialectic, crimes committed in the name of socialism were forgiven as contingent derelictions when they were not simply denied, and all attempts to hold their perpetrators to moral account were dismissed as an example of the "bad faith" to be expected from the bourgeois enemy.

There was a time, in the early 1950s, when this travesty of political morality met with some spirited resistance from American intellectuals, but for the most part that resistance proved to be ineffectual. In 1952, in his contribution to the symposium on "Our Country and Our Culture" in *Partisan Review*, Lionel Trilling wrote:

> The political situation, the commanding position of Stalinism in French cultural life, does not prevent our having the old

> affinity with certain elements of that life, but it makes the artistic and intellectual leadership of France unthinkable.

Yet even Trilling, when he came to reprint his essay in *A Gathering of Fugitives* in 1956, deleted this important passage. Others, like Sidney Hook, remained more stalwart in their criticism of Sartre and his cohorts, but however much their efforts were to be welcomed, they were without influence in Paris, where the Sartrean politics of fantasy and denial reigned supreme. So supreme, indeed, that even Charles de Gaulle at the height of his power refused to call Sartre to account when he was clearly in violation of the law. "You do not imprison Voltaire," the President of France famously observed—but then, of course, de Gaulle had an anti-American agenda of his own.

When American intellectual life was itself overtaken by a radical movement in the Sixties, this demonization of the United States in particular and of bourgeois democracy in general was swiftly established here, too, as the hallmark of political wisdom, and there was no more talk about the intellectual leadership of France being "unthinkable." In fact, a new wave of French radical influence was already taking possession of American intellectual life, and the Sartrean brand of anti-Americanism, now greatly augmented by homemade simulacra cut from the same ideological materials, became the dominant outlook of our own intellectual class.

It has remained so, moreover, down to the present day, and is now deeply embedded in public policy and pedagogy. Pronouncements that even in the Sixties could still stir a minor scandal—Susan Sontag's assertion in 1966, for example, that "the white race *is* the cancer of history"—have now been integrated into the school curriculum, and a racist fanatic like Frantz Fanon, whose influence is another of Sartre's lethal contributions to our political culture, is mandatory reading at our most prestigious universities. There is thus now a sense in which our students, too, have been pressed into the service of laying flowers on Sartre's grave. Only here it is a classroom exercise, not a sentimental ramble through the Montparnasse cemetery.

It will forever remain one of the ironic lessons of history that the moral force which finally shattered the influence of Sartre and the French Left on their own home ground came not from any effective dissent in the intellectual capitals of the West but from a heroic survivor of the very system whose evils they had long denied. It was the publication of Aleksandr Solzhenitsyn's *Gulag Archipelago* in France in the early 1970s that finally reduced this whole tradition of political falsehood to ideological rubble. Robert Conquest described the "immense shock" that Solzhenitsyn's epic work administered to the French intellectual elite:

> We have seen, for the first time, the crumbling of the old delusions of the intellectuals. The incredible deceptions and self-deceptions by which Sartre and all the others indoctrinated the intelligentsia had been impervious to the presentation of facts, and to the advancing of logical arguments by a handful of distinguished analysts like Raymond Aron or polemical attacks on their whole way of thinking by independent men like Jean-François Revel. It remained true that a climate of conformity pervaded the intellectual classes, that every *bien-pensant* professor, student, journalist, writer held, in a way too automatic to be called a belief, that even if the USSR or similar systems had their faults, they were nonetheless imbued with a central virtue which made them superior to the wicked West.

Publication of *The Gulag Archipelago* was the turning point that finally made it possible for the truth about the French Left's mythification of the Soviet system to be openly discussed as a historical scandal of huge proportions. "The sudden disintegration of this new Age of Faith, the swift dissipation of the tenacious miasmas which had hung over the French mind," Conquest wrote, "have been truly astonishing."

No less astonishing was what may be called Sartre's existential response to this long-deferred moment of truth, for with a symbolism almost too perfect to be believed, this momentous shift in the Zeitgeist found Sartre himself afflicted with physical blindness, the perfect correlative of the purblind political vision that had long characterized his analysis of every public issue. When he suffered the loss of his eyesight in 1973, the year of *The Gulag Archipelago*'s original publication, Sartre announced that "My occupation as a writer is completely destroyed." But, as was often the case with this writer, the statement turned out to have a larger meaning that the man himself was hardly capable of comprehending.

Now, a generation after Robert Conquest wrote about the effect of *The Gulag Archipelago* upon the "climate of conformity [that] pervaded the intellectual classes" in France in the days of Sartre's ascendancy, comes a detailed analysis of the first dozen years of this shameful post-World War II history. Solzhenitsyn's book is barely mentioned in Tony Judt's *Past Imperfect: French Intellectuals 1944-1956* (University of California Press), for the appearance of *The Gulag Archipelago* postdates the period under examination, yet the consequences of its publication in France in the Seventies obviously prepared the way for this new study.

One of the central perspectives that Judt (who teaches at New York University) brings to his examination of the ideological gyrations of the French Left in the early days of the Cold War is that of political developments in the Soviet Union and Eastern and Central Europe. "[I]t was precisely in this decade," he writes,

> that Soviet society expanded from its earlier containment within the frontiers of a distant and alien Russia and established itself in the territory formerly known as Central Europe. . . . The postwar establishment of totalitarian govern-

> ments in Budapest, Warsaw, Berlin, and Prague, with its attendant repression, persecution, and social upheaval, placed the moral dilemma of Marxist practice at the center of the Western intellectual agenda.

The story of how the French intellectual Left responded to this expansion of Stalinism, and specifically to the Stalinist show trials of 1947–53, occupies the moral center of Judt's book.

Thus, while *Past Imperfect* is first of all what Judt calls "an essay on intellectual responsibility, [and] a study of the moral condition of the intelligentsia in postwar France," it is several other things as well. It is an important contribution to the intellectual history of the Cold War as that war was conducted in the cultural capital of Western Europe. It is also, in part, an analysis of French anti-Americanism and the role it played in the Left's falsification of Soviet tyranny. And finally, it offers us an illuminating theory of French political thought that traces the origin of this tendency to falsify the facts of history to what Judt describes as "France's own revolutionary heritage and its ambivalent ethical message."

In particular Judt is interested "in an aspect of the modern philosophical tradition in France that has until very recently aroused little comment in France itself, the marked absence of a concern with public ethics or political morality." With this book we have certainly come a long way from, say, a work like David Caute's *Communism and the French Intellectuals* (1964), in which Sartre is described as "without doubt the most perceptive and morally responsible of the French philosopher-writers to have wrestled with the problem of Communism."

Sartre is not the only prominent figure in post-World War II French intellectual life to come under scathing scrutiny in Judt's study. Much attention is also lavished upon Simone de Beauvoir, Albert Camus, Maurice Merleau-Ponty, and sundry camp followers of Sartre's magazine *Les Temps modernes* as well as Emmanuel Mounier and his radical circle at the journal *Esprit*. It is, in fact, Sartre, Mounier, and their satellites who are at the center of this critical survey, for it was they who "controlled the cultural terrain, they [who] set the terms of public discourse, they [who] shaped the prejudices and language of their audience." As Judt says: "Their way of being intellectuals echoed and reinforced the self-image of the intellectual community at large, even those of its members who disagreed with them."

Foremost among the "prejudices" of this intellectual community was its devotion to the idea of revolution and its corollary rejection of liberalism and parliamentary democracy. This prejudice had a history that predated the war and the Occupation. It had already made itself felt in the squalid political battles of the 1930s that prepared the way for the complaisant ethos of the Occupation. On the Left, as Judt writes of the 1930s, "fascism might be the immediate threat, but liberalism was the true enemy"; and on the Right, represented by Charles Maurras and *Action française*, "an aggressive distaste for the compromises of democratic politics" was also "commonplace."

Judt is particularly good at tracing the intellectual genealogy of this prewar "intersection at the extremes of radical sentiment from Left to Right." "Like the Communist party of the postwar years," he writes, "Maurras and his movement constituted a sort of revolving door through which passed a surprising number of writers afterward associated with quite different political positions." (In other words, radical positions on the Left.) He cites the example of Jean-Marie Domenach, later the successor to Emmanuel Mounier as editor of *Esprit*, who in 1953 expressed his faith in the Communists' "sincere love of justice," but who in the 1930s had been, by his own admission, a "childish" follower of French fascism. What remained consistent in this shift from the radical Right to the radical Left was a hatred of bourgeois democracy.

For all but the most die-hard acolytes of French fascism, however, the Nazi conquest of France in 1940 and the establishment of the Vichy regime effectively eradicated the appeal of the extreme Right. Yet, contrary to popular belief, the Resistance did not prompt any wholesale alignment with the extreme Left. Memories of the Hitler-Stalin pact, though soon to evaporate, were still fresh. As Judt observes, "the political ideas and programs of the Resistance itself were not notably revolutionary." True, there was "the sense of being part of something larger than oneself—a circle of dissenting writers, a resistance group, a clandestine political organization, or History itself." But in the beginning, at least, History was not yet wholly identified with the idea of revolution. That would come with the Liberation and a return to party politics. "If there was a general sentiment" in the Resistance, he writes, "it was probably something along the lines of Camus's desire for 'the simultaneous instauration of a collective economy and a liberal polity.' "

Yet after the war, when faced with the political choices of the Liberation, "intellectuals directed criticism at the parliamentarians for betraying the ideals of a united national renaissance." It was in this situation of recoil from the politics of bourgeois democracy that "the Communists . . . mattered the most for the intellectual community." As Judt puts it:

> This is not because the Communist party could count on a significant membership among the haute intelligentsia—quite the contrary: the impermeable, deathless commitment of an Aragon . . . was only ever a minority taste. But for many younger intellectuals, not only had the party redeemed itself in action since 1941, but it represented in France, both symbolically and in the flesh, the transcendent power and glory of Stalin's Soviet Union, victorious in its titanic struggle with Nazi Germany, the unchallenged land power on the European continent and heir apparent to a prostrate Europe.

"It helped," Judt adds in a telling insight, "that Communism asked of its sympathizers not that they think for themselves, merely that they accept the authority of others." Moreover, what was most important about Communism's appeal for the intellectuals was that it was "about revolution"—not revolution here and now, to be sure, and certainly not in a way that would vitiate either their freedom or their status, but in some distant "future [that] could always justify passivity in the present."

What the idea of revolution signified for these intellectuals remained remarkably abstract, however. The keen identification with history engendered by the Occupation and Resistance never entailed a close examination of actual historical events—especially the kind of historical events that might cast some light on the way revolution really worked. What the idea of revolution seemed to mean, first of all, was "the natural and necessary outcome . . . of the hopes and allegiances of the wartime years." In this respect, the idea of revolution seemed to embody a kind of historical inevitability beyond the reach of individual volition.

Then too, notes Judt, "revolution meant order"—an alternative to "the unregulated mediocrity of the Third Republic" that derived "its political coordinates from the lessons of history and its moral imperatives from the recent experience of political struggle and engagement." The irony—or was it only the hypocrisy?—of the situation was that for most of these intellectuals, there had been no real "political struggle and engagement" during the war:

> Only a few of the men and women who are the subject of this book were ever exposed to real risks during this period; indeed, those who went to the most trouble to theorize this situation tended to be the ones whose position was least exposed and whose careers were least affected.

But what was finally most important for the intellectuals was a belief in revolution as a "categorical imperative." This was "Sartre's special contribution." For Sartre, Judt explains,

> revolution was not a matter of social analysis or political preference, nor was the moment of revolution something one could select on the basis of experience or information. It was an *a priori* existential requirement. . . . In short, action (of a revolutionary nature) is what sustains the authenticity of the individual.

With the idea of revolution thus transformed into an "*a priori* existential requirement" and its goal firmly tethered to the "authenticity of the individual," politics in the ordinary sense of the term tended to disappear in favor of a fantasy world in which actions and events were judged according to some purely subjective standard of ideological gratification. In Judt's words:

> The abstract and protean quality of revolution thus described meant not only that almost any circumstance could be judged propitious to it and any action favorable to its ends; it also meant that anything that qualified under the heading "revolutionary" was necessarily to be supported and defended.

In this realm of looking-glass politics, revolution was, in effect, whatever you wanted it to be, and it neither entailed sacrifice nor brought any malign consequences in its wake. The threat of real revolution was always elsewhere. "Thus it cost little to be for the revolution," Judt writes, "and was hardly worth the effort to be against it, in this abstract form."

Still, despite the best efforts of Sartre, Mounier, and other fantasists of the Left to reduce the politics of revolution to the rhetoric of existential posturing, historical reality persisted in producing actual events that required an immediate and unequivocal response to brute assertions of totalitarian power. It was in the face of such events that what Judt calls "the moral price that was exacted" by this commitment to revolution was made most explicit.

One of the first tests came with the Prague coup in February 1948, which Judt describes as "the last Communist takeover in Central Europe, [which] made little pretense of representing the desires of the majority or of responding to some real or imaginary national crisis." Even for readers inured to the obscene apologetics with which the radical Left in France championed Soviet tyranny in this period, it is still shocking to be reminded of what Mounier, for example, wrote in defending the Communist coup in Prague:

> In Czechoslovakia the coup masks a retreat of capitalism, the increase of workers' control, the beginnings of a division of landed property. There is nothing astonishing in the fact that it was not undertaken with all the ceremonial of a diplomatic move, nor that it is the work of a minority. None of this is unique to Communism: there is no regime in the world today or in history that did not begin with force, no progress that was not initiated by an audacious minority in the face of the instinctive laziness of the vast majority.

"As to the victims of the Prague coup, the Czech socialists and their social-democratic allies," Judt observes, "Mounier had no regrets. The social democrats in particular he described as 'saboteurs of the European Liberations.' Their cause is lost, their fate richly deserved—they belong to a dead Europe." And this was a sentiment widely shared on the Left. Judt cites "the disdain felt by Simone de Beauvoir, for example, at all mention of 'reformism,' her desire to see social change brought about in a single convulsive moment or else not at all."

The sum of Soviet horrors that had somehow to be explained—and explained away—by the French intellectual Left in these years was truly formidable, yet in every case, no matter what the extremes of violence and terror, what Judt characterizes as the "moral anesthesia" of the Left proved equal to the sordid task. In 1949 came the appeal of David Rousset in *Le Figaro littéraire* for an inquiry into the Soviet labor camps. "Rousset was a left-wing activist, a survivor of the German camps, a friend of Sartre, and a Frenchman," Judt points out, but what finally counted against him for Sartre was that his position on the Soviet concentration camp system placed him on the wrong side of the Communist issue: "*Les Temps modernes* broke with Rousset at the end of 1949, over what it saw as his anti-Communism, or more precisely his willingness to work with anti-Communists in pursuit of his revelations about the USSR." This was, in effect, a dress rehearsal for Sartre's more famous break with Camus, in 1952, over essentially the same issue.

Beginning in 1949, too, came the purges and show trials in the Soviet-controlled states of Central and Eastern Europe that culminated in what Judt calls "a final, sanguinary convulsion" when "the Czech Communist leadership and its Soviet advisers staged the trial of Rudolf Slansky and thirteen others in November 1952." Slansky had until recently been the secretary-general of the Communist party in Prague, and, like others among the accused, he was a Jew. The trial that was staged for Slansky and his colleagues, with what Judt describes as its "unambiguously anti-Semitic character," thus added still another dimension to the horror that the French intellectual Left was obliged to assimilate into its defense of the Soviet Union.

And then, in 1956, came the Hungarian uprising and the Soviet invasion. "It might be thought," says Judt, "that the Soviet invasion of Hungary constituted sufficient evidence of history's verdict upon the Communist illusion," but of course with Sartre and his circle mere "evidence" was never any match for dialectical prowess. For Sartre,

> Soviet actions had no bearing on the legitimacy of the Communist project. . . . On the contrary, Sartre insisted, the Soviet Union is privileged by its goal (liberty and justice for all) and by the fact that it differs from all other systems and regimes in this respect.

As for the West, tainted as it was by capitalism and bourgeois democracy, it had, according to Sartre, "nothing to offer in place of Communism." "It seems, then," writes Judt, "that for Sartre there was no conceivable circumstance under which we would abandon our faith in the Communist future, given our need to believe in something."

From such statements about "faith" and "belief" in Communism, Judt draws the obvious conclusion:

> In order to appreciate the belief system of postwar intellectuals, we need to grasp that what is at issue here is not understanding, the cognitive activity usually associated with intellectuals, but faith. To react as people did to the impact of Communism in the years following 1945, they had first to accept unquestioningly a certain number of the fundamental tenets of what amounted to a civic religion.

He then offers us a summary of "the fundamental tenets" of this "civic religion":

> [A]t the center lay the will and the desire to believe in Communism. Around this article of faith were wrapped various layers of argument deriving from specific Communist achievements in the recent past. In the next orbit was to be found a certain style of reasoning, a sort of epistemological double vision, which made it possible to explain Soviet behavior in terms not invoked for any other system or persons; this discourse, although especially applicable to the Communist case, did not derive from it and had older historical and philosophical origins and objectives. The same is true of the next layer, a longstanding habit of mind, hostile to various manifestations of modernity and individualism, which is sometimes referred to, in misleading shorthand, as "anti-Americanism." At a further remove, but still within the galaxy of established cultural practices, there was the peculiar com-

bination of preeminence and self-hatred that has marked the intellectual as a public figure in modern France and contributed to ambivalence in the face of a proletarian politics. Finally, and providing all the above with their political and ideological anchor, there was the indigenous anti-liberalism of the French republican intelligentsia.

One notable feature of this "civic religion" was its indifference to the increasingly blatant anti-Semitic features of Soviet power in the Fifties. In this matter, the French themselves had a good deal of blood on their hands. They had, after all, collaborated with the Nazis in rounding up French Jews for the extermination camps. But this, for the moment, could be—and was—attributed to the "reaction and fascism" that had overtaken France with the Nazi conquest. After the war, it was believed—in yet another act of faith—that, as Judt writes, "Nations that had undergone . . . a revolution—the Soviet Union and now the countries of Eastern Europe—were by definition freed forever from the scourge of racial hatred and persecution." In other words, "With Stalin's defeat of Hitler, anti-Semitism had ceased to be an issue." As a consequence, Judt observes, "the intellectual community in France was ill-prepared for the onslaught of anti-Semitic prejudice that surfaced in the international Communist movement at the beginning of the 1950s."

On this issue, too, Sartre remained consistent in his refusal to criticize the Communists even when openly challenged to deal with the Jewish question by no less an eminence than François Mauriac:

> [M]aking direct reference to [Sartre's] *Reflexions sur la question juive*, [Mauriac] demanded of Sartre a statement on the condition of the Jews in the Soviet bloc, the persecution of Jewish Communists, the deportation and murder of Yiddish writers, and the growing rumors of an impending pogrom in Moscow itself.

But Sartre had other priorities. "[T]his demand for a moral commitment, for a significant intervention by Sartre," Judt writes,

> came just at the time of his enthusiastic adoption of the Communist cause and the publication of his strongest statement in defense of the open-ended legitimacy of Communist practice; the first part of "Les Communistes et la paix" was published in *Les Temps Modernes* in July 1952, the second in November 1952. Not only did Sartre not comment on the Slansky trial, he attended the Communists' "World Congress of Peace" in Vienna in the days immediately following the mass execution of eleven of those convicted. His only reply to Mauriac was to issue the following characteristic warning: "The problem of the condition of Jews in the Peoples' Democracies must not become a pretext for propaganda or polemic."

Once again, it was far more important for Sartre to remain anti-anti-Communist than to address the truth. "An anti-Communist is a dog, I don't change my views on this, I never shall," he later declared; and he never did.

There are many more such episodes described in *Past Imperfect*, and many more statements of a similar kind quoted, analyzed, and annotated. This is a book dense with detail and documentation, and it goes further than anything else I have read in answering the question as to why, as Judt puts it in his introduction, "in the circumstances of modern French political culture, anti-Communism appeared to be excluded from the lexicon of nonconservative beliefs."

For anyone with a taste for macabre intellectual comedy, moreover, Judt turns up some very choice items. There is the case of Claude Roy, who, after his disillusionment with the Soviet Union, turned his attention to the achievements of Mao's China, out of a desire, he said, to escape the "stench" of

Stalinism! Roy is also cited as one (there have been others) who, in Judt's words, "was politically engaged on the Left in the postwar years [but] claims now to have retained an inner identity not wholly aligned with the public one presented to the world and to friends on the Left." And how does Roy explain this moral discrepancy? Well, by the usual leap into high-flown abstraction: "I voted for Jean-Jacques Rousseau and for Marx in the elections of History. But in the secret ballot of the individual, I opted rather for Schopenhauer and Godot."

About this whole phenomenon of fatuous self-exculpation, Judt offers some mordant observations:

> The apparently insouciant ease with which the French intellectual Left thus put the Communist moment behind it was bought at the cost of its credibility and prestige in the rest of Europe. . . . More than their past errors or the occasional air of overbearing superiority, it was the ineffable solipsism of so many French intellectuals that finally broke their hold on the European imagination. Uniquely, they seemed unable to grasp the course of events. Despite their best intentions, Sartre, Mounier, Merleau-Ponty, and their spiritual heirs did not see themselves projected onto the stage of history but rather saw history reduced to the categories and dimensions of their own intellectual trajectories.

As a result, Judt continues, "What was lost was the special meaning of the term French intellectual in continental Europe itself."

The sheer scale of the mendacity and bad faith of this "civic religion," by means of which French intellectuals turned Communism into a sacred cause, is still breathtaking and dispiriting to contemplate even when all the explanations are firmly in place. And it is all the more appalling when one comes to realize how much was owed to the example of Sartre and his French contemporaries by our own intellectuals when, beginning in the

Sixties, they engaged in a similar project to deify totalitarian regimes—only now in Havana and Hanoi instead of Moscow and Prague—at the expense of the West. Who can doubt that Sartre and his circle served as models for Susan Sontag and even Mary McCarthy, despite her earlier attacks on Simone de Beauvoir, in their political pilgrimages to Hanoi?

By that time, of course, Moscow was discredited even in Paris. After 1956, as Judt points out in an interesting analysis, "there began not so much a major shift in mood as a transfer of allegiances. The Communist question was not engaged, much less resolved: it was abandoned." This entailed an "escape from Europe" by the French intellectual Left, which now turned its attention to the third world. Yet not much had really changed:

> To the extent that *tiers-mondisme* [third worldism] required of intellectuals that they turn a blind eye to terror or persecution, it hardly differed from the price extracted from fellow travelers in the 1940s and early 50s; . . . If there was a difference it was this: in order to live with the turbulent news from Eastern Europe it had been necessary to deny it, to manipulate and launder it. In the case of the third world, however, many French and other European intellectuals positively gloried in the news of violence, persecution, and poverty coming from Latin America, Africa, and Asia; it took altogether less dissimulation and self delusion to justify the sufferings of non-Europeans.

In this respect, perhaps, the American intellectual Left from the 1960s onward can be said to have at last been brought into perfect alignment with its French counterpart and model.

As a result of the intellectual and moral debacle whose history is so brilliantly traced in *Past Imperfect*, the audience for French thought, as Judt writes,

> shifted quite noticeably from Eastern and Southern Europe to

> Britain and the United States. . . . The special claims to attention of the French intelligentsia were now channeled through more abstruse media, with [Claude] Lévi-Strauss, [Roland] Barthes, [Jacques] Lacan, [Michel] Foucault, and their heirs replacing the generation of Camus and Sartre.

With this melancholy observation, Judt brings his intellectual history into the present.

We have it on the authority of Foucault's latest biographer, James Miller, that he, too, "had been inspired by Sartre's example":

> Throughout the 1970s, the two men had marched side by side countless times: to protest the plight of factory workers, to agitate for better conditions in prisons, to demand that the French government pay more attention to refugees from Vietnam. Whatever their philosophical disagreements, which were many . . . they were cut from the same cloth.

Which is, alas, undoubtedly true. For what, after all, was Foucault's project for "a new kind of biopolitics" but Sartre's notion of revolution in the service of "the authenticity of the individual" transferred to the realm of sexuality? Grateful as we may be that Sartre's direct influence has now faded and his stature as a political thinker is now permanently discredited, the flowers on his grave continue to poison the intellectual atmosphere. In this sense, at least, the story told in *Past Imperfect* is one that will continue to haunt us for a long time to come.

July 1993

THE STRANGE FATE OF LIBERAL ANTI-COMMUNISM

What Was the Congress for Cultural Freedom?

I can think of no group of people who have done more to hold our world together in these last years than you and your associates in the Congress [for Cultural Freedom]. *In this country* [the United States] *in particular, few will ever understand the dimensions and significance of your accomplishment.*

—George F. Kennan to Nicolas Nabokov, 1959

Of the many important chapters in the history of the Cold War that are nowadays either forgotten, misremembered, or summarily consigned to a demonology that places them beyond the reach of rational inquiry, none has been entombed under a heavier burden of obloquy and distortion than the story of the Congress for Cultural Freedom, which emerged in 1950 as the West's most steadfast and effective focus of intellectual resistance to Stalin and Stalinism and went on to play a significant role in exposing the true nature of Communism and the fraudulent culture that had been created in its name. The reason for the dismal fate suffered by this once admired organization—the ostensible reason, anyway—is anything but obscure. For much of its seventeen-year existence, the Congress for Cultural Freedom—and thus its principal publications and programs—was covertly financed by the Central Intelligence Agency in

Washington. Exactly how many of the Congress's leaders were actually deceived about the CIA's subvention of their organization's activities is something we shall probably never know. (Michael Josselson, the executive director and presiding spirit of the Congress, was the only one to acknowledge responsibility in the matter.) How many would have been bothered by the CIA connection, had they known, is another question to which we have no answer. They were, after all, voluntarily serving the interests of the Western democracies in their fierce conflict with the deadliest and most powerful international tyranny known to modern history. The crucial point is, however, that the CIA role *was* concealed, and when that fact came to light in the dark days of the Vietnam War, the ensuing scandal had the effect of shattering whatever prestige the Congress still retained. More importantly, it also had the retrospective effect of discrediting some of the Congress's most exemplary accomplishments.

The political climate in 1967 was, of course, especially favorable to such a scandal. The New Left, with its vociferous revival of totalitarian ideas, was in its ascendancy, making swift inroads even among the many liberals for whom—until then, anyway—anti-Communism had been an article of faith. Owing to the war in Vietnam and the antiwar movement it spawned, moreover, everything about the United States—its political system, its culture, its prosperity, and its position as a world power—had become for many people, especially many young people from the middle classes, an object of hatred and derision. When the scandal erupted over the CIA's sponsorship of the Congress for Cultural Freedom, it was thus promptly turned into a double-edged weapon aimed at maligning American democracy and destroying the moral legitimacy of anti-Communism. The glorification of totalitarian systems had once again become not only acceptable but fashionable. The media, the academy, and the cultural world were quick to adopt the new line. Suddenly, as if a switch had been thrown, Hanoi and Havana emerged as the New Jerusalems, and "Amerika," as it came to be called in radical circles, was now likened to Nazi Germany. Hence the passion and the vitriol that were invested in decrying an organization that had led the way in stripping Communism of its every claim to virtue. Writers and intellectuals who now thought it wonderful that their counterparts in North Vietnam and Cuba were employed as the licensed servitors of regimes that had stamped out dissent by violent means purported to be horrified that an agency of their own democratic government had taken an interest in launching highbrow journals and international conferences designed to uphold the values of liberal culture and to expose the horrors of Communism and the mendacity of the organs that promoted its power. The Left had begun its "long march through the institutions" of the West, and Jean-Paul Sartre had defined the new political orthodoxy when he declared that "an anti-Communist is a rat." Not since the heyday of Stalinism in the Thirties had so many intellectuals in the West voluntarily repudiated the traditions of liberal democracy in favor of a totalitarian ideal.

It was precisely to forestall such an abject surrender to the totalitarian ideal that the Congress for Cultural Freedom had been founded in the first place—founded, it is important to recall, at a moment when the Cold War was transformed, at Stalin's instigation, into a hot war in Korea and immediately after the fall of the politically divided Berlin to the Communists had been narrowly averted by the Allied airlift, an effort that foiled the Kremlin's ruthless attempt to starve West Berlin into submission. The Congress was founded, in other words, at a moment when the struggle to resist worldwide Soviet expansionism—which was understood to mean the spread of Communist rule by means of terror and the Gulag—was in its formative stages and a victorious outcome for the West, which we are only just now beginning to witness some four decades later, was anything but assured.

One of the great weaknesses that afflicted the West in this fateful struggle was the long-standing tendency of its artists, intellectuals, and other opinion-makers to ally themselves with any regime, no matter how brutal and undemocratic, that claimed to rule in the name of socialism. Capitalism was generally, if not quite universally, abominated in this intellectual class, and one or another variety of Marxian socialism—ranging from the ostensibly "democratic" to the rigidly communistic—had acquired over the years the status of a sacred doctrine. It hardly seemed to matter that the rule of Soviet-style socialism had turned the societies upon which it was inflicted into despotisms of the most extreme and unrelieved cruelty and deprivation. Reality counted for little or nothing where belief in the ultimate goodness of the socialist ideal persisted; and that belief—hard as it may now be to understand or forgive—was a widespread phenomenon among Western intellectuals. As a result, Stalin and his criminal cohorts could still, despite the enormity of their crimes and the high visibility of their police-state methods, count upon the sympathy and support of "progressives" the world over in the drive for world domination. In France and Italy there were huge Communist parties, well-financed by Moscow, already in control of labor and the arts; and even in the United States, where significant defections from the Stalinist ranks had occurred in the aftermath of the Moscow Trials and the Hitler-Stalin pact, there was never any shortage of ardent fellow-travelers, not to say militant Stalinists, among the intellectual, scientific, and entertainment elites. At the notorious Waldorf Conference in New York in 1949—one year before the Congress for Cultural Freedom was founded—eminences on the order of Arthur Miller, Lillian Hellman, Norman Mailer, I. F. Stone, Howard Fast, and F. O. Matthiessen joined forces with Stalin's emissaries to defend the Soviet Union as the champion of "peace" while denouncing the United States as the promoter of war. At that conference the young Norman Mailer was thought to be tremendously audacious for announcing, after he had assured his listeners that he, too, believed that "so long as there is capitalism, there is going to be war. Until you have a decent, equitable socialism, you can't have peace," that "I am afraid that both the United States and the Soviet Union are moving toward state capitalism." Among true-believing "progressives," however, even this premature exercise in moral equivalence was considered an impermissible slur on Stalin's noble accomplishments.

Nearly twenty years later, Norman Mailer, summoning that gift for moral delicacy that is so much admired in the work of his maturity, described the intellectuals involved in the Congress for Cultural Freedom as "cockroaches in a slum sink." There was a lot of this sort of thing in the left-wing press in the aftermath of the revelations about CIA support for the Congress. Christopher Lasch spoke of these same intellectuals as "servants . . . of the secret police." Andrew Kopkind denounced them as "spies who came in for the gold." It is therefore worth recalling exactly who these "cockroaches," "spies," and "servants . . . of the secret police" actually were, and what sort of work they carried out on behalf of the Congress and its programs. After all, such figures as Raymond Aron, Nicola Chiaromonte, Malcolm Muggeridge, Nicolas Nabokov, Denis de Rougemont, Edward Shils, Ignazio Silone, and Stephen Spender—all of whom were deeply involved in the Congress's activities—aren't usually spoken of as "cockroaches" and "spies"; and *Encounter*, *Preuves*, and *Tempo Presente*—the three principal magazines that were launched by the Congress in Europe—do not represent the sort of intelligence that is commonly associated with the work of "the secret police" in any country.

The task of setting the record straight on these and other matters has now been greatly advanced by an Australian writer—Peter Coleman, the editor of *Quadrant*—who has written the first history of the Congress. *The Liberal Conspiracy* (The Free Press), as Coleman's book is called, is unlikely to be the last word on the Congress for Cultural Freedom—it has remarkably little to say, for example, about the kind of culture the Congress was created to defend and advance—but it nonetheless provides us with a readable and fairly detailed chronicle of the organization's history, its publications, its programs, its principal personnel, and the remarkably deep divisions and dissensions that determined the course of its history from the outset. Coleman, a barrister and former member of the Australian Parliament, does not pretend to write as an entirely disinterested observer. *Quadrant*, the cultural review he now edits in Sydney, was one of the many magazines launched by the Congress in the 1950s—though, like *Encounter* in London, it has long since been published as a completely independent journal. (Coleman was not, by the way, *Quadrant*'s editor when the magazine was supported by the Congress.) His political views, moreover, are essentially those that guided the Congress at the outset—which is to say, he is a liberal anti-Communist, or so I infer, anyway, from what he has written. He writes, in other words, as a champion of the Congress and its program who is also fully aware of the flaws and contradictions that haunted its history. His overall judgment on the Congress, implicit throughout *The Liberal Conspiracy*, is stated in the most unequivocal terms in the concluding paragraph of the book.

> The achievement of the Congress for Cultural Freedom [he writes] was in its time to have placed some severe limits on the advantages of Stalinist Russia. Today almost everyone (including Mikhail Gorbachev) agrees with the Congress's once lonely assessment of Soviet totalitarianism, and in particular of the Soviet failure to accept human rights (in other words, cultural freedom). In contributing in so brilliant and timely a way to this public awareness throughout the world in a period of great danger, the Congress for Cultural Freedom was a historic success.

Of the many important points to emerge from Coleman's history of the Congress, probably the most crucial is his insistent reminder throughout the book of the extent to which the organization and its program—indeed, its basic political orientation—was firmly and irreversibly tethered to the views of the international Left. Mailer's "cockroaches" turn out to have been, by and large, a band of liberals, socialists, and social democrats who were distinguishable from their brethren on the international Left mainly by their opposition to totalitarian rule. And in the end, so complete was this bias in favor of the political Left that even this distinction was abandoned by the Congress's chief executive when confronted by the war in Vietnam. It is positively eerie to discover in *The Liberal Conspiracy* that in 1967, when the United States was deeply involved in the war against Communism in Vietnam and the Congress's link to the CIA had been revealed in the press, Michael Josselson, still ringmaster of the whole operation, "approved [as Coleman writes] the antiwar positions of [John Kenneth] Galbraith, [Arthur] Schlesinger, and Richard Lowenthal, and disagreed with the Indian and Australian associates of the Congress who supported the U.S. commitment to save South Vietnam from Communism." In May 1967, according to Coleman, Josselson wrote in no uncertain terms to the head of the Australian Association for Cultural Freedom, which received its funds from the Congress, that on the war in Vietnam "I agree with Senator McGovern." Which, among much else, would have made the executive director of the Congress for Cultural Freedom an ally, albeit an unacknowledged one, of Norman Mailer, Christopher Lasch, and Andrew Kopkind.

This attachment to certain elements of the international Left had, of course, been fundamental to the Congress's political outlook from the beginning, and although it was bound to cause immense problems—and very quickly did—no other course was probably possible at the time. For it was only on the Left—which is to say, in the ranks of what came to be known as liberal anti-Communism—that eager and knowledgeable recruits for the intellectual struggle against Stalinism were to be found. Except for James Burnham, political conservatives played little or no part in this endeavor. (That some of these liberals and leftists reemerged, in the late Sixties, as conservatives or neoconservatives is a story that belongs to a later chapter of intellectual history.) At the time, the only opposition to Stalinism that counted for anything was a liberal opposition, which by the late 1940s was beginning to emerge as a coherent intellectual impulse. About this development and its role both in influencing the State Department in Washington and the formation of the Congress for Cultural Freedom, Coleman is very illuminating.

> [I]n the late 1940s [he writes] opinion on the Left gradually began to change, spurred on by the Sovietization and the purges of social democrats in Eastern and Central Europe, the Berlin Blockade, and the campaign against Tito. The year 1949 brought the publication of three books that indicated the new mood on the Left: *The God That Failed* (edited by R. H. S. Crossman), George Orwell's *1984*, and Arthur M. Schlesinger, Jr.'s *The Vital Center*. Schlesinger's book, a manifesto of the American "Non-Communist Left," also showed how quickly this movement had spread from the intellectual ghetto to high government office under the influence of such figures as George Kennan, Charles E. Bohlen, and Isaiah Berlin. "Under Byrnes and Marshall," Schlesinger said, recounting a "quiet revolution," . . . the State Department moved in the direction of a philosophy of the non-Communist Left. The very phrase, indeed, was reduced in the Washington manner to its initials; and the cryptic designation "NCL" was constantly used in inner State Department circles.
>
> It was the widespread adoption in the more intellectual U.S. government circles of the belief that the non-Communist Left could be the most effective response to the totalitarian Left that created a receptive atmosphere for the formation and support of what would become the Congress for Cultural Freedom.

Thus, when the first public meeting of the Congress for Cultural Freedom was convened in Berlin in June 1950, Coleman writes, "almost all the participants were liberals or social democrats, critical of capitalism and opposed to colonialism, imperialism, nationalism, racism, and dictatorship. They supported freedom of thought and the extension of the welfare state." The Congress's five Honorary Presidents—"whose names exemplified the spirit of the occasion," as Coleman correctly observes—were Benedetto Croce, John Dewey, Karl Jaspers, Jacques Maritain, and Bertrand Russell.

Was it inevitable that a serious split would develop at the very moment when the Congress was being formed? Probably. The intellectuals who gathered in Berlin were very largely veterans of the kind of political factionalism that had long been endemic on the Left, and there were genuine differences, in any case, about the goals to be pursued now that the Cold War had erupted into a military conflict in Korea. Arthur Koestler, whose novel about the Moscow purge trials, *Darkness at Noon*, had undoubtedly exerted a greater influence than any other book in winning converts to the anti-Communist cause on the Left, at least until the publication of *1984*, and whose political eloquence had dominated the Berlin meeting, believed that the Congress, in Coleman's words, "should be less a cultural organization and more a political movement, a 'Deminform' to counter the Cominform."

But Koestler's brand of militancy did not prevail, and Koestler himself promptly removed himself from the Congress's affairs. "The alternative strategy adopted by the Congress for Cultural Freedom," Coleman writes, "was to build a kind of 'united front' with the democratic elements of the European Left and gradually win it over to the Atlanticist cause." This meant, in practice, an attempt to win favor in so-called "neutralist" circles, which were not in any political sense neutral at all, and thus to blur, insofar as it was possible, the very deep differences that divided the founders of the Congress from, say, Sartre and his fellow-traveling allies. No doubt Coleman is correct when he observes that "it is impossible to separate this coup—at once ideological and pragmatic—from the decision of the U.S. Central Intelligence Agency to assume responsibility for the continuing funding of the Congress." In other words, the ban imposed on Koestler's plan for a militant anti-Communist political movement was very likely the result of a CIA directive.

This overt dependence on the political Left as the intellectual mainstay of the Congress may indeed have been necessary, given the realities of the moment, but it was only a matter of time before it became the source of considerable dissension—and the time was not long in coming. As early as 1955, only two years after the founding of *Encounter* in London, Josselson attempted to remove its American co-editor, Irving Kristol, and replace him with the more radical Dwight Macdonald in an effort to appease the anti-American sentiments of the English literary and academic establishment. This was a move enthusiastically supported by Schlesinger ("I could not think of a better American prospect for the job") and Kristol's English co-editor, Stephen Spender ("the most amazing piece of good luck and should be seized"), and if what was wanted was an American who could be counted upon to outdo even the English in voicing anti-American sentiments, Macdonald was certainly the right man for the job. But even Josselson changed his mind once he had met Macdonald, and under Kristol's editorship *Encounter* soon became, as he said, "*the* English-language cultural periodical," with a circulation of sixteen thousand. When the time came for Irving Kristol to leave, he was replaced by Melvin J. Lasky, who had been one of the principal organizers of the Berlin meeting in 1950. "By 1963," Coleman writes, "*Encounter*'s circulation had risen to 34,000, and it was a success." In his *Mémoires*, published in 1983, Raymond Aron described it as "the first, the best monthly review in English." Coleman also reminds us that, under Lasky's editorship, *Encounter* allied itself with the Hugh Gaitskell wing of the

Labour Party, and when Harold Wilson formed his Labour Government in October 1964, "his Ministry included half a dozen regular *Encounter* writers." Thus, the attachment to the Left, though not to the most radical Left, persisted well into the Sixties.

As for the Congress's role in advancing the culture which it had been founded to defend, that too proved to be a source of conflict within the organization's ranks. Part of the problem, which it would be a mistake to underestimate, was the sheer philistinism of so many of the intellectuals who had allied themselves with the Congress. Coleman points out, for example, that at *Encounter* Lasky "rejected an article by Malcolm Muggeridge that briskly dismissed all twentieth-century literature, music, and art; none of it, Muggeridge said, 'will be of any conceivable imaginative interest to posterity.' But this meant dismissing the Western culture that . . . the Congress for Cultural Freedom had been created to affirm." Muggeridge's was hardly an isolated case though, with his customary candor, he was more open in his expression of contempt for the high culture of his time than many of his like-minded colleagues in the Congress could bring themselves to be.

This tendency to dismiss the arts as either unimportant or, as in Muggeridge's case, utterly worthless was emphatically resisted, however, by the man who served as secretary-general of the Congress at its Paris headquarters. Nicolas Nabokov, the Russian-born composer and cousin of the novelist, had achieved fame, as Coleman reminds us, "in Paris in 1928 when Serge Diaghilev produced his ballet *Ode*. He continued his musical career in the United States, where the Ballet Russe de Monte Carlo presented his ballet *Union Pacific*, its first ballet with an American theme." He had become an American citizen in 1939, and worked as a translator for the government in Washington during the war. After the war, he worked for the U.S. Military Government in Berlin, where he had grown up after fleeing the

Bolsheviks with his family, and also worked for the Voice of America before joining the Congress for Cultural Freedom.

It was Nabokov's view that the Congress ought to live up to its obligation to foster the artistic life of the West as a vital alternative to the Soviet cultural model, and toward this end he organized a massive arts festival—the Festival of Paris—in May 1952 that lasted for thirty days. According to Coleman:

> Nabokov presented Paris with one hundred symphonies, concertos, operas, and ballets by about seventy twentieth-century composers. Paris had its first productions of Alban Berg's *Wozzeck* (by the Vienna Opera), of Benjamin Britten's *Billy Budd* (by Covent Garden), of Gertrude Stein's and Virgil Thomson's *Four Saints in Three Acts* (by Harlem and ANTA, with Alice B. Toklas attending), and of Arnold Schoenberg's *Die Erwartung*. Igor Stravinsky conducted *Oedipus Rex*, for which Jean Cocteau designed the set and directed the choreography. There were performances by the Boston Symphony Orchestra and the New York City Ballet. William Faulkner, Katherine Anne Porter, and Allen Tate came from the United States for literary debates. There was an exhibition of 150 modern paintings and sculptures. As well as celebrating the cultural freedom of the West, the Festival also made its anti-Soviet point indirectly by performing works by Sergei Prokofiev and Dmitri Shostakovich that were banned in the Soviet Union, and directly by arranging church services for the victims of totalitarian oppression.

You would think, if you didn't know better, that this extraordinary festival of the arts would be acclaimed in retrospect as one of the proudest accomplishments in the history of the Congress. But such it did not turn out to be in the eyes of those political stalwarts of the Congress for whom "culture" counted for very little. Arthur Koestler dismissed the Festival of Paris as "an effete gathering," and Sidney Hook went on denouncing Nabokov for wasting the Congress's money right into the 1980s. Unfortunately, Coleman is not really equipped to deal with this aspect of the Congress's history—he seems, for example, to be under the mistaken impression that Pierre Monteux and Charles Munch were composers—and he accords it very little attention. Even about the cultural aspect of the Congress's many magazines, he has remarkably little to say. The cultural history of the Congress for Cultural Freedom remains to be written; what we are mainly given in *The Liberal Conspiracy* is its political history.

Is Coleman right, then, in his judgment that the Congress was "a historic success"? On the whole, I think he is, especially in regard to its activities in the 1950s—the period when it made the greatest difference. By the time the Congress was dissolved in the wake of revelations about the CIA connection, its attachment to the Left was no longer politically viable. The anti-Communist Left was itself beginning to fall apart—which is to say, more and more divided in its response to Communism. Toward the end of *The Liberal Conspiracy,* Coleman turns to Edward Shils for an account of this political denouement—an account that makes even better sense in the light of events in Eastern and Central Europe today than it did when Shils first made his analysis some years ago.

> Edward Shils summed up the position . . . when he wrote that although the Cold War continued unceasingly, the "moral strain" of it proved too much for Western opinion, including, if not especially, that of the non-Communist Left, which increasingly grasped at the idea of "competitive coexistence" and emphasized the relaxing coexistence rather than the competitiveness. He found the source of the "moral strain" in "the burden of 1917," the liberal conviction that the Soviet Union, whatever its terrible imperfections, remains an "advanced" and "progressive" society, since it has abolished private property, capitalism, and the market. To eliminate that "burden," it is necessary to acknowledge that a free society is bound up with

> private property, capitalism, and the market, that there is "an inescapable affinity between socialists and communists."

It wasn't only the Congress for Cultural Freedom that came to an end in the Sixties. What also ended, by and large, was the old non-Communist Left to which the Congress had, for better or worse, tethered its fate.

January 1990

Life After Liberalism: The New Republic *at Eighty*

Reading *The New Republic* these days, I often think of the late Lionel Trilling. It was Trilling's fondest wish to remain, in everything he thought and wrote, a paragon of enlightened liberalism. He had, of course, sharply criticized the liberalism of his own generation—the liberalism that in the 1930s and 1940s had proved to be so easily captive to Stalinist influence. Yet it was never his intention to repudiate liberalism itself. He set out to reform it, to make it more responsive to the complexities of experience and less doctrinaire in its formulas of salvation. His models in this endeavor were Arnold and Mill—especially the Mill who had written about the conservative Coleridge and the radical Bentham with such undeceived intelligence.

That his own criticism of liberalism was likely to meet with resistance and opprobrium from the radical Left was a risk that Trilling was willing to take. Indeed, to incur the wrath of the Stalinists was in those days, for a liberal of Trilling's persuasion, a badge of honor. It seems not have occurred to him, however, that he might be put down as a conservative by non-Stalinist liberals because of the very nature of his attack on liberalism. When the charge was made—and not by any Stalinist hack but by Joseph Frank, a critic of impeccable liberal credentials—Trilling was stunned. There is a sense in which it can truly be said that he never recovered from the demoralization he suffered as a result of this attempt to characterize his whole approach to culture and politics as essentially conservative in spirit. Trilling died without responding to the charge, and the debate over the exact nature of his conservative liberalism—or, if you like, his liberal conservatism—has continued to haunt his posthumous reputation.

The reason I think of Trilling while reading *The New Republic* is that this celebrated journal of liberal opinion nowadays offers us almost weekly bulletins on what might be called the Trilling dilemma: how to function as a critic of liberalism without being stigmatized as a conservative. *The New Republic*, which this year observes its eightieth anniversary, still presents itself to its readers as a bastion of liberal thought. Yet its expression of that thought, which on many issues is now all but indistinguishable from certain aspects of neoconservative thought, is frequently marked by an obvious dread of being seen—especially by liberals further to the Left than *The New Republic*—to be deviating from the permissible limits of liberal orthodoxy. In the vain hope of warding off such charges, the magazine conducts a sort of intermittent border warfare against some of the neoconservatives who are its natural allies—often, in fact, its only allies—against the radical Left. At the same time, however, the magazine publishes certain neoconservative writers—usually in its book-review pages—on subjects that are safely distant from party politics. The editors do not mind borrowing a little intellectual authority from the neoconservative camp so long as it is not seen to compromise the magazine's liberal loyalties.

As to what those liberal loyalties now consist of, it is sometimes difficult to say, especially since the departure of Hendrik Hertzberg and Sidney Blumenthal for Tina Brown's left-wing political salon at *The New Yorker*. For the better part of twenty years—since Martin Peretz acquired ownership of *The New Republic* in 1974—the magazine has seemed deliberately to organize its staff and its contributors into opposing liberal factions, some more liberal, some more conservative, some merely more facetious, than others. This carefully modulated deviation from liberal orthodoxy, which is mainly but not exclusively confined to the realm of foreign policy, inevitably brought cries of protest from the magazine's Left-liberal constituency when it resulted in outright support for some Reagan administration initiative—as it did, for example, in the case of the Nicaraguan *contras*. But since Hendrik Hertzberg, who alternated for a time with the peripatetic Michael Kinsley in the editor's chair, could always be counted on to supply the requisite take-no-prisoners assault on Reagan himself, the protests of the loyal opposition at the magazine never amounted to much. Kinsley himself generally assumed the lighter burden of amusing the magazine's yuppie liberal constituency—a group more interested in style than substance—with his flippant patter on domestic political affairs. While Hertzberg's liberalism wore a frown of scornful disapproval, Kinsley's displayed the self-satisfied smile of the perennial undergraduate scoring points against his elders.

Even if these upscale liberals had really wanted to break with *The New Republic* over its much-discussed turn to the Right, where could they have gone? *The Nation*, which had long been *The New Republic*'s principal rival among Left-liberal weeklies, had further degenerated into a sectarian organ reminiscent of the bad old days when radicals still worshiped at the altar of revolution. *The New York Review of Books*, now *The New Republic*'s only real competition for the loyalty of campus liberals, was already oversupplied with anti-conservative savants, and in any case preferred writers with more glittering intellectual credentials. Sidney Blumenthal did a stint at *The Washington Post*, to be sure, but he soon hurried back to the more salubrious purlieu of *The New Republic*, where he waited for something better to show up. Until Tina Brown made it safe—and far more lucrative, too—to practice radical-chic journalism without risk or restraint, the opportunities were somewhat limited for the Left-liberal mandarins at *The New Republic*. When it came time for Kinsley to decamp, he at last found his true vocation, bringing his Ivy League brand of liberal facetiousness to the world of the television talk show, where it is accepted practice for glib phrases to serve as a substitute for thought. By and large, when the folks on Marty Peretz's Left flank departed the magazine, it was more a matter of opportunity than of political principle.

Still, it must be said that, whatever the magazine's flaws, failures, and contradictions have been during the last twenty years of publication, Marty Peretz has succeeded in breaking the mold of the traditional liberal weekly by the changes he brought to *The New Republic*. He has weaned the magazine away from its infantile Leftism, closed the door on any doubts as to what the Cold War was really all about, cast a critical eye on the new politics of racial quotas and preferments and the judicial arguments supporting them, kept a prudent distance from the excesses of feminist radicalism, and in general purged the pages of *The New Republic* of its abject obeisance to the political and cultural legacy of the Sixties. While allowing his Left-flank editors and contributors plenty of space in which to vent their dissent from the magazine's new course and vilify those outside the magazine who uphold views that in some cases are virtually identical with those that had now become central to *The New Republic* itself, Peretz went a long way toward disembarrassing the magazine of its disreputable political past. Not the whole way, to be sure, but a large part of the distance to be traversed, given the appalling political history of *The New Republic* since the Thirties.

From Malcolm Cowley's praise of the enlightened "jurisprudence" governing the Moscow Trials in the 1930s to Richard Gilman's pusillanimous surrender to black nihilism in Eldridge Cleaver's *Soul on Ice* in the 1960s, the old *New Republic* had a pretty dismal record when it came to resisting or even comprehending the nature of the Left-liberal fashions of its time. Under three of its most notoriously compromised editors—Bruce Bliven, Michael Straight, and Henry A. Wallace—the magazine remained, with only occasional exceptions, a complaisant supporter of Soviet foreign policy during the worst years of Stalin's murderous reign.

It is one of the merits of *The New Republic Reader* (A New Republic Book/Basic Books), which Dorothy Wickenden has edited to mark the magazine's eightieth anniversary, that it acknowledges the reality of this shameful political past both in the introduction and in the selection of texts. It doesn't, to be sure, attempt to give us a comprehensive account of this history or dwell on the role played by *The New Republic*'s pro-Soviet line in the political life of the Thirties and Forties—a role that was finally reduced to macabre political comedy when, in 1946, the year in which Churchill issued his warning about the "Iron Curtain" that Stalin was then imposing on Eastern Europe, the magazine's proprietor, Michael Straight, appointed as editor the most eminent fellow-traveler in the country, Henry A. Wallace, who had been Vice President during F.D.R.'s third term.

Straight was not lacking in Stalinist credentials of his own. As Wickenden delicately points out, Straight "fell in with the Soviet agents Anthony Blunt and Guy Burgess" during his student days at Cambridge University in the Thirties. She never actually explains that Straight was inducted into the Blunt–Burgess spy ring and for a time reported regularly to his Soviet "control." In a parenthetical aside, she acknowledges that while Straight claimed to have become an ex-Communist by the Forties, his "own loyalties, however, remained a little murky. . . . In March 1951 [while the Korean War was still raging], Burgess ran into Straight in Washington, D.C., and admitted that he had passed along to Moscow the U.S. plans to advance into North Korea." Yet Straight, who had once served as one of F.D.R.'s speech writers, did not disclose this betrayal to American authorities until long after the event, and then only because disclosure was a condition of securing a job he wanted with the Kennedy administration.

Wickenden, who was formerly *The New Republic*'s executive editor and is now the national affairs editor of *Newsweek*, is sometimes a little murky herself in explaining, or failing to explain, how the magazine's liberalism adjusted to the shocks of the Hitler-Stalin pact and the outbreak of the Second World War. She professes astonishment that the *The New Republic* "counseled fatalism and restraint"—in other words, non-intervention—"in the face of Hitler, Mussolini, and Franco" at the onset of the war, as if this had not been the Communist Party line as a result of the Hitler-Stalin pact right up to the day in 1941 when Hitler's armies invaded Russia. Then, of course, the party line changed, and so did *The New Republic*'s. But then, Wickenden isn't very clear about the war itself. She seems to be under the impression that in September 1939 "the war began with Germany's invasion of Czechoslovakia." Apparently she is still unaware of what happened to Poland in September 1939.

Notwithstanding these egregious confusions, however, Wickenden has included just enough in this *Reader* to give newcomers to the subject a glimpse of what *The New Republic*'s liberal fellow-traveling line entailed in the heyday of Stalin's influence on American intellectual life. In this department, the *Reader*'s prize exhibit is undoubtedly Bruce Bliven's "Letter to Stalin," from the issue of March 30, 1938. As the infamous Moscow Trials were completing their course and the Great Terror continued to sweep millions of lives in its path, this abject liberal acolyte of the Soviet experiment made an open appeal to Stalin to, as we would say today, *improve his image*!

Bliven was worried, you see, that, as he wrote to Comrade Stalin with a heavy heart, "the series of trials of traitors, spies and saboteurs has had a bad effect on world public opinion." To remedy the situation, Bliven made four proposals. "I suggest, first," he wrote, "that in future treason trials, a procedure should be followed more compatible with that of countries under the Anglo-Saxon or the Roman law tradition." Then, in an attempt to soften so bold a suggestion, Bliven added: "It may be unjust of the Americans, for example, to suspect that torture is used in these cases; but in the United States there is a nationwide and long continued tradition of police brutality, of extorting confessions by torture in every sort of case from petty larceny to murder. It is inevitable that this country should look with suspicion upon confessions obtained in secret hearings, however plausible these confessions may be on their face."

It gets better, for Bliven's second point, or plea, was to suggest "that in the future you shall not merely present to the world testimony which many people in all countries find incredible, without some attempt to make its credibility apparent." Then, getting really desperate, Bliven added: "If these proceedings are not convincing, there is no point in holding them"—an observation that tacitly acknowledged that the Moscow "treason" trials weren't judicial proceedings at all but political show trials which were proving to be embarrassing to the faithful. What liberal acolytes of Stalinism like Bliven could not bring themselves to comprehend was that the trials were never meant to be convincing—not about the defendants' guilt, anyway. They were an instrument of terror, and they served their purpose with all the cold-blooded efficiency that Stalin meant for them to have.

Bliven's utter incapacity to understand the world he was writing about was made fairly explicit when, in his third recommendation to Comrade Stalin, he urged him to "abolish the death sentence for these and all other crimes." By March 1938, Stalin had already caused the deaths of millions of innocent people, and in the years that were left to him he would cause the death of millions more. This was something that the editor of the great liberal journal simply could not fathom—and neither, apparently, could the magazine's loyal liberal readers. By such people, Communism was still looked upon as a somewhat more militant variety of the liberal vocation, which itself was believed to have an exclusive patent on political virtue. Those who served in the underground Soviet apparatus knew otherwise, of course, but that was one of the reasons they were obliged to remain underground—from which position they were able to manipulate fellow-traveling fools like Bruce Bliven with the skill of expert puppeteers, no matter how contradictory or embarrassing the twists and turns of the Moscow party line might be. In Bliven's mental universe, it was unimaginable to be opposed to Communism, for such opposition would have constituted a violation of the liberal compact.

And so Bliven persevered, blind as a bat to the moral implications of the policies he espoused, advising Comrade Stalin in the fourth of his recommendations that he "offer an amnesty to all opponents who have not yet been guilty of any crime under the normal civil code, on a pledge on their part of future good behavior." He then added a further suggestion: that Stalin withdraw, as he wrote, "from the public life of your country for a stipulated length of time, perhaps a year or eighteen months," to prove to the world that he was not, after all, like the other dictators on the world scene. The sheer idiocy of the entire document is still astounding to contemplate, yet this was the kind of thinking that held the liberal Left in thrall during one of the periods of *The New Republic*'s greatest influence.

It is Wickenden's view that one of *The New Republic*'s "saving graces" in the Thirties was its "cultural criticism." "[Malcolm] Cowley's and [Edmund] Wilson's myopia about Soviet communism did not extend to the arts," she writes, "where they exuberantly explored modernism and its relation to the cultural legacy of the West." This is partly true, but it is by no means the whole story—especially where Cowley was concerned. The fact is, Cowley consistently used the literary pages of *The New Republic* to advance the reputations of writers favored by the Stalinist Left and discredit writers who opposed it. Which was why, in 1940, James T. Farrell published an article in *The American Mercury* attacking Cowley for turning *The New Republic* into what he characterized as a literary mouthpiece for the Communist Party, and why Edmund Wilson, in a private letter written around the same time, criticized Cowley's Stalinism along the same lines. Wickenden makes a brief and not altogether intelligible reference to Wilson's letter to Cowley in her introduction to the *Reader*, but never mentions Farrell's attack, which ought to have been taken account of.

In the realm of literature and the arts, however, Wickenden does not seem to have either a keen interest or a firm grasp. As a result, that whole side of *The New Republic*'s history, which in certain periods *was* one of the magazine's chief glories, is given little more than token acknowledgment in this new *Reader*.[1] From reading this new *New Republic Reader*, you could have no idea that the magazine employed two of the finest theater critics writing in this century—first Stark Young and then Eric Bentley—or that in Otis Ferguson it could boast of one of our best movie critics or that there had ever been a time when writers as distinguished as Léonie Adams, Conrad Aiken, Van Wyck Brooks, Kenneth Burke, Horace Gregory, Paul Rosenfeld, and Delmore Schwartz were regular contributors to its literary and arts pages. Rare contributions like T. S. Eliot's review of Julien Benda's *The Treason of the Intellectuals*, in 1928, and Scott Fitzgerald's obituary memoir of Ring Lardner, in 1933, have likewise been dropped down the memory hole, as have George Santayana's essays from the earliest years of the magazine's existence. Clearly, contributions of this sort are of no interest to Wickenden. Instead she treats us to a report dispatched to *The New Republic* for the issue of February 14, 1933, by H. V. Kaltenborn, who offered the magazine's readers the following assessment of Adolf Hitler: "He is sworn to obey the Constitution and is likely to do so. The time for a Fascist coup d'état is past.

[1] It isn't even true, by the way, as the dust jacket claims, that this *Reader* is "the first major anthology of essays" drawn from *The New Republic*. At least two earlier collections have been published—*The New Republic Anthology, 1915-1935*, edited by Groff Conklin, with an introduction by Bruce Bliven (Dodge); and *The Faces of Five Decades: Selections from Fifty Years of The New Republic, 1914-1964*, edited by Robert Luce, with commentary by Arthur M. Schlesinger, Jr. (Simon & Schuster). Both give better accounts of the periods they cover than the new *Reader*.

Hitler himself had definitely lost prestige and power before he won the chancellorship. Whatever the result of the March fifth election, it will not give Adolf Hitler the opportunity to establish his long heralded *Drittes Reich*." As one turns the pages of this *Reader*, there are times when one almost suspects Wickenden of harboring a wicked sense of humor.

Or is it that, from the perspective of Washington, even the most mistaken political analysis inevitably commands an interest for the editors of *The New Republic* that a cogent criticism of culture and the arts cannot claim? In any comprehensive historical account of *The New Republic*, the implications of its move from New York to Washington in 1950 would have to be closely scrutinized. The magazine had been established in New York by a circle of intellectuals that had a serious interest in the arts. Its founding editor, Herbert Croly, was a writer on architecture. Even a writer as deeply immersed in political affairs as Walter Lippmann, another founder of the magazine, was capable in the early days of producing first-rate literary commentary, as he did in essays on Sinclair Lewis and H. L. Mencken. Edmund Wilson's tenure as literary editor was closely tethered to New York literary life in the Twenties and its involvement in European modernism—a tradition that was continued by Malcolm Cowley until the effort foundered on the shoals of Stalinist orthodoxy.

When Michael Straight moved *The New Republic* to Washington, in the aftermath of the Wallace debacle, the nation's capital was still a cultural backwater, and in many respects it has remained one. Only in a capital as intellectually provincial as Washington could a president like John Kennedy earn a reputation as a supporter of the arts simply by inviting André Malraux and Igor Stravinsky to dinner. (And it's been downhill since then, for such invitations nowadays go to the likes of Oprah Winfrey and Maya Angelou.) Two of Cowley's successors in the literary editorship—Robert Richman (no relation, incidentally, to *The New Criterion*'s poetry editor) and Robert Evett—did a creditable job of keeping up a high standard in the magazine's coverage of literature and the arts in the Fifties and early Sixties, but in the aftermath of the Kennedy assassination and the eruption of the counterculture and the codification of the "new sensibility" in the period of the Vietnam War, the magazine's cultural pages suffered a descent into radical chic almost as devastating to sound judgment and high standards as the Stalinism of the Thirties.

Given this history, it has been disappointing, to say the least, that *The New Republic* under Marty Peretz has never seen fit to appoint a literary editor whose primary intellectual interest is literature and the arts. This, I think, has something to do with the magazine's entrenched Washington orientation, which predisposes it to favor a philistine perspective, and a lot to do with its failed liberalism, which values the arts only when they can be seen to be an appendage to social policy. As a result, criticism of the arts has for some years now been relegated to a marginal status in the magazine. There are occasional articles of considerable interest, but little or nothing in the way of sustained attention. The principal exception to this rule has been the magazine's abiding attention to the movies—that sacred staple of yuppie culture, which years ago supplanted literature as the lead item in the magazine's back-of-the-book and, more often than not, has virtually nothing to do with serious artistic interests. Literature still fares better than most other fields in *The New Republic*, but that may be owing to the fact that the work of so many of the writers who are nowadays highly regarded is itself an expression of social policy, if not indeed of social pathology.

About the present literary editor of *The New Republic*, however, I cannot speak in an entirely disinterested spirit. For one of the longest essays that Wickenden has thought it appropriate to reprint in her survey of *The New Republic*'s first eighty years—and the only one that makes even a feeble attempt to comprehend the arts in the age of modernism—is Leon Wieseltier's "Matthew Arnold and the Cold War." This is the salvo that Wieseltier fired against *The New Criterion* upon the publication of its first issue in September 1982. Of course it is immensely flattering to find that the debut of our journal exactly a dozen years ago is deemed to be the only cultural event of the last eighty years important enough to merit a nine-page essay in this *New Republic Reader*. Yet the pleasure which this remarkable judgment affords us is somewhat allayed by the misrepresentations and unconscionable bad faith exhibited in the essay itself.

In this essay Wieseltier had some disparaging things to say about several of the writers who contributed to the first issue of *The New Criterion*, and falsely accused us of attempting to foster what he described as "the political delegitimation of doubt." If anything, of course, that first issue of *The New Criterion* may have been somewhat overloaded with expressions of doubt about a whole range of current cultural orthodoxies. But these were not the kind of doubts that Wieseltier's liberal pieties could easily countenance, for they put into question the received opinions then dominating—and, for that matter, still dominating—the academic Left. To this first accusation Wieseltier added another that was equally false. This was the charge that we had somehow set out to undermine Lionel Trilling's call for "variousness, possibility, complexity, and difficulty" in critical debate. What was interesting about this charge, false as it was, was the unacknowledged restrictions that Wieseltier clearly wished to impose on what was now permissible to question in the name of "variousness, possibility, complexity, and difficulty."

Let me illustrate. Wieseltier took fierce exception to the essay called "Postmodern: Art and Culture in the 1980s," which I contributed to that first issue of *The New Criterion*. In that essay I was attempting to restate the theory of the modernist avant-garde, which I had first put forward in my book *The Age of the Avant-Garde* in 1973, and to amplify it in the light of the so-called "postmodern" assault that had been mounted against modernism in the interim. It was my view that the historical relation which obtained between the avant-garde, on the one hand, and its bourgeois antagonists, on the other, had been unduly simplified by radicals and reactionaries alike. As I wrote in the introduction to *The Age of the Avant-Garde*: "The history of the avant-garde actually harbors a complex agenda of internal conflict and debate, not only about aesthetic matters but about the social values that govern them. If the bourgeois ethos may be said to have both a 'progressive' and a 'reactionary' side, the avant-garde is similarly divided." In the "Postmodern" essay of 1982, I restated the point this way: "The modern movement was always, perhaps, a more complex and pluralistic phenomenon than its more doctrinaire champions—and, for that matter, its more doctrinaire enemies—could ever bring themselves to recognize."

Yet this attempt to bring the principles of "variousness, possibility, complexity, and difficulty" to bear on the study of modernism was firmly rejected by Wieseltier, who, donning the dunce's cap of the classroom radical for the purpose of slaying a suspected neoconservative dragon, insisted that "Modernism *was* a cultural insurrection," pure and simple. "The most unsatisfactory aspect of Kramer's analysis," he wrote, "is his failure to face up to the contradiction between the marriage of modernism and capitalism, on the one hand, and the history of their relations, on the other. These relations have not been harmonious." As if anything I have ever written had claimed that they were!

This categorical refusal to entertain the "possibility" of "variousness" or "complexity" in the discussion of modernism made Wieseltier a pretty lame advocate of the principle of "difficulty" he wished to claim in Trilling's name, but it *was* a perfect example of what I have called "the Trilling dilemma": the affliction suffered by disabused liberals out of a fear of being stigmatized as conservatives. And in Wieseltier's case, moreover, it represented an unacknowledged intellectual reversal on his part, for when he reviewed *The Age of the Avant-Garde* in the pages of *Commentary* in June 1974 he had nothing but praise for what he described as "not only a thoughtful and provocative statement of a revisionist view of avant-garde art, but . . . a comprehensive theory of modern culture as well." But that was before he fell victim to "the Trilling dilemma" as a member of *The New Republic*'s highly conflicted editorial board. In 1982, *The New Criterion* and its editor clearly looked like the easy targets for a writer eager to renew his liberal credentials in the face of charges by the Left of a turn to the Right at *The New Republic*, and it hardly seemed to matter that the claim to uphold "variousness, possibility, complexity, and difficulty" in critical debate got rather mangled in the process.

At *The New Republic*, the troubled afterlife of liberalism has often proven to entail more in the way of contradiction and denial than of anything resembling real complexity. Take, for example, the November 9, 1992, editorial endorsing "Clinton for President," which Wickenden has proudly reprinted in *The New Republic Reader*. Pronouncing the Bush administration "degenerate," a word seldom employed in liberal political discourse, the editors dismissed "the question of character"—"We believe it tells in Clinton's favor," they wrote—and cited the Democratic candidate's "Arkansas record" as a sign of the wonderful things he could be expected to accomplish in the fields of education and health. In fact, no more than the rest of the liberal media did *The New Republic* bother to scrutinize Clinton's Arkansas record before the election. Like a lot of other wounded liberals at the time, the editors of *The New Republic* turned Bill Clinton into a fantasy candidate, praising his "integrity," his "moral intuition," his grasp of "the cultural reality of today's America," his "internationalism" and "deep understanding" of foreign affairs, even his "marriage," as if on every one of these questions there were not already grave doubts to be entertained.

Which is why, since the election, as more and more has come to be known about the President's political and personal past and his conduct of the Presidency itself, *The New Republic* has been obliged, like the rest of the press that favored Clinton, to explore all of the questions that were studiously avoided during the 1992 campaign. Only now—in the issue of August 22/29, 1994—does the magazine speak of "the general foreign policy vacuum at the center of the Clinton administration," for example, and this is but one of the many other issues—the health-care proposal, the Whitewater affair, the Paula Jones lawsuit, sundry conflict-of-interest cases, etc.—on which the magazine's fantasy candidate has proved to be an immense political embarrassment. In the afterlife of liberalism at *The New Republic*, the magazine's so-called turn to the Right always comes to a halt at the voting booth, at which point the critical faculty is furloughed to make way for the same old political sentimentalities.

The New Republic deserved a better book than Wickenden's patchwork anthology to mark its eightieth anniversary— the kind of book that at least made an attempt to define the magazine's mission in the aftermath of liberalism's failures now that those failures are once again so vividly on display in our political and cultural affairs. But the fact that the editors have settled for such an intellectually inept account of the magazine's own history is no doubt a reflection of the troubled and conflicted choices that continue to beset *The New Republic* itself.

September 1994

Reflections on Partisan Review

WALTER Bagehot, writing in 1855, observed that "it is odd to hear that the *Edinburgh Review* was once thought an incendiary publication." That was approximately half a century after the *Edinburgh Review* had been launched by Francis Jeffrey, Henry Brougham, and Sydney Smith on its career of critical controversy and political partisanship. Younger readers of *Partisan Review*, coming to that venerable journal in 1996, more than fifty years after its founding by William Phillips and Philip Rahv, might be forgiven for entertaining a similar sense of wonder about a magazine that has enjoyed the status of an established institution for as long as they can remember. Its days as an "incendiary publication" have likewise passed into history.

As a consequence, attempting to explain to younger readers in the 1990s what it meant in 1937 to launch a literary magazine in New York that was at once Marxist, pro-modernist, and anti-Stalinist is likely to entail a feat of historical elucidation not unlike that required to explicate some of the more arcane mysteries of medieval Christian theology for a modern audience of the heathen. The lineaments of an entire historical epoch need to be reconstructed for even a minimal understanding of its impulses and orthodoxies to be grasped. It is not only that the pillars of Marxist belief have now crumbled beyond repair. Modernism, too, though it still accounts for the greatest artistic achievements of the twentieth century, has itself become an object of deconstructivist orthodoxy.

As for Stalinism and the fierce political and intellectual resistance it met with in the era of its greatest influence in this country—a resistance in which *Partisan Review* played a significant role—that is another phenomenon that is nowadays only vaguely understood. About the cultural as well as the political consequences of Stalinism, our historians are only now—thanks, in part, to the opening of the Soviet archives—beginning to tell the full story of what amounted to a massive and largely successful campaign of ideological brainwashing, conspiracy, and intimidation. Add to all this the general level of historical ignorance about matters large and small that obtains even among the so-called educated classes, and you have a situation in which almost nothing about the cultural life of this century can any longer be taken for granted.

It is clearly as an attempt to correct this situation as far as the history of *Partisan Review* is concerned that Edith Kurzweil, who now serves as an editor of the magazine, has assembled a new anthology called *A Partisan Century: Political Writings from Partisan Review* (Columbia University Press). There have, of course, been several earlier anthologies drawn from the pages of *Partisan Review*: *The Partisan Reader*, edited by William Phillips and Philip Rahv, with an introduction by Lionel Trilling, published in 1946; *The New Partisan Reader*, edited by Phillips and Rahv, in 1953; and *A Partisan View: Five Decades of the Literary Life*, edited by William Phillips in 1983. *A Partisan Century* differs from these in being wholly drawn from the magazine's political writings, which, because *Partisan Review* was always primarily a literary magazine, may in some respects be considered the most perishable part of its history. That this turns out not to be entirely the case is itself a reflection of the special position that *PR* (as it came to be called) has occupied for a good deal of its history.

For *PR* is a literary magazine that was founded as a consequence of a decisive political quarrel, and it was in the nature of that quarrel that it did much to determine the way the journal subsequently conducted itself as a literary magazine. The original *Partisan Review* was a quarterly created in 1934 as a publication of the John Reed Club, itself an organ of the American Communist Party. Its program—the Party's line at the time—was largely devoted to the promotion of so-called "proletarian" literature. This first *Partisan Review* proved to be short-lived, however. Two of its young editors, William Phillips and Philip Rahv, were soon discovered to be unacceptably critical of the "revolutionary" writing favored by the Party hierarchy. They were promptly accused of "bohemian individualism"—a serious charge in Communist circles—by the literary editor of the weekly *New Masses*, the Party's principal cultural journal.

Before that dispute could be resolved, however, the Party received orders from Moscow to shut down its network of John Reed Clubs. These were now to be replaced by another creation of the Party—the League of American Writers—signaling a shift in the international Party line. The call for a literature that supported a Soviet-style revolution and stigmatized bourgeois writers as class enemies was suddenly abandoned in favor of an alliance with "antifascist" liberals that included a good many of those very same bourgeois writers.

What had happened, of course, was the emergence of Hitler as a credible threat to Stalin's plans for the Soviet Union. Stalin now needed allies in the Western democracies for his "antifascist" crusade. In 1935, the new line was proclaimed by the Comintern as the Popular Front, which effectively supplanted the earlier "united" front in the service of the revolutionary proletariat. None of this had anything to do with an interest in literature, of course, but it completely altered the way literature was now to be assessed by the Communists and their literary fellow travelers.

As a Trotskyist critic sardonically observed at the time: "Sinclair Lewis has been miraculously transformed from a petty-bourgeois writer, who turned his back upon the revolutionary struggle of the proletariat, into a literary hero of the Popular Front." Many other middlebrow talents, theretofore denounced in Communist circles as reactionary lackeys of capitalist exploitation, were now similarly embraced as progressive exponents of the Kremlin's "antifascist" crusade.

Liberals flocked to this new progressive banner. The Comintern's Popular Front proved, in fact, to be an immense success. To this day, moreover, the history of its role in shaping the future course of American cultural life—not only in the 1930s but for a considerable period thereafter—has never been written. The Popular Front mind—intellectually middlebrow, artistically philistine, politically "progressive," and both sentimental and simplistic in its views of human nature and the nature of the Soviet Union—became a staple of American cultural life. It exerted enormous influence on Hollywood movies, the Broadway theater, popular fiction, mainstream journalism, the academy, the liberal clergy, and the liberal weeklies. "What had happened," wrote Robert Warshow in an essay called "The Legacy of the 30s" (1947), "was more than the defection of one part of the intelligentsia. The whole level of thought and discussion, the level of culture itself, had been lowered." It was in this sense that a good deal of American cultural life may be said to have been Stalinized, and at certain intervals—in the cultural revolution of the 1960s, for example, and with the imposition of political correctness and multiculturalism in the 1980s and 1990s—has been repeatedly re-Stalinized ever since.

It was the distinction of the new *Partisan Review*, which was relaunched in 1937 as an independent left-wing literary journal, that it set itself in open opposition to this Stalinization of culture and politics. The magazine's literary, artistic, and critical loyalties were now more openly highbrow and modernist. Its general political orientation remained Marxist, but what this meant in practice was to be a source of conflict within the magazine itself for some years to come. The new *PR*'s political identity was, in any case, more clearly established by the magazine's enemies—the Communist Party and its literary fellow travelers—than by its own political avowals.

Even before its first issue was off the press in December 1937, the new *PR* was castigated in the *New Masses* and *The Daily Worker* as "fascist," "Trotskyist," "slanderers of the working class," "agents provocateurs," and so on, and it wasn't long before the liberal weeklies joined the Stalinist chorus, with Malcolm Cowley denouncing the magazine in *The New Republic* as "anti-Soviet" and a perpetrator of "literary crimes." By the time the latter charge was brought, *PR* had already published fiction and poetry by Elizabeth Bishop, Delmore Schwartz, Wallace Stevens, James Agee, Eleanor Clark, Louise Bogan, and Dylan Thomas, and criticism by Edmund Wilson, Meyer Schapiro, and William Troy. Cowley had meanwhile written a rousing defense of the Moscow Trials for *The New Republic*. It was a measure of the power enjoyed by Stalinist orthodoxy at that moment—1938—that Cowley could bring the charge of "literary crimes" against *PR* without being thought ridiculous. On the other hand, it was the rhetorical violence of the Stalinists' attack on the revamped *Partisan Review* that instantly established it as an "incendiary" journal. This was not something that the somewhat equivocal political content of the new *PR* could have achieved for the magazine on its own firepower.

On the new board of editors at *PR*, William Phillips and Philip Rahv were joined by Dwight Macdonald, Mary McCarthy, F. W. Dupee, and George L. K. Morris. The latter was a classmate of Macdonald's at Yale and a painter who helped to organize the American Abstract Artists group in 1936. Macdonald was in some respects the most militant in his political radicalism, espousing a brand of Trotskyism with which, for better or worse, *PR* became identified for a time. It is one of the disappointments of *A Partisan Century*, by the way, that Edith Kurzweil has not felt under any obligation to clarify the editors' rather muddled relation to Trotsky and his ideas in these early years. He was clearly a much respected figure in *PR* circles—rather too respected, considering his political crimes in the early years of the Bolshevik regime. He was published in *PR*—Professor Kurzweil reprints a piece on "Art and Politics" from 1938—and his assassination in 1940 was treated as a momentous event. (*A Partisan Century* reprints James T. Farrell's eulogy to "the Old Man," as Trotsky was affectionately known among his admirers. Omitted, unfortunately, is Dwight Macdonald's even more effusive tribute to Trotsky.) The exact extent to which the Old Man served as a political mentor for *PR* remains as blurred as ever in this volume devoted to its political history.

By the early 1940s, however, *PR* had already won a firm place for itself as a literary magazine of considerable distinction. In its issues for 1941, in quick succession it published T. S. Eliot's "The Dry Salvages," W. H. Auden's "At the Grave of Henry James," and Elizabeth Bishop's "Three Key West Poems," and began a regular series of "London Letters" by George Orwell. The following year, it again published Eliot—this time an essay on "The Music of Poetry"—as well as Marianne Moore's memoir of *The Dial*, fiction by Saul Bellow and Edmund Wilson, and reviews by Robert Penn Warren, Weldon Kees, and Randall Jarrell. The magazine was well on its way to being the premier American literary journal of its time.

Owing, however, to conflicts among the editors as to what a properly Marxist or socialist response to the Second World War should be, the political course of *PR* in the early years of the war was a good deal more problematic. These conflicts ripened into a full-fledged factional dispute when, in the July-August issue of 1941, the magazine published "10 Propositions on the War," a socialist manifesto drafted by Macdonald in collaboration with Clement Greenberg, who was now a member of *PR*'s board of editors.

This hopelessly obtuse political declaration, which Professor Kurzweil reprints in *A Partisan Century*, confidently predicted that "in the war or out of it, the United States faces only one future under capitalism: Fascism." It was therefore firmly believed that "to support the Roosevelt-Churchill war regimes clears the road for fascism from within and blocks the organization of an effective war effort against fascism outside." It thus followed that "all support of whatever kind must be withheld from Churchill and Roosevelt."

And what, in the view of these militant socialist theorists, would "an effective war effort against fascism" consist of? "The only way this conflict can be won in the interests of mankind as a whole," the manifesto concluded, "is by some method of warfare that will transfer the struggle from the flesh of humanity to its mind. Such a method is offered only by the cause of socialist revolution."[1]

This exercise in utopian Trotskyite nonsense proved to be too much for Philip Rahv, who, though still nominally a Marxist, promptly dismissed the Greenberg-Macdonald manifesto as "a kind of academic revolutionism which we should have learned to discard long ago." (Rahv's "10 Propositions and Eight Errors" response is also reprinted in *A Partisan Century*.) "The orthodox Marxists," Rahv wrote, "thought that the imperialists of both camps will exhaust themselves and then they will take over." He pointed out, however, that "there has been no stalemate; England has survived, but her continental allies have all suffered total defeat. Now Russia is next, and if Stalin fails to stem the invasion it won't be a Trotskyite but Hitler's Gauleiter who will be installed in the Kremlin."

No sooner had Rahv's response been published in the November-December 1941 issue of *PR* than the United States was indeed at war, thanks to the Japanese attack on Pearl Harbor, and in its first issue for 1942 *PR* now took the position of

[1] It is worth recalling that the United States was not yet officially at war when this was written. Yet most of continental Europe was already under Nazi control, Japan was advancing in its conquest of Asia, and Britain was still conducting its lonely struggle for survival.

having, in effect, *no* position on the war. In a statement signed by the editors, the magazine acknowledged that "for some time . . . the editors have disagreed on major political questions" and would henceforth "express themselves on the [war] issue as individuals." *PR*'s main task now, said the statement, is to preserve cultural values against all types of pressure and coercion."

Yet even this concession to socialist piety failed to satisfy Macdonald, who was intent upon playing the academic revolutionist. The issue was settled for Clement Greenberg—for the moment, anyway—when he went into the U.S. Army. Macdonald proved to be recalcitrant. He quit *PR*, declaring that the magazine was no longer political enough, and promptly started his own magazine. It was called, appropriately, *Politics*, and its position on the war might best be described as high-minded pacifism, while its views on other political matters cleaved more to a variety of libertarian anarchism than to Marxist socialism. After *Politics* folded in 1949, Macdonald took a sabbatical from politics to write for *The New Yorker*, a magazine he had hilariously ridiculed in the first number of the reborn *PR* in 1937. It wasn't until the 1960s, when the Vietnam War and the emergence of the counterculture provided yet another absolute he could pursue with impunity, that he returned to the political wars.

It may well be asked: Why, more than half a century after these sometimes solemn, sometimes comic-opera contretemps, is it still worth recalling the political twists and turns that animated them? In retrospect, after all, Dwight Macdonald was never a serious political thinker—nor, for that matter, was Philip Rahv. Compared to its brilliant contributions to literature and the arts, moreover, *PR*'s contribution to political thought was, with one exception, never either clear-headed or dependable. Its single shining virtue as a political journal was the anti-Communism that derived from the editors' early rejection of Stalinism, yet even that great virtue was severely compromised in the radical uproars of the 1960s. As Professor Kurzweil discreetly acknowledges, in the 1960s there was "a lessening of the magazine's anti-Communism." That is putting the matter very delicately indeed.

Yet it is precisely in such surrenders to political and cultural accommodation, whatever the pressure that prompted them, that the history of *Partisan Review* and its literary circle does so much to illuminate the moral temper of the period the magazine has traversed. A more thorough examination of *PR*'s political history than is provided by *A Partisan Century* would be obliged to address itself to a grim paradox: that the literary journal which established its political and cultural independence in the days of the Popular Front and carried the anti-Communist banner in the Cold War of the 1950s so readily succumbed once again to the totalitarian temptation in the 1960s.

Among the editors who guided the breakaway *PR* in 1937, three thoroughly disgraced themselves in the Vietnam War period: Dwight Macdonald, who made common cause with the anti-intellectual, anti-democratic radicals whose pop-culture values he had spent his whole professional career ridiculing; Mary McCarthy, who volunteered her services as an apologist for the Communist regime in North Vietnam, going so far in the process as to vilify George Orwell for *his* anti-Communist writings; and Philip Rahv, who ended his days as what Frederick Crews aptly described as a "born-again Leninist," and capped the debacle of his career by mounting a Stalinoid attack on one of the writers—Henry James—to whose work he had devoted some of his own best writing. By the end of the 1960s, the betrayals perpetuated by these writers were more frequently to be found in *The New York Review of Books*, but *PR* was clearly doing its best to keep up with the radical momentum already established by *The New York Review*.

In this connection, it isn't entirely accurate to claim, as Professor Kurzweil does in her introduction to *A Partisan Century*, that *PR* always "eschewed trendy politics." However true this was in the late 1930s, when *PR* was bucking the Stalinist tide, it was no longer the case after the Second World War. By the 1950s, certainly, its politics were distinctly "trendy." To its great credit, *PR* went very far in embracing the pro-American, pro-Western "trendy politics" of liberal anti-Communism during the Cold War years of the 1950s, and to its discredit it gave warm welcome to the anti-American, anti-Western politics of the Vietnam War period in the 1960s.

To the re-Stalinization of the political Left in the 1960s *PR* offered a lot less resistance than it had mustered against the original Stalinist assault thirty years earlier, and to the re-Stalinization of culture in the 1960s it offered scarcely any resistance at all. Over time, to be sure, the magazine has fortunately recovered some of the ground it had ceded to the radical Left in the darkest days of the anti-war movement and the counterculture. Its symposium on "The Politics of Political Correctness" in 1993, for example, is one of the best discussions of the subject that we have. (*A Partisan Century* reprints Steven Marcus's valuable contribution to that symposium, an essay called "Soft Totalitarianism.") Yet there is no denying that the 1960s caused great damage to the magazine. Its position of intellectual leadership fell hostage to the authority of the new radicalism and the "new sensibility."

All of this would have been made a lot clearer to readers in 1996 if Professor Kurzweil had not omitted certain watershed contributions to *PR* from the late 1960s. Take, as an egregious example, Susan Sontag's contribution to the magazine's symposium on "What's Happening to America?" in the Winter 1967 issue. This was the piece that contained the never-to-be-forgotten assertion that "the white race *is* the cancer of human history; it is the white race and it alone—its ideologies and inventions—which eradicates autonomous civilizations wherever it spreads, which has upset the ecological balance of the planet, which now threatens the very existence of life itself." In a volume purporting to trace the course of *PR*'s political history, this remarkable pronouncement—the most extreme expression of racialist ideology ever to appear in the magazine—certainly merited a prominent place. This wasn't Malcolm X or Eldridge Cleaver speaking. This was the doyenne of the "new sensibility." Yet this historic utterance is passed over in favor of Sontag's better-known "Notes on 'Camp.'"

Frankly, I think this omission represents a failure of nerve—to use a phrase that *PR* once made famous. So does the omission of that other emblematic expression of the "new sensibility" —Richard Poirier's essay, "Learning from the Beatles," in the Fall 1967 issue of *PR*.[2] By that time, alas, it was no longer very clear to the readers of *PR* as to who was actually in charge of the magazine's affairs. Rahv, though his name still appeared on *PR*'s masthead, had decamped to a professorship at Brandeis, and was very outspoken—among friends, anyway—in his bitter denunciation of the "swingers" who had seized control of the magazine. *PR* had meanwhile moved to Rutgers, where Richard Poirier was installed as an editor. William Phillips remained as chairman of the magazine's editorial board, but it was no secret that he wasn't entirely happy with *PR*'s new alliances.

It wasn't until he was able to take the magazine to the more conservative intellectual environment of Boston University that *PR* began to regain some of its old footing. Yet by then the magazine, with Phillips still in charge, faced a different kind of challenge: how to remain a recognizably liberal journal when so many of its actual intellectual affinities now lay with writers and artists whose loyalties are more conservative than *PR* wished to be seen to be. That, it seems to me, remains the dilemma of *Partisan Review* at the present time.

For certain writers and intellectuals of my own generation,

[2] "Well, sometimes they are like Monteverdi," wrote Poirier, "and sometimes their songs are even better than Schumann's." And: "It could be said that they know what Beckett and Borges know but without any loss of simple enthusiasm or innocent expectation, and without any patronization of those who do not know." In the end, the Beatles were firmly placed among "the very great."

however, the earlier *Partisan Review*, the magazine we were first drawn to in the late 1940s and early 1950s, will always occupy a special place in our experience. At that moment in our lives, *PR* was more than a magazine. It was an essential part of our education, as much a part of that education as the books we read, the visits we made to the museums, the concerts we attended, and the records we bought. It gave us an entrée to modern cultural life—to its gravity and complexity and combative character—that few of our teachers could match (and those few were likely to be readers of or contributors to *PR*). It conferred upon every subject it encompassed—art, literature, politics, history, and current affairs—an air of intellectual urgency that made us, as readers, feel implicated and called upon to respond. If, later on, we began to question the perfect confidence that *PR* seemed to bring to its pronouncements on every issue, and to understand the unacknowledged contradictions that lay concealed beneath its style of apodictic authority—well, that too was an essential part of our education.

Elsewhere, to be sure, there were critics who did more to shape our comprehension of the disciplines that interested us—B. H. Haggin and Virgil Thomson on music, Edwin Denby on dance, Stark Young and Eric Bentley on theater, and the New Critics on poetry. (About the New Criticism, *PR* could never bring itself to be entirely forthright. For while it tended to condemn what it took to be the "politics" of the New Criticism, the magazine nonetheless availed itself of a good deal of the literary talent that had been shaped by the New Critics.) On political matters, too, Elliot Cohen's *Commentary* soon outdistanced *PR* as the principal intellectual organ of liberal anti-Communism. Yet well into the 1950s, despite the quarrels and recantations and expulsions that marked its history in that still misunderstood decade, *PR* retained its authority for us—and not only for us, as I quickly learned when I made my own first contribution to the magazine as a critic.

In the spring of 1953, I sent an essay on the contemporary art scene to Philip Rahv, whom I had met the summer before at the School of Letters in Indiana. (I had gone there to study Dante with Allen Tate and Shakespeare with Francis Fergusson.) Much to my astonishment, Rahv accepted the piece and promptly published it in the July/August issue of *PR*. I had already published some literary criticism elsewhere, but this was my debut as an art critic and I quickly discovered that, owing to the intellectual authority which *PR* then enjoyed, publication in the magazine was in itself a ticket to a career I wasn't yet certain that I wanted. Invitations to write for other publications—including one from Clement Greenberg to contribute to *Commentary*—soon came pouring in, and I woke up one fine day to discover that the world, or at least the part of it with which I was now becoming acquainted, considered me a professional art critic.

It was then that I began seeing a good deal of Philip Rahv, first in New York and then in Boston when he took up his appointment at Brandeis. I liked him—when the spirit was upon him, he could be very generous and wildly funny—but I never quite trusted him. Listening to the scurrilous things he habitually said about his closest friends and colleagues, I never doubted for a moment that he was likely to be saying the same sorts of things about *me* to *them*. I somehow knew the day would come when I, too, would be classed as an enemy.

And so it did in the early 1970s, not long before his death. A few years earlier, when he had broken with *PR* to start his own magazine, called *Modern Occasions*, he asked me to write something for it, and I did—an essay on art and politics. He then asked me to join his staff as managing editor. This I declined to do, and not only because I was then happily employed at *The New York Times*. The prospect of placing my professional life in Philip's hands was simply unthinkable. By that time, it was plainly evident that the principal mission of *Modern Occasions* was the settling of old scores, real or imaginary, with Rahv's former colleagues at *PR*. I was horrified by the attacks he published on Clement Greenberg and Lionel Trilling, and told him so. Yet he continued to importune me for further contributions, and the end came when I told him I would be sending my essay on "The Age of the Avant-Garde"—the introduction to my first book—to Norman Podhoretz at *Commentary*, not to *Modern Occasions*. He never spoke to me again, though I gather he had much to say *about* me to his circle of young acolytes in Boston.

I did not get to know William Phillips until after Rahv's death. We've had our disagreements, and will no doubt continue to have others, but I nevertheless consider him a friend. And the feat he has achieved in keeping *Partisan Review* going, through good times and bad, is unequaled, I believe, in the entire history of American literary journals. It is doubtful, moreover, that *The New Criterion* would be what it is today if *PR* had not been what it was when I discovered it more than half a century ago. Let me close, then, as I began, by quoting Walter Bagehot. "If in the [preceding] pages we seem to cavil and find fault," wrote Bagehot, "let it be remembered, that the business of a critic is criticism; that it is *not* his business to be thankful; that he must attempt an estimate rather than a eulogy." That is what I have thought important to attempt here.

September 1996

Index

A NOTE ON THE AUTHOR

HILTON KRAMER was born in Gloucester, Massachusetts, and attended the public schools there. He received a bachelor's degree from Syracuse University and studied at Columbia, Harvard, and Indiana Universities before teaching at the University of Colorado, Bennington College, and the Yale School of Drama. Mr. Kramer became editor of *Arts Magazine* in 1955 and art critic of *The Nation* seven years later. In 1965 he was appointed art news editor of the *New York Times*, then its chief art critic, a position he held until 1982, when he left to found *The New Criterion*, which he now edits. He is also art critic of the *New York Observer*. Mr. Kramer's other books include *The Age of the Avant-Garde* and *The Revenge of the Philistines*. He lives in Westport, Connecticut.